Start Something Good

STORIES OF ORDINARY PEOPLE BECOMING LEADERS THROUGH FAILURE AND PERSEVERANCE

Bart Skorupa

D1508916

Printed in the United States of America

First Printing, 2019

Hardcover: ISBN 978-1-7326304-0-6

Ebook ISBN: 978-1-7326304-1-3

Audiobook ISBN: 978-1-7326304-2-0

Paperback ISBN: 978-1-7326304-3-7

Start Something Good Foundation
335 Cascade
Fairfax, CA 94930

www.startsomethinggood.org

Dedicated to my grandfather,

who taught me to

build humbly,

upwards and onwards.

Contents

Contents

Foreword

One thorn of experience is worth a wilderness of warning.
~ James Russell Lowell

This is a story about failure and perseverance as keys to success.

When you start something good, bad things can happen. The good intentions you pour into your creations and passions do not always lead to good outcomes. When this disconnect happens, it is called failure, a state wherein the expected reaction never materializes.

Failure is inevitable.

You will pick up the bat and you will strike out.

The more important thing is what happens *after* you fail. Transforming failure into purpose requires perseverance, a tenacious toil rooted in an honest reflection of what went wrong. Then, after ceaseless improvement and iteration, a home run will eventually sail over the fences.

When I began writing this book in 2015, failure and perseverance were not meant to be the foundational pillars of this narrative. When the first words were written, a nonprofit organization I co-founded was growing quickly. At the height of our impact, Groundwork Opportunities (GO) supported 20 organizations with a wide array of services in 13 countries. Leaders from all corners of the world invested their counsel and expertise. Growth seemed limitless.

Then, things began to fall apart.

GO transformed into something beyond my control. Two years into my writing, the organization and the original narrative of the book began to crumble. After eight years of building a startup nonprofit that invested millions of dollars into a swath of global development projects, the organization that connected leaders around the world collapsed. People I loved and worked with acted in curious ways. Relationships fell apart, feelings were hurt, and people lawyered up.

While our rise was faster and bigger than I could have imagined, it was the magnificent free-fall at the end that brought the greatest learning lessons.

So the book began to evolve. The same facts were present yet the vital lessons to be gleaned took on a new light. I wrote erratically and unconfidently as the narrative of the organization and the book unfolded in real-time.

Then a little miracle happened.

I became a father to a daughter whose soul radiates selfless giving.

A definitive end to the narrative revealed itself to me in a lightning strike. My passion returned and I committed myself to daily sprints of writing that began at 5:30 a.m. and ended when her first murmurs entered the day. She gave me the clarity of purpose and resolve to finish.

After three years, the book was finally done. The final copy was shared with dozens of people most closely associated with GO to ensure the validity and accuracy of the content. Most responded with enthusiastic positivity, a few expressed concerns, and a handful requested their names to be changed for legal and personal reasons. For those that responded with cautious reviews, I doubled down on my efforts to reflect the truth of what transpired. I researched thousands of emails, read documented reports and blogs, and interviewed many people to ensure the facts and tone I had captured was accurate. I re-lived the countless triumphs and reflected over the moments of human darkness when our work went awry.

In retrospect, the path of a beautiful and wondrous failure appeared inevitable.

When GO began, we were idealistic and ambitious volunteers who wanted to make a difference in the field of international development. Early on, we found success by working with like-minded leaders. Then, lots of money, support, and attention entered. First slowly, then suddenly. Our work focused on areas of extreme poverty, where economic disparity created an environment fraught with cultural misunderstanding, politically motivated actions, or devious behavior. A mix of hopeful intent cast against an unequal divide grew a rose bush adorned with countless thorns.

And when the scope of our work grew beyond our control, situations sometimes got ugly. Contracts, lawsuits, and non-disclosure agreements became the norm. To tell the story of everything that happened would cause reputational damage to people I love and expose my family and me to legal action. So after extensive legal and personal reviews of this book, I decided to include certain controversial material while leaving out the crucial details that would cause further pain and anguish. Additionally, some names have been changed to protect reputations of people I admire and respect.

This book is meant to teach, not hurt. Failure is where we find our greatest learnings and I have done my best to reveal what lies behind the curtain when organizations and the people behind them break down. This intricate balance of finding truth through the fog of emotions that envelopes the painful experiences I researched is challenging, especially while protecting the reputations of those involved.

Right up to the moment of publication, I debated with myself continually whether or not to publish certain material. Then I remembered that the same people who warned me against writing about what transpired had also cautioned me against starting something like GO in the first place. There were *countless* reasons not to quit my job and start something that I thought could make the world a better place. Statistics undeniably underscore the point that most new ventures fail. Anyone who would seriously consider becoming a social entrepreneur and attempt to change the world is far beyond the sway of reasoned argument.

By doing something beyond yourself, you risk that the thorn of experience will sting. But for a meaningful and rich life experience, it's far better than succumbing to the wilderness of warning. Life is too short for regrets. By following this uncharted path, I was party to the rise and fall of something truly special. I worked alongside some of the wisest and most humble leaders that came from the most remote corners of our Earth. Despite the hardships, thousands of lives were transformed for the better. Our humble organization proudly improved the wellbeing of people and made a lasting impact.

I'm a person crazy enough to think I can change the world. That belief requires me to chart a different course in life, one where risk and folly inevitably have many seats at the table. The plain truth is that starting something good and publishing a book about doing so is a risky endeavor. I am mindful that these experiences will bring feelings of noble pride from the accomplishments and painful reflections from the failures. The latter weighs heavily on my conscience but to not share my truth will weigh far greater.

My ultimate hope is that contents herein educate and empower future changemakers to improve their lives, their communities, and the world around them. The narrative is framed with specific lessons learned at each stage of development to prove that every tool you need to become a changemaker is already within your grasp. Learn from these words and stories. Find your meaning and purpose in them.

Then go out and push the boundaries of life, helping anyone that comes across your path to do the same in an authentic, transparent, and dignified manner.

This book will be there with you, every step of the way.

Bartlomiej Jan Skorupa
Fairfax, CA
October 2018

CHAPTER 1

THE LAWN

*The city must disappear from the surface of the Earth. No stone can
remain standing. Every building must be razed to its foundation.*
—SS chief Heinrich Himmler, October 17, 1944,
SS Officers' Conference[1]

In January 1945, Henryk Skorupa walk into the gray, blank slate that
used to be the city of Warsaw. He was an officer in the First Polish Army,
returning to his Motherland. After six years of German occupation, a
city he had once called home lay destroyed and abandoned. Rubble and
silence ensued. A war of unprecedented scale had razed everything from
his past. Physically, nearly nothing remained of Warsaw. The concept,
justified by the rules of engagement in times of war, was to destroy a
nation's entire morale and culture by destroying her buildings. And
so, Warsaw was burned to the ground during the final year of World
War II. Fully eighty-five percent of her buildings were destroyed; her
cultural heritage was deliberately burned to the ground.

Henryk looked at his burned homeland alongside nearly one million
Poles who had lost their homes, possessions, and countless friends and
family. Nazi Germany had plotted to remove Warsaw and her culture
from the face of the Earth. Yet Henryk envisioned a different narrative
in his mind. He began to build.

For the next seventy years, Henryk labored beyond a bitter past
by focusing on prudently functional buildings (homes, apartments
and nursing homes) that would help his nation rise again. He found
his purpose as a builder and erected steadfast structures that not only

helped Poland rise from the ashes, they catapulted her into the sky. While writing this book in Poland in 2015, I heard many people remark that times have not been this good since the Jagiellonian dynasty during the 15th century. Yet back then, nearly everything had to be rebuilt. No one could foresee happiness; they only experienced misery. In the rubble of 1945, this vision of a thriving Poland could only be embraced by the mad.

Yet the craziest thing you could do was nothing.

So Henryk started doing.

After the war, he worked for various construction companies in Poland and Greece, learning the trade while doing the work that would rebuild a nation scarred by war. As his skills grew, he ventured off on his own by starting something small in scale yet vastly profound in impact: building his own home so he could raise a family. In this home, my father, Piotr Skorupa, was born. Henryk instilled his passion for building into young Piotr's mind, who would become a civil engineer himself. Throughout the 1970s, as Piotr matured, he and Henryk started constructing a second home. Materials were hard to come by and funding was scarce but with grit and determination they continued to build. As Poland began to cast off the yolk of Communism in the 1980s, Henryk kept building. He began to build his first apartment building in Warsaw with more skill and resources.

With the advent of Capitalism in the 1990s, new financial capital began to trickle into Poland and she embraced her widening economic resources. Henryk leveraged these opportunities to expand his small operation, increasing the size of existing properties while starting new developments. Nursing homes were built for the elderly. Older homes were sold to raise capital to build new ones. Henryk's love of building transcended the distinction that many held between business and personal affairs. He treated everyone he worked with like family and everyone was treated as an equal. There was no greater value in his life than the bonds of family and community.

In 1992, Henryk manifested these values physically by conceiving a much larger home: a large duplex that would provide enough space for his wife, the parents of my mother, and their growing family of grandchildren spread across Poland and the United States. Till their final days, all four grandparents lived together under the same roof that they had built. Family members and growing grandchildren came and went as the kaleidoscope of time kept turning.

During the roaring economic growth in the early 2000s, Henryk kept pace with the opportunities that flooded into Poland. Despite entering his eighties, he continued to seek new plots of land and found new ways to expand a room, add a new roof, or build something new. I watched his earlier creations transform with the times as his apartment building in Warsaw began to house immigrants from Ukraine, Bulgaria, and Romania as they sought to take part in Poland's economic miracle. Modern Poland had come of age, miraculously becoming a provider of opportunities for my family, my country, and our wider world. Through his eyes, Henryk once saw rubble and gray. Today he sees blue skies and growth.

I went to pick up my grandfather from his latest development on a balmy and strikingly blue sky August afternoon in 2013. I pulled his beat up station wagon over to the side of the road. Remaining out of view, I approached the gate and watched him mow the lawn of his latest property. He worked alone. His once powerful frame stood diminished by age in faded shorts, blue socks, and leather sandals. A three-story yellow building destined to be a retirement home further dwarfed his stature. He did not see me approach. I watched and waited. He stopped the mower and surveyed the beautiful lawn. The air was dense with the sweet scent of fresh cut grass. He removed his faded cap that protected his bald head from the glaring sun. He sighed and looked content. The gate made an audible creek as I opened it, and he caught sight of my presence. Smiling, he walked over to me.

Nie jestem skonczony he said with raspy laughter.

I am not finished.

I was not surprised in the least. My grandfather said this phrase throughout my entire life. I nodded and watched him amble back towards his small mower to finish his mowing job. He pressed the button and the mower began to lightly hum. He pushed forward and kept going.

At 87, he was mowing the lawn of his newest property. This was not a job that you retire from. This was a man determined to complete his work and to finish his project; a means and a goal that are irrelevant to age, deaf to the word impossible, and blind to impeding walls. He was completely in the moment, fully immersed in his task, and achieving a state of flow that created a continual sense of calm and happiness.

The mowing was an integral piece of work and stood equal in importance to the summation of his vision and the wider pursuit of his calling in life. The retirement home had to be visualized. This was where the work began. The bricks were laid. The work continued. The grass had to be mowed. This is work we must not devalue. There must be no concept that any piece of work is beneath you; all parts are equal in the creation of the whole. This is how you turn things around, from individual to nation, to the course of humanity. The work is the purpose, the existence. This is the final memory I have of my grandfather, standing in the sun, appraising his work, clear eyes and a full heart.

At times, I do my best to see this resolve and determination in my own mirror.

And it's the same look I see in the eyes of social entrepreneurs around the world.

TURN IT AROUND
INTRODUCTION

We can imagine anything inside ourselves. The hard part of life is creating a continual practice of getting those imagined nations of thought out into the world. Time and again, an amazing idea lights our brains right before the precipice of sleep drifts over our bodies for the evening. In the morning, it's gone. Frustration sets in as our expectations of what "could be" do not align to "what is." As we grow older, we become afraid of acting out and trying things that are new. We fall into a marched rut of desolation.

Through my grandfather, I learned the utter satisfaction of doing things fearlessly. I can scarcely imagine the hardships that his long life encompassed though I do embody the confidence that keeps things in motion, even in dire circumstances. I am not afraid to try and fail. This does not mean I do not have anxiety when trying something new, lapse into depression when things fail, or lack an ego that craves attention.

I have all of these things.

Through pivotal life experiences, I designed a life that is fulfilling for my family, my greater community and myself. I passionately love my wife, am blessed with a strong family, have traveled to well over 100 countries, started social ventures big and small, driven successful careers, conferred with world leaders, and built wealth. I have also been sued, lost friends, depressed, failed in most things I attempted, blown small fortunes, and engaged in substance abuse. Different means, same person, and the same end. I am incredibly grateful for all of these things and strive to find beauty in all present moments, whether they are broken and miserable or whole and fulfilling.

I wrote this book to share these ideas and lessons so that they will unlock the possibility inside every individual. Through my travels, I have seen far too much injustice and poverty to not act, to not try. My grandfather saw his home demolished. He did not wallow. He built.

Early on in life, I lacked the character to follow in his footsteps, only finding my stride through a medical emergency that literally and figuratively changed my vision on life. That incident led to a transformational journey that completely changed my perspective on life. I met remarkable leaders from all walks of life. They lived in a variety of geographic regions, including some of the world's most remote locations. Like my grandfather, these individuals worked tirelessly to rebuild their communities. I sought out ways to help them and they continually reciprocated; together we strived to alleviate suffering from abject poverty.

This book is my way of aggregating and sharing the precious lessons that I have learned while in the field. My hope is that it will serve as a guide for you—the reader—to create a life of meaning and purpose. Each section of the book begins with a short narrative and then follows with a moral takeaway. These takeaways, referred to as "Turn Arounds," are meant to highlight specific values and methods that empower change makers to lead fulfilling, mission-driven lives. Ultimately, the goal is to support your professional and personal commitment to designing a better life experience for you and your community by becoming a social entrepreneur.

For the foundation of our discussion, it is critical to establish a shared language. What exactly is a social entrepreneur? I define it as a leader that starts something—whether a project at school or a disruptive startup in the marketplace—which empowers others to lead healthy, productive lives. It is my passionate belief that anyone can be a social entrepreneur. We are all able to contribute to the betterment of humanity in our own unique way.

Throughout our *Start Something Good* journey, I will introduce you to a handful of standout characters. Peter Luswata, a man born into poverty on a banana plantation, created middle-class jobs in his community. John Dau, an awakened giant, fled his homeland by foot. After walking hundreds of miles in the desert, he persevered and raised millions of dollars to support South Sudan. Similarly, Costa Ndayisabye has endured the tremendous pain of fleeing from two genocides, yet he remains one of the most joyful and resilient humans I've had the pleasure of meeting. We will also talk with students like Kyle Miller and backpackers like Sarah Sowden. Kyle and Sarah met these local leaders and helped raise funds and awareness to their ventures. United together, they transformed themselves and the world around them for the better.

All of the aforementioned individuals would qualify as social entrepreneurs in my eyes. They navigated an unfamiliar path to start something good. Our world needs more of them, which is why I've written this book as a tool for aspiring influencers. It is my fundamental worldview that all beings are interconnected. I exist because you exist; I am because you are. If you are unwell, then I am not well either. My grandfather knew this, which was why he selflessly built in places where others destroyed. He continues to inspire me to build something great with you.

CHAPTER 2

BEING AN OTHER

We're in the back of the bus. The bumps in the road spike their words.

"You know you're a follower, right?"

"Yeah, why do you just follow everybody around?"

The words cut deep and echo sharply against the yellow metal walls. The morning began so normal and like any other day in that weirdly magical time of being a seventh grader. I sat in Trigonometry and doodled spirals in my notebook. I had lunch with Tyler and Casey, and made obnoxious jokes over barking laughter.

Then the bell rang and the day was done.

Latchkey kids like me escape so we can watch Fresh Prince of Bel Air *before our parents come home.*

I board the bus, head to the back, and zone out with bad sitcoms on my mind.

Then Ryan (a girl) and Jamie (a boy) go ahead and fuck up my entire day with a dual confrontation on the ride home.

"You realize that you follow everyone around right?"

"Yeah, man. You realize that no one really wants to hang out with you?"

"No wants you around. You just follow everyone."

"Why are you even back here? This is where the cool kids sit."

The ride is deathly quiet outside of these resoundingly apt observations about my being.

Everyone hears. Everyone listens.

I sit quietly and stare out the window. I count the seconds till my neighborhood rolls into view.

But it's already too late. My secret fear is out into the world. Everyone now knows I am faking it and pretending that I fit in. My life is over. I thought I had been clever, perhaps even cool.

*Ryan and Jamie are ruining it all, tag teaming back and forth on my inability
to be anything other than a follower. I am being socially exterminated from the tribe.
Everyone knows.
I'm a loser, an outcast* Other.

~

Like many raised in the prosperous west, I won the ovarian lottery.
No one chooses his or her parents or where they are raised. Some claim
the winning ticket and are raised in the coddled nests of rich countries.
Some hold the losing ticket and are raised in poverty, hunger, oppression,
or war. I am cognizant of this privilege since I did not win the lottery
merely by the virtue of my birth. My winning ticket came through the
sacrifices my parents made during my youth.

I was born in Warsaw, Poland in 1979. The yolk of many unfortunate
circumstances predicated by the Second World War incessantly lingered
across Europe, and a particularly heavy burden held fast to Poland. The
end of World War II ushered in the occupation by the Soviet Union,
a stranglehold that began in the late 1940s and reached well into the
1980s. The repressive echoes born out of that war were still on active
display throughout my first years of life.

After the birth of my sister Ania, my parents put an ambitious plan
in motion to give their children more opportunities in life. With torn
hearts, they made the profound decision to leave family, friends, and
country behind so their children could iterate freely and grow their
lives in the privilege of freedom.

We moved to America.

We left Poland during a time of political upheaval and began life anew
in quiet Urbana-Champaign, twin cities in the agricultural heartland of
Midwest America. We arrived in Orchard Downs, a housing complex on
the Urbana side, which offered affordable housing to the large immigrant
community. And while the apartment standards were economical, the
community was rich in culture. Snaps of the Mandarin language chimed

with the terse, guttural vocalizations of Arabic. My first baby-sitter was Nigerian and her similarly aged son became my first friend.

Emulsified in this melting pot of immigrants, my new American life was spent amongst this group of strangers from strange lands. We were all *Others* seeking to belong, to live the American Dream, and grow a better life. Families depended on each other even if they could not quite exactly understand each other. They worked hard and hustled. And while I witnessed these sacrifices all around me, I had more selfish designs in my head. I had no idea how to visualize this dream. I didn't remember the chokehold of a repressive Polish government that threatened the liberties of my people. All I cared about was learning how to fit in. And that socially-minded goal brought numerous hardships.

Why?

Because I was different and a dork.

I learned this fact while in middle school and once we left Orchard Downs for the suburbs of more conservative Champaign. The move to strips malls and college football country made me desperately want the normal American life and I shunned my immigration façade. I pined for the apple-pie suburbia embodied by the Seaver family in *Growing Pains* and yearned for the urban coolness of the Huxtables from the *Cosby Show*. I lived in their virtual worlds, trying to decipher the magic secret of uniting with the American tribe.

I witnessed.

I mimicked.

And I failed.

The bus ride home taught me that.

Ryan and Jamie's words still echo in my brain, reaching with a faint sting all the way back to that seventh-grade bus ride home. The memory is so vivid that I will never forget their names and that fateful afternoon. I am sure they, like myself, have grown up, matured, and become good people. Yet at the time, being outed by the cool kids did set a trajectory that radically transformed my identity. I grew addicted to loneliness and isolation, which to me generally had less to do with being alone and more to do with not having other people around. I began to relish in the feelings of isolation. Ironically, my ability to travel allowed me to stay in a state of isolation.

The political situation in Poland began to calm during my teenage years. Our economic situation improved, and my family started making annual trips back to our homeland. Entire summers were spent back in the motherland and our lives began to continually shift between central Illinois and Poland. Summers in Poland meant endless hours of exploration and my prized alone time. No television to watch, no video games to master. No striving to fake friendships. My time was spent with my family and in the joy of reading anything I could get my hands on. I read entire books in one sitting, not moving for hours on end as the words streamed from the pages. I got exposed to new ways of thinking during epic three-hour family dinners that encouraged political debate.

The Skorupas traveled frequently across Europe as many of our clan scattered during the grayness of Communism to new homes in France, Germany, Portugal, England, and Switzerland. Their doors and couches were open for our travels and their dinner tables exposed me to new thoughts about social adaptation. While staying at my uncle's home outside of Zurich, I learned that one could not simply arrive in Switzerland and immediately call themselves Swiss. Only after working in Switzerland for twelve years could you *attempt* to establish residency. And residency is only a legal term, as my uncle could never consider himself as truly 'Swiss'. The culture would not allow that and he would always be an *Other*. His families' only hope of truly belonging was delegated to his children, born onto the neutral soil of pastures, mountains, and cuckoo clocks.

I considered how lucky I felt since, despite being a dork, at least I could call myself American. Like any pizza joint in America, that identity came with instant delivery. The ideals of this modern nation-state founded by immigrants and for immigrants still hold fast today. The title of "American" is equal and open to all. This liberating ideal influences so many Americans—whether new immigrants or those from deeply-rooted families—to be what they want to be, to shape their own destiny, and both define and control the narrative of their lives. You just have to be adaptable, resilient, and have the determination to make it happen. It's an unbelievably powerful thought and one that can empower virtually anyone to create their own realities.

Over time, I became steeped in self-confidence because of my travels and explorations. I became proud of the differences that set me apart and grateful for the open-minded lessons that multiculturalism fostered. Jamie and Ryan be damned, I slowly and surely began to realize the power of being an *Other*. I was humbled by the fact that I could be so globally interconnected at such a young age. I learned to "think different". I learned the powerful value of standing out during my transformative teenage moments.

As I matured into college, my travels abroad set me apart in a positive light. I got my first real girlfriend, joined various social clubs, and worked hard to save for backpacking trips. Travel became my favorite addiction. It helped me better understand the rules of social engagement and allowed me to create an inner and external acceptance of my European background. I embraced my multiculturalism and realized the many advantages.

In short, I stood out and thereby the follower began to take roles of leadership. I embraced my *Otherness* and its allure to draw people into my thinking while finding others that shared those values. I was blessed to have a family that empowered me with the ability to explore a wide array of tribes at such a young age. Their sacrifices eventually allowed me to blaze a path across 100 countries. Through those travels, I met amazing leaders from all walks of life that showed me the profound power of stitching people together with the needle of identity and the fabric of core values. I learned to lead with humility, to stay in the back, to eat last, and gently yet confidently encourage *everyone* forward, whether *Other* or *Same*.

Even in the bleakest of upbringings, we can all find the strength to create, or perhaps grow into, a positive identity. This baseline of self is the necessary foundation to start fomenting a calling and a purpose in life that will drive our lives into greater states of wellbeing. Some find their calling early in life with ease and doggedly pursue their passion at all costs. For others, it takes decades to uncover. Yet it's never too late to re-invent yourself and no matter how dire your previous circumstances, you can find strength in your past and leverage your stories to develop a better life experience. This is the first step towards becoming a social entrepreneur.

Trust me that you will not find your sense of completion through fame, wealth, and material gain. That is not the "American Dream" my parents bestowed upon me. That ideal does not fit within the lessons I learned from local leaders from around the world. No, I was shown a different path to happiness in life. I was taught that the effect you have on others is the most valuable currency that exists. How will you serve the world? What does the global community need that your talent and calling in life can provide? This is all you need to figure out to start living a meaningful life as a social entrepreneur.

And I believe that anyone can achieve wellbeing and economic gain by following this path. Let me prove my point by providing a stark counter-example that greatly contrasts with my sanguine Midwestern youth.

Meet Costa Ndayisabye, a dear friend and mentor. Costa was also continually marked as an *Other* over the course of his life. He was born in Burundi as his parents fled from their native Rwanda's first Tutsi massacre and genocide in 1959. They subsequently settled in the Democratic Republic of Congo. He and his siblings grew up in extreme poverty after his mother was widowed at a young age. War, hunger and famine permeated his life. As an *Other*, he was imprisoned three times in Congo, Burundi and in Rwanda. He witnessed the second genocide of his life in his early thirties. Like a horrific skipping record, the genocidal tune of death played again in Rwanda in 1994. Nearly one million innocents lost their lives during 100 days of a destruction of self and community. After unspeakable acts of violence and hatred ravaged his homeland, Costa returned to Rwanda in 1995 to help rebuild the nation and the heart of the people. How could one soul possibly endure two genocides in the course of their life while finding hope, purpose, and perseverance?

And now, more importantly, how could this *Other* now living outside of Austin, Texas, with his wife (a survivor of the Rwandan genocide) and their two beautiful children be the happiest person I know in my life? Authentic and deeply permeating prosperity radiates out from his wide smile and infects everyone around him with joy and laughter.

Sharing this metamorphosis of poor hatred into rich peace is his calling in life. Today, Costa is an international presenter, author, and facilitator who shares his miraculous journey from hatred to peace as a means for individual healing and interpersonal reconciliation. I have watched him help turn around the lives of countless individuals from various countries, races, and creeds.

Costa is happy because of his purposeful life that drives empathy and peace. He turned around a tragic upbringing and moved towards a deeper purpose that foments his wellbeing. This purpose gives strength to his family and value to his international community. His life path to his calling is similar to mine. I did it in the coddled west. He did it through the nightmare of genocide. If I can do it and he can do it, then we all can do it.

I have met and worked alongside countless social entrepreneurs over the past decade that, like Costa, helped me foster an innate belief that anyone can find a calling in life and manifest purpose into their career. Whether you are launching your own company, starting a nonprofit, or driving a project at work, what lies herein are the tools that will move your calling from being haphazardly found through manifest destiny, and shift it to be designed by willful purpose. This path only requires grit, determination, and belief of self. And this belief of self comes from the only truly unique thing we all share and that sets us all apart: our life story.

Our lives are the stories that we tell ourselves and share with the world. They can be designed and sharpened into a powerful tool that can be leveraged to influence meaningful change. Awkward bus rides are given meaning. Genocides are given purpose. Some are meant to make people laugh, others to cry, and the best stories instruct us about what it means to be human. Our life stories can empower us to shape the experiences of the past to create a better future.

Whether born hungry into extreme poverty or spoon-fed in an industrialized nation, we all have the power to design a better human experience. After a medical emergency that literally changed my vision in life, I started an organization with my best friends to fund social entrepreneurs like Costa who were ending poverty in their communities. I had no idea what I was doing nor any money to launch a company. I was living in a closet and sleeping on a pile of clothes in San Francisco with no job to my name. Yet I started something good, and with continual failure and iteration, this organization ended up raising millions of dollars. More importantly, inspiring leaders who taught me how to lead a meaningful life surrounded me.

Through this experience, I witnessed impossible things being done by awe-inspiring people that rocked me to the core of my existence. I gave these social entrepreneurs my *everything* and did whatever I could to help them succeed. Some thrived and some failed. Some stabbed me in the back and ripped apart my heart. All of them made an impact, gave me wisdom, and instilled humility into my being. In turn, this giving also greatly expanded my choices in life by growing wealth that now enables my family to achieve their dreams in life. I can now look into my daughter's eyes and see the world through her, while also deeply understanding how amazing our lives are, and will be, because of the life choices I made to be different. I chose to do something, acted, and created things that other people could use to improve their lives.

Your life will never be the same once you start down this altruistic path and watch it grow beyond your wildest dreams. So let's start something good together and take that first step, no matter how small it may be, and see what grows from there.

TURN IT AROUND
DISCOVER YOUR CALLING

Others surrounded me as an immigrant growing up in the multi-cultural melting pot of Orchard Downs, Illinois. Like my parents, those *Others* sacrificed their love for their motherland for a higher purpose. Ironically, their children, myself included, tried desperately to wrest away their differences by trying to fit in. Yet like any well-planted seed, the bounty of fruits can takes years to sow.

I am indebted to my parents for the opportunities they provided by shifting my life to a free country. The heterogeneous neighborhoods of America and Europe that I explored during my formative years greatly opened my eyes. Perspectives of the world surged into my young brain.

Foremost, I learned that we are all different and all the same. There is no other perspective like mine in the entire world and there is no other perspective in the entire world like yours. Combining this into an identity and finding pride in the experiences that shaped your unique worldview is the first step towards realizing something great: you are different. You may not like it, you may spend a lot of time fighting it, but you can never really escape it. That being said, it is fully in your power to shape it, now and in the future. Embrace your inner *Other* as it's the most unique and scarce thing in the world. Don't worry, everyone else is doing it too, whether cognizant of the fact or not. And in that scarcity you can find extremely high value.

So who *are* you?

There is no one path to discovering the answer to this question nor is the answer permanent. The paths to discovery change and the roads taken lead to different locations. As a teenager, you would be hard-pressed not to discover you were, at times, a jerk. As a parent, you would be hard pressed not to discover you had an innate capability to give. You always evolve. So here are two tools to help you design a better life experience:

1. Discover Your Calling

When your passion intersects with your employment, then you have found your calling in life. Like my grandfather, there is no concept of retiring from your calling. You will be "mowing the lawn" until the final days and will find joy in (almost) all moments. So ask yourself:

- If you did not have to worry about money, what would you do with your time?
- What kind of work would you want to do?
- What cause would you serve?

You will discover a path of fulfillment that will enrich your life when you honestly ask yourself these questions. My father told me at a young age that work is one-third of your adult life so figure out something that brings you joy. I did not even need to hear that from my grandfather. I witnessed it throughout his life. Personally, I love starting projects from scratch and rapidly scaling their impact. I am very good at thinking about something and then watching it *become* something. I excel at being the person that spearheads new projects whether through roles in my own companies or by working in corporate America. This can often lead to tireless hours of failure and repetition, but I don't care since the work flows through me. I eat, sleep, create, and repeat.

I am obsessed with people so I must work in a healthy team dynamic. I also need to do something that helps improve the lives of others. I craft these pursuits into a vision and mission statement (which will be covered in more detail later), which then guides me towards something that transcends beyond a job or a career. I don't care about the money involved in doing these things. I thrive in the chaos of starting something new, and ironically get compensated handsomely for my efforts. And this higher amount of wealth makes me a more ardent philanthropist.

At some point in our lives, we will have to work, earn money, and share our talent with the world. This begins with a job, which then evolves into a career, and if we are lucky enough, will evolve into a calling in life. Visually, this path looks like a mountain, as shown below.

Chip Conley who we'll learn more about later taught the above concept to me. As Chip showed me, jobs form the base of the pyramid. It is a blessing to have an occupation that provides for you and your family. I have worked in areas of the world where jobs were scarce so I am fully aware of the luck involved to even get to this stage. Equally, once we are fortunate enough to get a job and start building our skills, we can leverage that experience to climb up the career ladder. Jobs and careers can both be part of the same path as getting to your calling. Indeed, my own journey followed this path of serendipity. But many people begin jobs with little clue about why they are doing them and then those jobs blossom into careers they do not like. That then leads to dreaded Monday mornings and anxiously watching the minutes on the clock ticking by. We ultimately become bitter and unhappy.

The danger of not living a meaningful life is that the career ladder you are climbing does not make you passionate about work. If your answers to the above questions resonate with your current occupation, whether you are volunteering to gain experience at your first job or getting paid a salary in a field that clicks with your heart, mind, and soul, then you are truly blessed in life. You are quickly on a path towards a state of wellbeing and self-actualization.

If your answers don't resonate with your current occupation, can you better shape them to fall into your calling? Do you have the power, influence, and skills to be able to bend your job or career into something better? If the answers are no, then it's time to move on. Don't worry;

there will be plenty more explanation ahead about why this is not as scary as it sounds.

2. Identify Yourself

We are born with a certain nature that is sculpted by our environments. My memories that began in Poland and continued on in America formed countless frames of how I viewed my past. Humans by nature are sentimental and empathetic animals that collect and keep memories that shape their self-images. Even if the memories are painful, they can be fashioned into gratitude for the present and hope for the future. I have witnessed this transformation in people suffering immense pain in their lives including survivors of genocide, rape, and disease. I learned how these people created purpose out of their suffering and found meaning in their pasts. Take stock of your situation, regardless of whatever the past may hold on your present life, and ask yourself:

- Who are you in terms of your memories?
- Who are you in terms of your closest friends?
- Who are you in terms of your possessions?

Your memories are a story you are telling yourself and are a perception of reality that you simply happen to believe in. If you ceased to exist, then the true reality of the world would continue on. Yet you cannot cease to exist. You think therefore you are. You can take hold of your story and shape your memories to achieve wellbeing in life. As you master the story of your life, which is covered in more detail later, the next most impactful influence of your identity comes through your immediate circle of friends and family.

Only form bonds with positive and determined people who you can learn from and who will not drain your valuable energy with uninspiring attitudes. You will feed off their energy and their sheer presence will inspire you to do more. This may seem like a painful purge if your current friends are negative, bigoted, or deceptive. Yet this will become unavoidable as you attain success in life. I attempted to avoid conflict with people who held uninspiring attitudes and poured energy into unhealthy relationships. This led to a massive emotional calamity that disrupted my startups, struck my marriage, and resulted in a great loss of friends. We will explore these stories later though realize that removing negativity around you is instrumental for starting something good.

Be sure to maintain perspective. While mingling with admired leaders and celebrities, also associate with inspired individuals who, like you, are also just getting started on launching their next big thing. This prevents exasperation when you compare yourself to the idols you admire. And never forget to mentor those below you in terms of experience of development. Connect with inspirational people and your whole world will literally change.

This path to "inner Zen" all leads to the most difficult question:

Who *are* you in terms of *your* being?

No "one size fits all" exercise exists that can answer such a profound question. I employ various methods in my coaching sessions including ideas covered in this book to help others find their calling in life. It's a challenging process though one with immense impact. Even when you discover this inner drive, it's always temporal. Finding your reason to exist is a process of discovery that continues through every present moment that occurs throughout your life. We iterate and we evolve.

Bart Version 1.0—the baby born in potato-fed Poland—is not the same as Bart 2.0—the youngster raised in corn-fed America. Bart 7.0 ran an internationally recognized nonprofit. Bart 11.0 coaches others on how to do the same. The terms of my being are constantly negotiated against the opportunities presented by the universe around me. And those opportunities grow exponentially because of the people I associate with and the environment that surrounds me. It continues to leap and grow, unfolding in exciting new ways that make every morning vibrant and fresh. I am not bound. I am free.

I say this not to impress you though to impress upon you that this can also be achieved in your life. Sharing this ability with others is my calling and determines the terms of my being. Inspiring others to design a better life experience stems from my fundamental worldview that believes "I exist because you are". I understand that to improve my condition then I must also improve your condition. I believe that humanity and wellness are qualities we owe to each other.

Throughout this book are the tools and stories from social entrepreneurs that equally believe in the righteousness of sharing wellbeing. These leaders are my community and have shaped my identity. Their stories and lessons are to be used as a compass to draw your map towards purpose.

After all, you and I are one so it only makes sense that I ensure your wellbeing along with mine.

CHAPTER 3

TRIBAL RECOGNITION

It's Monday morning in downtown Chicago. I'm standing in the middle of it all. People walk fast and horns honk loud. Stillness is not a virtue. I keep looking up. I'm a small town kid that is becoming a big city adult. I swish through the door and enter the glass and steel colossus of a building. It's the revolving kind—a carousel that swings the past away when you push and circles you into the present as you enter. I walk with uncertain purpose and nervous anticipation. Things around me move fast but the moment is slow, full of weight, yet void of a deeper meaning.

The receptionist looks up at me.

"I'm here to report for the first day of the rest of my life," I quip.

She laughs and my introduction to big time consulting begins. This is the place where I will learn the skills that pay the bills. Power dwells in these hushed hallways while influence swirls around vapidly white conference rooms. I do not understand what is happening around me, I am not sure I belong here. I long for a manual, a vision and a mission to guide me like the North Star, so I can find purpose and intention in my senseless steps forward.

I have none of those things. I take the temporary security badge in my clammy hand and mindlessly pass by the receptionist's jerked thumb indicating the elevators.

I press the button for the 44th floor.

The elevator lifts me up. People move slowly and quiet rules the moment.

The monitor inside flashes weather updates and useless headlines. There is a traffic jam somewhere, a war somewhere else, and a new product everyone must buy.

The door hushes open.

My career at Accenture begins.

For the wise, the first day at any job should be treated as a paid scholarship towards a career, which should then hopefully manifest into a calling later in life. It's the place where the real world slowly reveals itself; the inner workings of tribalism, capitalism, market forces, and political gain all expose themselves. Some find meaning in their efforts yet most believe they have no other option and so are left unhappy in their jobs.

I fell into that latter category when I left the tribes of college. I encountered wide-open spaces for wide-open thoughts as I drove from the small town to the big city. And I tried to picture what my life would look like. My first real job awaited and I had a starting salary higher than most of my professors—those very mentors who had decades of experience that shaped my thoughts and outlook on life were economically thwarted by the free market. Welcome to management consulting.

I marveled that my services—fresh out of university with a face healing from acne scars—commanded $175 per hour. Few can do fruitful things at that age to merit such a bill rate. Yet that's the leverage model and how management consulting firms make themselves profitable. Take young, doe-eyed, and ambitious graduates who like to learn fast and cast them out to the clients. Imagine the gall of the system that had me speaking to people twice my age about how to improve their business. I spoke about industries I did not understand while recommending unfamiliar technologies. I failed often and learned quickly. I did everything I was told during the first two years before protesting what I began to see as inefficiencies. I was hyper-competitive and had the patience of a gnat with a massive caffeine addiction. I could not stand when time was wasted.

I began my career by editing an training manual for enterprise-level accounting software that I had never used before. After eight months, I told my manager this was dumb and got promptly fired from the project. My next role had me doing software quality testing which meant executing prewritten scripts of very specific instructions in front of a keyboard. I doodled endlessly in the paper-based scripts to keep my brain from evaporating.

Eventually, I started spending time in meetings talking about the status of work. I noticed the other managers scribbling doodles in their notebooks while pretending to listen. Work was dull so I devised hacks to finish my tasks quicker. I created musical playlists with tracks specifically tailored for 30, 60 and 90-minute work sprints that steeped my brain into deep focus. I ate the right diet and worked out constantly to relieve stress while positively stimulating my emotional energy. I scheduled my day around my energy levels versus my time. This approach made me appear chipper at work and I got quickly promoted. I began managing teams that focused on productivity management. More importantly, it created space for me to work on my passion projects outside of work.

I rose up quickly, shifting industries, and working in both the USA and Europe. I consulted across a byzantine world of verticals: banking, health care, construction, manufacturing, e-commerce, retail, government and nonprofit. This bouncing around industries was done with purpose. I met the CEO of Jack in the Box on a pivotal hunting trip during a time in my life when climbing the ladder became "a thing" for me. He heard a rough summary of my career, pointed directly at my chest, and barked out, "Keep doing what you are doing. But whatever you do, don't pigeonhole yourself." The pigeon analogy seared itself into my brain as we fired shotguns upon fleeing quail.

With words of wisdom in hand, my career blossomed across industries. I kept asking *why* questions and paid more attention to *how* a person responded in addition to *what* he or she said. How they answered gave clues to their experience of leadership. Did they give an answer to every question, no matter how difficult? This probably meant they were making stuff up so I should be wary of the information presented. Did they apologize too much or never at all? This likely meant they were weak and uncomfortable in my presence. Did they offer opinions and set boundaries? If so, they were confident and important. Their opinion *mattered*.

Foremost, I learned that there is a vast difference between truth and the perception of truth. In the pursuit of a career and working your way up the corporate ladder, the perception of truth is an important rule of the game. I began to realize that people actually monitored time-stamps of emails (the later you send something, the more it appears you are working hard), and that the ability to sway opinion with key influencers was far more important than coding the right algorithm or designing the perfect status report. I watched how senior vice presidents of major companies often placed their key-chains on the conference room table, their intent being to show their BMW key to the group and thereby command the attention that "Alpha" deserved. They took up space at their designated areas with their designer sunglasses and expensive pens. Power, and the reflection of power by using open body language, can move mountains. My career thrived once I understood how to convey the secret code of power and began to master the art of social fluency.

By 26 years of age, I co-led a team of 60 people, earned a six figure salary, and lived free of any expenses in the heart of San Francisco's Financial District. No rent to pay, food for free, and earning big money, I convinced myself that I was running the jewels.

Yet these fancy externalities lacked a purposeful core. My work wasn't fulfilling and I hid my misery by working harder, drinking more, taking drugs, exercising daily, and surrounding myself with people to get away from myself. And then one day my body gave out, pressing an internal reset button on a random Monday afternoon. While walking down the hallway to a large weekly meeting that I ran, I noticed the hallway lights going dim on a cloudless sunny day.

The vignette of life shrank into a tiny hole of light.

Dizzy, I looked at my boss.

"I…. don't…. feel ……right," I mumbled.

Things went dark.

The next thing I remembered, I was on a couch in our office wellness room. I was given Gatorade and somebody called for a cab to take me to the emergency room. The ER nurse took my pulse and looked at the caved out black holes surrounding my eyes:

She muttered, "Get some rest, drink more fluids, and stop wasting my time."

My campaign to leave the world of big time consulting began that day. While it would take months before I officially cut loose, my mind began to plot the path. More importantly, I wrote the plan down with pen and paper, sketching a map to freedom. That pivotal morning, my body had told me what my mind was too scared to figure out. Life is a gift—every second, every minute.

It's temporary not infinite.

So I quit my job and bought a one-way ticket to Africa.

TURN IT AROUND
DEFINE CORE VALUES

Few come straight out of the gate as a leader or change-maker. It takes thousands of hours of perseverance, grit, and determination to learn the necessary skills that make you a leader. So get paid while you learn. Jobs are excellent scholarships to teach skills while figuring out the maze of your career. Whether it's learning how to smile while taking down reservations for a restaurant or how to tweak that TPS report *just* right, these skills matter. Realize the nobility of hard work. Instead of thinking of your current job as shitty, see it as rich compost that will help you grow your career. Always deliver impact and your income will scale exponentially as your career grows. Tim Morris, a professor of Management Studies at Saïd Business School in Oxford, proved the logarithmic return on investment when people focused on building stellar reputations.

Graphically, it looks like this:

His international research on professional services plots closely to my own personal experience. My ability to deliver impact builds my reputation and grows my income. This grew slowly then quickly.

Fortunately, I also was lucky enough to work in management consulting which exposed me to the inner workings of a wide variety of industries, business verticals, organizational management techniques, and people management roles.

Once my professional reputation became established, I became unreasonable when being pushed into areas that did not fulfill my curiosity. I challenged the status quo to follow a specific path in life. I sought mentors outside of my career to keep my saw sharp. These mentors were all entrepreneurs working towards something above and beyond themselves. They inspired me to make bold decisions.

Many will consider this easier written than done, especially when composed by a person with a large support network who lives in the heart of Silicon Valley. After all, I had encouraging parents, a university degree, and a high paying career in an economically vibrant city. So let's parry with a stark counter-example.

"Impossible is what you won't do."

John Dau, a towering figure in the social entrepreneurship world, taught these words to me. John was born into the Dinka tribe in war-torn Sudan. In 1987, his village of Duk Payuel was attacked and he fled on foot for three months until reaching Ethiopia. His reptilian brain faced true dangers: starvation, thirst, and the fear of being killed by other local people or wild animals. He eventually reached the Kenyan Kakuma refugee camp where he learned to read, write and speak English and received a basic education. In 2001, John was luckily selected to immigrate to the United States and settled in Syracuse, New York. Powering through culture shock, he regularly worked 60 hours a week at two or three jobs while earning a Bachelor's Degree from Syracuse University.

Today, he is an awake and actualized giant. John took his degree and went on to start three non-profit organizations that raised nearly $3 million for healthcare and economic development in his native South Sudan. He's earned many awards for his public achievements and charitable work. His life story is featured in the award-winning documentary, *God Grew Tired of Us*. The title references a thought John had while his people starved in the desert. Under such hostile conditions, this prodigal man of deep faith questioned whether his Maker forgot about his sheer existence. Yet he persevered and now carries these words like a torch, expanding light into the dark.

Together, John and I screened this film at the African American Arts and Cultural Center in San Francisco to raise money and awareness for his work at the John Dau Foundation. He graced the presence of my home with his near seven-foot frame dwarfing the air mattress on my floor. Yet he did not complain. Instead, he cramped his body draped in saintly white pajamas into a tight ball while thanking my wife and me for our hospitality. He taught me gratitude for the little things, even when the little things do not temporarily fit into our bigger aspirations. More importantly, he taught me to never stop striving towards my calling in life, even when all odds are against me.

John transcended jobs and careers into a wider calling: a place where purpose, livelihood, and wellbeing intersected. He is a noted leader in the field of international development, a devoted father, and one of the most humble and hardworking individuals I have ever met. And he made these leaps despite having nearly every bad card dealt against him.

I have met many leaders like John. Even when God seemingly forgot about them, they strove upwards and onwards.

They have proven to me that no matter what card you hold in your hands, the *only* impossible play is the one you won't consider. Once you realize that power which is innate in every human being, the next step is getting help from others. You must find or build a tribe. Leaders like John Dau drive change via their core values. One of the first things you need for explosive growth of your good idea is the *right people* in the *right seats*. The former is measured by their values and the latter by their skill sets. Blend that together under an inspiring vision and mission (more on that later) and then you can make anything possible.

Leadership must set, reflect, and drive the adoption of core values across the organization. This fundamental exercise became clear to me when I got invited to Summit Series, a gathering of the world's top entrepreneurs, artists, movers and shakers. Given the quick growth of my first startup nonprofit, I got introduced to this tribe by Mike Del Ponte, a serial social entrepreneur and investor. Their members included Richard Branson, Kendrick Lamar, Peter Thiel, Scott Harrison, and other leaders of risky, trailblazing businesses.

As I scanned my invitation to join these folks on a three-day cruise sailing to a private island in the Caribbean, I became starkly anxious. The seventh-grade dork had just been invited to sit at the cool kids' table. I had little idea on how to act. My first nonprofit had become a living and breathing company. We had traction, attention, and early seed funding to help leaders like Costa or John alleviate poverty in their communities. Because of that growth and my connection to Mike, I got invited to join Summit at Sea, wherein the only thing that could stop me from striking up a conversation with any of these disruptive thinkers, was my own timidity.

At the time, the responsibility of growing my nonprofit weighed on me greatly. I kept asking myself, "How in the world did I get here?" I needed to hire people and form a proper board of directors. How could I ensure that I enlisted the right people to grow the idea further?

Since no better place existed to solve this riddle of leadership than Summit Series, I swallowed my fear and signed up. Unsure of my next steps as a leader of a growing tribe, I needed access to people that knew how to launch ideas and drive them to fruition. This struggle of how to get my idea off the runway also empowered me with a great conversation opener.

Walking around the ship, I bumped into Tony Hsieh, the founder of Zappos, a startup online shoe company that Amazon bought for about a billion dollars. He told me that nothing helped shape the spectacular growth of Zappos more than writing down the core values of his business. Later that evening, I met Greg Zlevor, an executive leadership development coach who vigorously supported the same view. Over dinner, he warned me that once the culture leaves the Petri dish, it grows and evolves on its own. Having clearly articulated values mitigates the risk that the organization will enlist the "wrong" people.

Tony and Greg's counsel was spot on. The right people are everything when it comes to starting something good. Any idea can flourish if you have the right support around you that is empowered to make the right decisions. Cultural and tribal ties matter in business and life because they lower transaction costs. Tribal loyalty fosters trust and we need each other to exist. Movements that scale begin by finding a group that's disconnected but already has a common yearning. Once this group congregates around a set of core beliefs, they provide vital services to the whole by:

- Giving greater energy and strength than one could ever possibly generate alone
- Providing support when a member feels like giving up
- Creating an engaging community that allows them to make their passion their livelihood

Whether you desire to start a project at your company or launch your own business, the guidelines below can assist you in creating and leading a tribe. I guarantee this documentation of both personal and organizational core values, done in that order, will fundamentally shift your trajectory upwards.

1. Discover your personal core values

Look back into your past. Remember the stories that shifted the direction of your life. Look honestly at failures like being fired from a job and dig deep to see what lessons can be inferred. Don't forget the seemingly trivial moments like your first trip away from home or constantly debating with your parents have a large impact on the values that drive your life. My personal core values, and how I discovered them, are shared at the end of this book.

2. Discover an organization's values

Defining the culture of an organization is one of the most inspiring acts a company will do in its lifetime. These values produce goose-bump feelings of pride from the founders and coalesce leadership towards a shared vision. There are many methods to capture the values of a living, breathing body of people and it depends on the size of the organization. I've done this via emails with founders, over beers with leadership teams, and as part of leadership retreats. Whether formal or informal, the most important thing is to keep it fun and inspiring. Think big. You are writing the creed that may be read by millions. No matter what the organization's goal may be (sell more widgets, save more puppies, etc.), *why* everyone is involved is the single most important thing to get right.

My first foray into this game-changing aspect of organizational growth happened over a series of emails that would launch a nonprofit named Groundwork Opportunities (GO). Before countless eyes came to our work, we wrote down the following values:

Do more with less
GO seeks leaders who, despite having few resources, build their ideas into successful projects.

Build trust through life-long relationships
Family needs to build trust in one another and trust is the engine of our growth.

Be passionate and determined
Remember that impossible is what you won't do.

Build something special
Approach every task as something that will scale.

If you, as a leader, are still hesitant about the need of documenting values, here's a scary thought: the tribe you create will eventually grow beyond your ability to control it. This happens all the time. I have been voted off the board of directors of organizations I have started. I have had my creations, products, and services bought and then used in ways I never anticipated. I am fine with that. After all, the only constant is change. And if the values were correctly and honestly documented, they will transcend any perceived turmoil.

This transcendence of thought via values becomes acute during the most challenging of times. Eventually, anything we start and grow will reach a point of turmoil. Funding will cease, support will drop, and people will do crazy things. When an organization faces crisis, the values established by its leadership serve as enlightenment during dark times. The words that embody the values give us clarity on how to act.

No one captured this thought better than Mahatma Gandhi, who said:

"Your beliefs become your thoughts. Your thoughts become your words.

Your words become your actions. Your actions become your habits. Your habits become your values. Your values become your destiny."

CHAPTER 4

EVACUATE

The elevator hushes open for the last time.

"I quit."

The words simmer with more heat this time around. I've been here before but this time I mean it. This is the third time stepping up to the plate, ready to get ejected from the game. Every prior iteration resulted in a promotion or a raise. "Don't go", they'd say. "Here's more money, a greater title, and more entitlement." Just more. Today, I hold a trump card. I want less. Less responsibility, less definition, and less stuff.

My hands are clammy. Not nervous, just the anticipation that comes when not knowing what's next. "Next" is vague. "Next" means no job and a one-way ticket to spend a frigid winter at my Grandfather's home in Poland. "Next" is a reset button to go back to where everything started. "Next" is leaving a prodigious career as a management consultant so I can fill in the blank.

I wish I knew what that blank really was.

I wish I knew what would unfold.

Yet knowing prevents faith.

Faith thrives in the uncertain and is the purpose of the journey.

So the blank remains empty.

~

The blank eventually took shape into a rough plan penciled in my notebook. Poor drawings of the globe with arrows pointing to distant destinations filled the pages of my journal. The first arrow pointed to Poland, a place I knew and with experiences I could imagine. Walking down the quiet hallway of power to leave the security of corporate America, I already felt so close to home.

Wonderful tomato soup from my Grandmother would nourish my soul. I would listen to my grandfather tell stories about the Second World War. I would devour book after book in the cold silence. Countless cups of black tea would be gulped down over simmering political debate.

Home. Family. Comfort.

Then I'd quickly grow restless. I'd open my journal once again and trace the next set of arrows south to Africa. One arrow pointed to South Africa, another to Madagascar, and many culminated together in Rwanda. My analog pencil drawings transformed into digital searches on Google to form the plan. During my search queries, I saw an ad for Blue Ventures, an English based nonprofit that casts volunteer divers to collect coral and fish data in a remote region in Madagascar.

I filled out the form for their upcoming cohort of divers without hesitation and began the interview process via Skype the next day. After getting accepted into the program, I forked out the cash to join the next expedition and signed a massive waiver of various health and mental dangers that lurk while working in remote tropical regions.

I'd set the reset button on life for a while and see what would happen. So I quit.

Paradise Lost
Easter Sunday 1600

A few months later, after an epic five-day journey including a 4x4, bus, truck, ox cart, wading through rivers, trudging through bogs, and a blissful speedboat, I finally arrived in Andavadoaka, Madagascar. I spent the next three months there diving, researching, and working in a remote paradise. The expedition began wonderfully, diving or boat marshaling in the morning, studying in the early afternoon, capped off by soccer matches on the sandy white beaches. Our expedition numbered about 24 people, mostly Europeans and Americans exploring the depths of the sea. On my second dive, we discovered a new coral reef site no one had ever found before, though our GPS system ran out of batteries and we were unable to record its location.

During the third week, on Easter Sunday, the local villagers challenged our expedition crew to a full field, full-length football game. After 29 expeditions compromising 29 separate research teams, the locals had never lost, due to the fact that after the first half, the Europeans just could not keep up in the unbearable heat. Fortunately, an oncoming hurricane clouded the afternoon, bringing a cool air that leveled the playing field. The match was the best game I had ever played though we lost 0-1 in the 89th minute. Still, the locals were deeply—perhaps politely—impressed. Diving had been cancelled for the next few days due to the turbulent weather, so we all heavily celebrated through the night drinking obscene amounts of beer and *togagash*, a lethal, and I think maybe illegal, Malagasy home brewed spirit. My right eye began to twitch with pain early in the evening but I attributed it to the dusty playing field and early morning dive.

I awoke the next morning with a dull headache and an inability to open my right eye due to an intense pain that had nothing to do with a hangover. Even opening my left eye caused excruciating pain to the right. My hut-mates Kyle and Derek guided my blinded and weary body to our on-site medic. Craig, a paramedic and ex-military doctor perfectly suited to deal with illnesses in remote areas, struggled to rouse himself that morning though eventually sat me down in his make-shift clinic. Examining my eye with fluorine, he saw a volcano shaped crater in my right cornea.

Obviously concerned, he immediately satellite phoned a specialist in London. As Craig suspected, I had a corneal ulcer and was to be administered antibiotic eye drops to dissipate the bacteria, and was also given Codeine for the pain. With drops and rest, we were assured via our specialist in London that the ulcer would dissipate, making me fit to resume work in about a week. Craig taped both eyes shut and I spent the next 24 hours completely blind, honing my abilities to hear and groping my way about camp with the aid of my friends.

Things Got Worse
Tuesday 1400

Since I had been administering eye drops hourly throughout the night, I awoke with no pain in the eye but was very tired and under slept. I spent the day in darkness, adjusting to being blind, with time slowly sloshing by in the way it does when humans get no rest. Things seemed to be getting better and I was optimistic. Craig replaced my eye dressing later that afternoon and cleaned out all the, medically speaking, "gunk" in my eye. Once cleaned, I looked at Craig with my good eye shut.

I saw a world of only lights and shadows.

"Craig, I can't see anything," I said.

"You are shitting me," he responded, grabbing the satellite phone to call London.

I was done. Expedition over.

I called a quick meeting with the staff to let them know I was being evacuated. In spite of some really heartfelt condolences, I felt sadness and dismay more than anything else at that point. As I ambled my way back to my hut to gather my things, I saw Craig out by the football pitch on the phone. I went over to overhear the diagnosis, in vague hope that this was expected and might somehow still be handled locally. I was dead wrong, and instead heard words that I will never forget in my life:

"Right...I see...Right...And when you say 'urgent', what exact time frame are we talking about?"

I froze. Being thousands of kilometers from any hospital in a remote, desolate area, the skies darkening by an oncoming hurricane, the word "urgent" had no meaning.

Craig hung up.

"You have hours," he said.

Mission Critical
Tuesday 1600

I ran back to my hut to get my medical information and then ran to Jenny and Tristan's hut, the expedition managers. They took out their emergency procedures folder, full of evacuation contacts and available medical staff in Madagascar and South Africa. The four satellite phones were distributed between us to start going down the list of available aircraft that could make it to the site and evacuate me.

My first call was to United Healthcare to get information on coverage for this medical evacuation. With the now very real possibility of never seeing again being front and center in my mind, I wanted to skip this step. Costs became meaningless in a medical emergency. Jenny, however, being the prudent manager, pointed out that it was the first step in the medical evacuation process. It said so, she pointed out, on the weathered yet colorful PowerPoint slide, detailing all necessary steps for an emergency medical evacuation.

So I rang.

A chipper woman from an Indiana call center picked up the phone. Here was a phrase that would confuse any call center operator:

"Hello. My name is Bart and I am in an emergency situation. I am in a remote expedition site on the southern coast of Madagascar. I need a helicopter or seaplane to evacuate me immediately. I have GPS coordinates of a nearby football pitch to use as a landing pad. Is this covered by my insurance?"

"Um, right...You need to...Wow.... I need to speak to a supervisor. Please hold," she responded.

Placed on hold, I started listening to Elton John's *Rocket Man* while standing in the pouring rain at the rate of 3.50 Euro per minute. After about the 280 Euro mark, I realized I was not getting anywhere trying to explain my grievous situation. These are all the real answers to the most inane questions I had ever heard:

"Madagascar... M-A-D-A-G-A...."

"Yes, the country."

"No, it's on the continent of Africa."

"I don't know what type of certifications they may have. Did you hear I just said *Africa*"?

"Well, how the fuck does your ambulance fly?"

I hung up the phone and gave Jenny the "thumbs up" on insurance, anxious to get to the next step of calling various aircraft providers.

The storm hit full on, with the rain coming down sideways in sheets. To receive reception, we needed to be outside in the open. Holding a useless umbrella, drenched to the bone, I spoke to a pilot named Lionel, yelling out the GPS coordinates of our football pitch. His response:

"Sorry sir. With the hurricane, we cannot fly that far south until Thursday. Again, deeply sorry but there is no way we can fly."

Everyone got the same response. Nothing could fly here for another day and a half. I looked out into the black, turbulent ocean. My left eye was beginning to twitch. The infection was spreading and I was stuck, thinking the dark ocean would be one of the last things I would ever see.

The Search Party
Tuesday 2000

Search parties of two were organized. Any vehicle found in the area was to be commandeered and brought back to the site. I could not go, due to my lack of sight and had to resort to packing and thinking of alternate plans. With help from the staff, I began to stuff my things into two separate packs. One pack had all my non-essential clothes and dive gear. The second pack had one set of clothes, a medical kit, my knife, money, and travel documents. Evacuation may now be on foot or ox-cart to the nearest airstrip, near Morombe, where a plane *may* be landing. The hike could take eight hours, which could feasibly mean that I would be there by morning to await any evacuation aircraft. Ordinarily, that is not a difficult hike for me though given an ulcerated eye and a hellfire storm it seemed impossible. Derek, my Scottish hut mate, swore he would get me there on his back if he had to and we laid out plans for the hike.

The search parties came back empty handed. A 4x4 had left earlier that morning to Morombe, only to disappear in the storm. A ride to Morombe should only take 2-3 hours by 4x4 and 12 hours later, no one knew what happened to the car or its passengers. Most likely, it had broken down along the way and was waiting for the storm to pass. Hiking was immediately ruled out due to the weather and lack of any sort of map. All options were spent for that evening and we awaited dawn for the last resort, evacuation by boat.

The Last Resort
Wednesday 0530

Boat evacuation was always the last resort in all the planning, as the ocean was swirling from the storm. If the boat capsized then, well, that would have been the end. I did not sleep again and prayed that the morning would be calm. Upon first light, I saw the sun, indicating a passing of the storm. I grabbed both packs with Derek's help and trotted down to the beach. A few staff members and friends loaded one of our dive boats with bottles of water and three reserves of petrol. Two local Malagasy staff were to accompany me and I refused my other friend's touching offers to join us on the trip. The trip would take two to four hours depending on conditions, being rough in the best case scenario and quite dangerous in the worst case scenario. Our dive boat was a rickety, wooden affair with little to say for safety measures. I donned an orange life vest and put on my dive mask to protect my eye bandages. I looked like an aquatic dork.

After quick hugs and words of encouragement, the boat motored out into the swells of the ocean. The first hour was pretty solid travel but the further out we got, the worse the waves became. Some sounded like they were pounding the wood frame with steel hammers. One wave hit with such force that all three of us fell backwards. My back was sliced against the satellite phone box and warm blood trickled down my back. We stopped twice along the way, once to refuel and once to let the skipper violently vomit from seasickness.

After three hours, we eventually floated up to Morombe. I waded through the waters towards shore, carrying my bags over my head. The plan from there was sketchy at best. Once on shore, I set out to find some way to get myself to the airport. I had no idea how far it was, or exactly how I would get there. Finally, my luck changed.

A Savior
Wednesday 0830

I observed a family eating breakfast on a terrace by the beach. I quickly went over to explain my situation, hoping the eye patch, a blood stained shirt, and the medical kit I was carrying would be a universal sign that I needed help.

I was wrong.

My boat guides had disappeared without a trace and had carried off the satellite phone with them. Baffled and furious, I made my lonely walk towards the family. Not being able to speak the local language, I resorted to my basic French to communicate my situation. I desperately tried to explain to them in my awful French that I needed a car or directions to the airstrip, but nothing was getting through.

I needed immediate transport for evacuation. They smiled and nodded, and served me coffee and a baguette. As I sat down to eat, I took out a pad and paper to draw some pictures of a car, a plane, and then a hospital. Suddenly, a voice rang out

"BART!!!"

Shocked to hear my own name in literally the middle of nowhere, I jumped up towards the direction of the voice. With my dilapidated vision, I saw a petite blonde woman running towards me from the beach.

Great, I thought, not only am I losing my vision, I am also losing my mind.

She hugged me and then started asking what had happened with my eye since I last saw her on Sunday. A ray of light hit the recesses of my memory. I had met Heather at the local village bar three nights prior. She was working on a separate octopus conservation project in the area, and had left the morning prior in the 4x4 that everyone thought had wrecked somewhere en route.

She led me back to her room where she bandaged my back, changed my eye dressing and cleaned me up a bit. I still had fluorine dripping through the bandage yellowing my face, and for the first time in days, I saw myself in a mirror. I looked like death. Bic, her 4x4 driver, appeared at the door. Heather rapidly explained to him what was happening and sternly told him to find a car as soon as possible. Without a word, Bic jumped on a bike and pedaled off towards the village. As we waited for his return, she started gathering her things and stuffing them into her bag.

"What are you doing?" I asked.

"Bart, you can barely see and have no real idea where you are going. You can't speak either French or Malagasy. I am not going to leave your side," she responded.

I started to believe.

Air Rescue
Wednesday 0930

Bic not only found a beat up pickup truck with fuel, he also found my two guides and our satellite phone. All of us jumped in the back of the pickup and took off for the airport. I could not help but smile for the first time in a long time as Bic gave my errant guides one hell of a bitching out session for stranding a blind me while our crew drove to the airport.

Upon arrival, the airport proved to be nothing but a long concrete runway and a run-down white shack harnessing an antennae. Bic, Heather, and I jumped off the back of the truck and its driver sped off without waiting for payment or showing any concern over what would happen if this place was deserted. No planes, cars, or people were about.

Dead silence hung in the air.

We walked up to the shack, which had a worn down brown door. Above the doorframe, I saw the word "Deptarture" crudely and incorrectly written in blue paint. I opened the door and saw a small

Malagasy man sitting at a desk with a VHF radio. By the looks on our faces, I do not know who was more surprised to see the other. He spoke no English, so Heather took over in French. This was literally the entire conversation:

"This man needs to be flown to a hospital. Is there a plane coming today?" asked Heather.

"Yes, Madame," he responded.

"When?" she asked.

"Sometime," he responded.

"Where is it going?" she asked.

"Somewhere," he responded.

Heather and I looked at each other and shrugged. Both of us had been in Africa far too long to argue with this impeccable logic. We went back outside and sat in the shade, awaiting a plane to arrive sometime and to take us somewhere. I still had the satellite phone but decided to wait an hour or so before calling back to camp. After all, no "Plan B" existed anyway and I needed to conserve the battery.

After 30 minutes, the tiny drone of a small jet pierced the air. Air rescue! The three of us ran to the tarmac, watching an ancient Cessna hobble towards a landing. Heather squeezed my hand.

"Here's your plane, Mr. Bond!" she yelled, laughing.

Out of the plane popped a shaggy looking pilot named Josh. Josh was a Canadian working for Mission Air Force; a Christian based organization specializing in small aircraft delivering aid supplies to remote areas in Madagascar. Unbeknownst to me, Jenny back at camp had continued sending SOS signals for my evacuation and MAF caught wind that I needed to be extricated from Morombe to Tulear, a larger town where I could connect to the capital.

At first, he rejected taking both of us, saying he only had room for one person. I explained the full extent of my injury, claiming that without Heather, I would be dropped off in Tulear with poor vision needing to find urgent medical care. Seeing this, and being a good Christian, he forced room for three in a plane meant for two. I got strapped to a large cargo box with a five-point buckle and Heather took the co-pilot seat. Away we went, flying two quick-land reconnaissance missions en route so that Josh could test out dodgy dirt runways as potential drop-off points for medical supplies. Both landings failed but we aborted quickly, and all survived another day. One hour later we landed in Tulear, a city underwater after the hurricane.

The Mystery Man
Wednesday 1100

Heather and I jumped off the plane, carrying our bags down the runway. I was trying to form some sort of mental plan for getting tickets to the capital city of Antananarivo when a 4x4 literally cut us off and drove up on the runway before we could get into the terminal. An older white man with crisp white hair, chewing a cigarette came towards us. He looked at my patch and in a thick Belgian accent said:

"Bart, I assume? I have a ticket for you to get to Tana at 1700 today. You owe me $130. We have six hours here in Tulear to find you a doctor till then. Get into the car."

I looked at Heather and we threw our bags in the car. She asked if I knew who this was. I had no idea. He wasted no time and I never got the chance to ask his name, how he knew I would be there at that moment, or any question that would explain his baffling entry into an already bizarre journey. He just happened to appear.

The Belgian went straight to business and I showed him my list of medical contacts in Tulear. He shook his head at all of them.

"Sheet...sheet..all dees are sheet. You egg-*spect* to see again with these dackters? Ha!"

He put the 4x4 into gear, said he had a better idea and proceeded to make calls on his mobile phone. Driving through puddles the size of swimming pools; he made multiple calls, fluidly switching from French to Malagasy. We pulled up to a clinic where he made some inquiries. He shook his head and we got back into the car.

More calls, another clinic, another shake of the head.

Finally, he spotted a nun driving in the opposite direction. Cutting her off with his car, he started asking her questions. He finally nodded and said that the Catholic Mission had an eye doctor that would arrive in a few hours. He dropped off Heather and I at a small hotel and I paid him the $130. He scribbled the name, "Doctor Moray" and the address of the Catholic Mission on a scrap of paper. I thanked him profusely and he just shook his head and lit a cigarette.

As he drove off, I realized that I never caught his name.

To this day, neither I nor any of the Blue Ventures staff know who this man was or how he knew about my arrival to Tulear. All I know is that he saved my vision. For that, I thank him with all of my heart.

My Eye Gets Cut Open
Wednesday 1400

After dropping our bags into our room, Heather grabbed a cab to the Catholic Mission. We had nothing else to do but wait, so we figured we might as well do it at the clinic. The cab, a 1960 Renault hatchback, waded slowly through the sea that was once Tulear. Water began to flow into the car. Amazingly, the car made it the entire way to the mission without breaking down.

A yellowing building with boarded up windows greeted us. With all the doors and windows closed, I decided to take a quick nap on the front stoop, exhausted from three nights without sleep. Using my backpack as a pillow, Heather and I passed out only to be awakened by the same nun from earlier in the morning. She pointed to a small white building with an open door.

I walked into a room lit only by the sunlight, housing a bruised looking desk and an old shelf. In the corner, a Malagasy man in faded blue overalls hobbled over. His arm was held firmly to his side and he spoke with a pronounced stutter, most likely the result of a recent stroke. His broken English was surprisingly good and he pointed us in the direction of Doctor Moray. I opened a metallic green door to find another Spartan room, this one housing a few diagrams of the eye, a faded eye chart, a sterile metal table, and an ancient ophthalmoscope. I sat in front of the ophthalmoscope, awaiting the doctor to examine my eye.

To my surprise, the man in the faded overalls sat on the other side. The man I took to be the janitor was actually Doctor Moray. Heather pulled out my medical documents from Craig, which outlined the chain of events that had led to my evacuation. Dr. Moray shoved these aside and told me to put my chin on the ophthalmoscope. The light went on and he muttered a few things to himself.

"You have an un…. (*pause*). An…Un…ulcer," he said matter-of-factly.

Relieved that he at least got my problem correctly diagnosed, I said yes.

"It n-n-needs to be removed," he said, slowly rising to his feet.

"Now? Here?" I exclaimed.

"N-n..n….(*pause*)…Now," he stuttered, beginning to wash his hands.

I looked again at the desolate room and at Heather. She smiled weakly. I ran through the corridors of my mind, seeking another option. I could bolt out the door…but to where? I still had *hours* until the flight to Tana and hours counted. And once I arrived in Tana, I did not know what I'd find there. Heather had no ticket, so I would be going alone.

"Fuck it," I thought. Let's make this happen.

I laid down on the metallic table. Heather came up and took my left hand in hers and pressed it against her chest.

"Be brave, baby," she said.

Popsicle sticks were placed in my mouth to bite for the pain, and numbing drops were put into my eye. I realized then that I would still be awake to watch a knife go into my eye. I heard the faint, sterile clicks of instruments being placed on a metallic plate.

"What kind of instruments does he have?" I asked.

I felt Heather turn around. She squeezed my hand tighter.

"Sweetheart, you really don't want to know," she answered.

Nothing prepares you for watching your own eye be cut open.

Nothing prepares you for an operation in an unlit, unpowered room in the frontier of the world.

And nothing prepares you for having it done by a doctor partially paralyzed by a stroke. The next step just happens.

"L...L...Look but duh...duh...*(pause)*...do not move your eye," commanded Doctor Moray. His nurse switched on a cheap flashlight.

"Jesus," I thought. "This place doesn't even have working lights."

White light flooded my eye. I saw the faded glint of a knife. I bit down hard, held my breath to keep absolutely still, and looked forward with the fury and passion to see again. The knife flicked once. Then again. And again. My eye recessed into my skull under the pressure. White pain seared my brain. Heather squeezed my hand tighter and tighter.

"All done," said Doctor Moray.

I sat up and looked at Heather.

I could see nothing out of my left eye.

TURN IT AROUND
SETTING FEEL'D GOALS

I never doubted that my vision would return. I took a long nap immediately after surgery and hours later, awoke in the dark. I flicked on my head-torch, and holding out both hands in front of me, I fully expected to see both. When reality returned the vision of only one arm reaching out, I did not despair. I embraced the present. I nudged Heather off the bed and took her out to dinner and to a nightclub. And nightclub is the best word I can think of for a shack powered by a generator that blasted the same five Malagasy pop songs over and over. The eye patch got looks and prompted questions. People bought us drinks spiked with *logagash*. We danced. The night became early morning and things got hazy. We shared laughs. I refused to be down on myself.

Heather left me the next morning to return back to London. I was left alone. I started a daily positive affirmation routine to encourage recovery. Despite no power in the town and the unbearable heat, I became fixated on training both my mind and my eye to a state of positive encouragement. Mind and body are one system so I trained aggressively to keep both healthy by exercising frequently and reading often.

Despite the difficulties, I considered the opportunities. I had been given the greatest challenge in my life. I could have chosen to sit and cry or thrive and defy. I chose the latter. There is an actual science to this, a method that separates those who see the glass always as half empty versus half full. Fortune in life benefits those who think in the latter. They are the ones who find opportunity in the direst of circumstances. When they fail, they get up, dust themselves off, and try again. Only this time, smarter.

In the late 1970s, John Grinder and Richard Bandler started working on a model of social interaction by studying geniuses in the field of communication and change. By observing renowned hypnotists, psychiatrists, and psychologists, they developed a model of helping people from all walks of life operate at their maximum potential. From failing athletes that suffered from doubt, chronic gamblers embroiled in debt, or people with 'incurable' stutters, they watched how language and thought patterns could turn these same people into Olympic athletes, productive citizens, and fluid speakers. This field is known as Neurolinguistic Programming (NLP) and it is a cornerstone of my ability to see clearly to this day, literally and figuratively.

As John Dau taught me, "Impossible is what you won't do." There is nothing outside of my grasp if my mind and body are completely aligned in focus.

This one *Turn-Around* of a chapter cannot capture the depth of NLP and the wondrous impact it has had on my life. Yet there are essential facets in this rich body of science that are vital to me, which cannot be intellectually separated from the fact that my vision did return. The return, and expansion, of my vision came slowly. My recovery taught me powerful lessons of opportunity, grace, and empathy. It was not easy and at moments, I nearly lost my sanity. Yet like the 23-mile marker of a marathon where you are so close and yet feel *so far*, where everything appears to be a limitless hell of exhausted despair, the emotional payoff at the finish line is closely within sight.

The profound idea behind NLP is that once one person can do it, others can follow. Here's how this worked in my situation:

1. Know what you want

Well-formed and visualized outcomes are the most vital aspect of ensuring we get what we want out of life. The human nervous system is goal-oriented and we tend to get what we focus on. For the blinded me, that meant waking up every morning and staring at an old Coca-Cola can with my good eye shut. The first few mornings were black. Then one day I saw the outlines of a shape shrouded in gray. By the end of the week, I made out the letters C-O-C-A against the familiar red hue. By week two, I was reading again.

2. Take things literally and set a "Feel'd Goal"

Humans and their minds are engineered not to want to lose things. Nature has taught us to crave having things that provide us food, security, and the approval of others. So it's neurolinguistically insane to say, "I want to lose weight" if you are overweight. That goal will *never* work as our minds focus on what it *doesn't* want rather than on what it *does* want to achieve. We need to have that positive, self-reinforcing image of the person we want to be and anchor it in our minds. So if you are trying to lose weight, you need to *see* yourself as a slim, athletic version of your future self. You must *feel* how good it will feel being that healthy you. Emotion is motion and motion is emotion. I refer to these as "Feel'd Goals," the ability to set within yourself the specific feelings that you want to feel once you reach your desired end state.

In the weight loss example, you must experience the same feeling in the present moment as in the future state of when the slim athletic body stands fit for attention in the mirror. Or in my case, seeing the full me in the mirror with fully regained eyesight that reflected back in both directions. In both cases, the feelings of confidence and satisfaction anchor the mind towards that "Feel'd Goal." And your literal language will guide you and help you move towards the target.

Examples:
"I lost my vision."
Wrong.

"I want a new way to see."

Better.

"I want to lose weight."

Wrong.

"I want to see myself as a runner."

Better.

3. "Feel'd Goal" your language

Notice how in the above example regarding my vision I wrote about wanting a "new way" to see in a vague manner. Perhaps my physical vision in my left eye would never return. So what? I could now see in a new way and have my mind opened up to new ideas and new challenges. I would have the ability to explore a new way of thinking about depth perception. So in either case, the "Feel'd Goal" of the confident state of me and the feeling of what it would feel like once I reached a certain end-state, with or without an eye-patch, would still manifest itself.

This same pattern of thought applies to nearly every interaction I have with myself or with other people. When meeting with close friends or family, I set a "Feel'd Goal" of 'happiness and comfort' for the phone call with Mom or the barbecue with friends. When emailing bad news to a client, I set a "Feel'd Goal" of 'calm under duress.' I set this goal in my mind before I even start writing that email so that when I must send the bad news, I convey confident language that highlights the least worst resolutions: yes, things are not great, that didn't work out as planned, and here is a plan to get things back on track.

I know my language, whether oral, written, or via body cues, will be guided by that end-state feeling I set in my mind and will shape itself naturally in whatever the means of communication I choose to deliver the message. Think about your last phone call with anyone. Do you remember what you were going to say before you said it? Of course you didn't. Thought and speech just manipulated itself in a stream of consciousness, just as it always does. However, your unconscious mind definitely played a role in how the conversation went since even if you were not actively thinking about your feelings, your unconscious mind certainly was steering the emotional content of your message.

So why leave it to chance? Language generation, word selection, and grammar are already subconscious functions. We cannot make them conscious functions. It's neurologically impossible to think about what and how you will say something when you are actively speaking. What we can do is set a feeling target to steer our unconscious mind's language production automatically towards that communication goal.

If you want fruitful relationships with others, go there first and set a "Feel'd Goal" of that outcome. The quickest way to get a smile from someone is to start distributing them first. So set a "Feel'd Goal" of:

- Happiness and gratitude when calling your parents or loved ones
- Confidence and trust when presenting your business to a prospective client
- Empathy and solace when learning that your colleague's friend just got killed

4. Motion is emotion.

None of that is easy and I have been through all of the above examples, many when my mind could not fathom capturing the feeling I wanted to convey. Sometimes it's hard to "go there first." My heart pounds when I need to get on stage to speak to an audience, and moving my mind to being comical and confident is always a challenge. While in isolated recovery, I often slipped into ruthless despair. Sometimes I work well into the wee hours of the night and wake up feeling like shit. It happens.

Yet when I get on that stage or walk into a room of people that I am coaching, I know I have to 'go there' first so value and impact are delivered. So I shift my state and "fake it till I make it." NLP practitioners call this a state-shift; the process of moving the current state of the way one person is thinking and feeling to another. Guiding people, or yourself, into these state-shifts is among the most powerful tools on the planet. Here are a few ways to get started:

- Motion is emotion. Get out of your seat and jump around. Stand up and with arms fully out-stretched; clap them together, fast and furious in cadence. Do push-ups. These quick motions will break you out of undesirable states.

- Adopt the posture of the confident to fake it till *you* make it. When I have to get on a stage in front of thousands of people, I am terrified. No matter how many times I do it, my mind is never at ease. Yet I know if that I hold a Superman-pose for two minutes—legs apart, arms on hips, head held high—then my body will increase Testosterone (a hormone associated with feelings of confidence) by fifteen percent, and reduce Cortisol (a hormone associated with feelings of stress or nervousness) levels by twenty percent.

- Hug a loved one for at least ten seconds. Hugging increases levels of the "love hormone" Oxytocin and reduces levels of Cortisol simultaneously. This dual benefit cascades into a series of longer-term benefits such as lower blood pressure and a calmer heart. Trust me, the hippies have it right on this one.

We will all be pushed into states of emergency during the course of our lives. Tragedies happen, homes are burned, and dear friends and family weave in and out. That is not in our control. Yet the framing of the story and the perception of the reality within the truth are ours to control. When the mind begins to understand how it can be controlled, working lockstep with a healthy body, then anything is possible. The blind can see and the ability to understand, share, and harmonize with the feelings of others maturates. At that point, we are all empowered to create a better and more just world.

CHAPTER 5

THE RECOVERY

At first glance, the Les Passage hotel passes as a fitting place to recover. A building of rectangular appearance, white in its color and simple in its presentation, its structure faintly resembles a hospital detox resort for the wealthy. Glance right; the effect is heightened when you consider the wooden lounge chairs pockmarking lush green vegetation sprouting red and pink flowers. Worn and choppy brick paths guide guests to their rooms. Turn left, the intoxicating fantasy continues, as Zebu steaks are served rare with crispy fried potatoes. Adding the final touch of glamorous recovery are the rather abundant number of overweight and elderly Frenchmen who pass by the common areas in unbuttoned white linen shirts, adorned with snake coils of gold on their necks and wrists, sunglasses shielding their eyes, and their intentions.

They are not here to recover from any addiction. The fat men are here to feed their foul desires. Shattering the illusion is the reality of prostitution in a desperately impoverished community. I can hear the faux giggles accompanying shuffling feet into closed rooms and pretend that each is benefitting from their temporary relationships.

~

These abstract thoughts permeated over the weeks that I laid alone in bed, eyes lightly covered with bandages and sweat gleaning down my back. Light shined just a bit into one eye while the other eye remained stubbornly in the dark.

I removed the bandages every few hours to place antibacterial drops in my eye to prevent further infection. I removed the bandages again a few hours later, and then left my room and pointed at the food I'd

been served. I could not yet speak Malagasy however; my fingers were fluent when in need so I gestured towards the rare, bloody steaks that had been served for blood red men. I returned with a plate of food and ate it in blinded and heated silence.

"God, it's hot here," I thought. The fan died the first afternoon when the power got cut. I laid in bed with the same shirt and shorts I'd been wearing for the past week. I took a cold shower from a bucket of water and laid back down in bed. The unseen hours passed by into days with no distinguishing markers of events. A fine boredom blanketed my mind, lulling my grey matter into new territories of thought; melancholy remembrances of times past appeared from the basement of my memory.

I dreamed and nightmares of blindness flooded my subconscious. I drifted to sleep every night confident in my belief that a haze of vision would appear the next time I woke. A few hours later, I bolted up in bed as the shocking knife of doubt pierced my heart again. I switched on the light and took off the bandages. The bad eye refused to see the light and I found myself thinking I would never fully see out of that eye again. A nearby prostitute laughed in the dark and I tried to go back to sleep. Day in, day out.

~

A week later and I could finally make out the letters of C-O-C-A-C-O-L-A when holding the bottle within a few inches of my face. The familiar cursive font of home was legible. I was healing. I saw Doctor Moray every other day and he was encouraged by my progress. I sat in the hospital and despite the fact I was often encouraged to cut in front of the line by the Malagasy population—I was the only white person that visited that clinic—I refused and waited for my turn. This caused awkwardness as people beckoned me to the front because I was holding up the line by not cutting. White privilege still reigned even when we tried to pretend it did not.

A routine began to form as time continued to pass. I needed habit to attain a level of achievement and find occupation during the long hot days. I started a workout regimen and ran in the mornings before the city began to bake. This was followed by push-ups, pull-ups, and various other strengthening exercises. I rinsed with cold water from a bucket. Then I took my breakfast with a French grammar book I had found at the Catholic Mission. Over eggs, I taught myself grammar of a language I did not know.

Je suis Amercain.

Nous sons Amercains.

And so it goes.

~

Next came my mid-morning laundry routine. I had few clothes, so I washed my precious pile incessantly in the bathroom with my trusty bucket. I hung the clothes meticulously in the common garden area. For the first time in my life, I began to do things slowly. Laundry ceased to be a chore. It became a wonder.

Lunchtime brought more grammar and exercises for the eye. Then I would depart the hotel to wander, to speak with locals, and to take part in their presence of being. I discovered what appeared to be a makeshift cinema: a wooded shack beckoning people inside. As I approached, I heard the distinct sounds of cinematic gunfire coming from within. Next to the swinging wooden door that barely kept its grasp on the shack, I saw a chalkboard that featured the name of the film being shown. Scrawled in English, I saw the word "Commando". I rushed in, paid a small fare, and watched an awful Chinese film about flying ghosts that bore absolutely no resemblance to the aforementioned Schwarzenegger masterpiece. The show ended after 30 minutes when the generator that powered the television ran out of gas. I made daily visits to this 'cinema' and despite their wide collection of DVDs, I had yet to see a film begin since no schedule was published nor see one actually end since they never seemed to have enough gas to power the generator for more than an hour.

I walked by scenes of poverty that used to rush by in blurs. I had seen these same scenes of daily struggle on my prior travels though only distantly from the windows of the bus that was taking me here and then there. Now, I walked alongside the people and became more immersed in their lives. Despite my limited vision, I was strikingly aware of being very present in the here and now. I could see more than ever before. The smells of garbage, the sight of raw meat baking in the sun, and the coarse feeling of the endless dirt in the air made me wonder how this poverty came to be and how it could be fixed.

My daily walks ended as the sun fell. Flickering kerosene lamps lighted my path home through the dense communities of the markets. After a week, the townspeople became restless as frequent brownouts fizzled into indefinite blackouts. I absorbed the mounting tensions as I walked the streets. The people of Tulear were not happy.

~

As my sight neared perfection, I got restless. The town was still blacked out and the frustration of the people was palpable. Riots began in the streets and tension manifested into action as the locals demanded change. They wanted power, light and opportunity in the darkness. The shouting and fighting in the streets kept me awake at night.

The violence turned my mind south and I carved out a plan to get back to the dive site. Simultaneously, I met a white man from Zimbabwe named Garth. Garth was an odd cat that also worked for Blue Ventures and arrived in Tulear after taking a weeklong break traveling the coast. He spoke thoughtfully and drank like a fish. He got violent when drunk, often attempting to break random objects (tables, pitchers, my face) with his prominent forehead. Still, he knew the lay of the land so we joined forces. We needed to urgently depart so we started sharing ideas about how to find transport. I made a hasty goodbye at Doctor Moray's office during one final visit and packed my bags to be ready for any transport opportunity headed south.

Word got around one evening that a local seafood distributor named Copefrito was sending a truck of frozen octopus south to a town within striking distance of the Blue Ventures project. Garth and I negotiated our way on board and under the tension of night, scampered into the back of the truck. We laid down on massive plastic containers of frozen octopods. To keep from freezing, I wrapped myself in a sleeping bag. The overnight journey brought no sleep, many passengers hopped on and off, and the sheer vinyl of my sleeping bag slid on the plastic like skates on ice. I ping-ponged against the iron railing at every frequent bump.

Morning came, the truck shuddered to a stop as I awoke. We climbed out the back and the drivers were nowhere in sight. I stared past the empty truck and saw a few huts poking out of the sandy beaches. We abandoned the truck and blearily marched towards the town already baking in the hot sun. Together, Garth and I located the local village chief with hopes that he could help furnish transport for the last 50 kilometers of our journey. We found the chief in the biggest hut and he was a man in mourning as one of his sons had just passed away that week. He assented to helping us and requested our humble presence at the funeral. We attended the ceremony with the grieving families, the chief thanked us for our empathy, and he then secured a boat transport for us to complete the journey. Two men approached me with torn shorts and open shirts. One had a briefcase that was handcuffed to his arm. It was full of shark-fins.

Our only ride back to a sustainable marine project was at the mercy of two men who profited from the cruel shark trade. We hopped on their boat and quietly rode away as we had no means—perhaps no want—to communicate. We picked up their wives along the way. Their dark faces were adorned with yellow paste in the shapes of beautiful circular flowers. The men lovingly exchanged affections with their kaleidoscope colored wives. I realized they were just families doing what they could to get by. There wasn't any other work in the area and one fin could bring $100USD. Who was I to judge their choice of occupation? I would see situations like this play out in my career over and over again. For example: indigenous communities in oil ravaged areas that worked for the same oil companies that polluted their land, or farmers that grew food for foreign companies that processed those same foods into higher value items that were sold right back to the farmer.

We pulled into a very familiar bay and I leaped off, skipping through the water, awaiting a celebratory party that never came. Our Blue Ventures base camp had been entirely deserted. Every hut was empty. Garth noted that the team must be out on a hike and trotted off without a glance to his hut at the other end of camp.

I stood alone and watched the shark fin traders putter off into the distance over the crystal blue water. I walked into my old hut and saw that my bed had been transformed into something resembling a grave. My long sleeve shirt and pants were laid out neatly on top of the sheets with arms crossed and legs outstretched. My straw hat and broken sunglasses were placed on my pillow. Next to this deflated version of myself was a sign written in crayon that said "Goodbye Bart". I started to cry as I felt that an older version of Bart had indeed died. Yet like all deaths, something could be reborn. A chance to start something new, something good.

I awaited the return of my colleagues by taking shelter in a shaded dive boat. If today was a hiking day, that meant a day full of diving the next morning which required cleaning the boats before sunset. I knew they would find me here and so I hid my backpack under the bed to properly prepare the element of surprise.

But it would be hours before the team returned from their hiking expedition, and hours before I would hear Craig cry out, "Hang on lads, there's someone in that boat!" while hugging my sunburned shoulders.

Until that moment came, I considered what my return to the developed world would look like. I recalled how during my high school days in Champaign we got hit with a massive ice storm that knocked out power for a week. Though our home lacked power, our family drove to various restaurants to find heat and food. We were able to watch films in eye-popping clarity at a massive multiplex. The high school had an industrial sized generator to keep students learning. After six days, the municipal government fixed the broken power lines. Life continued on in comfortable complacency. I wondered why certain places worked and others didn't. I contemplated why some people saw this mind-boggling poverty of humankind and then deliberately chose not to exert human kindness. I wondered if I would be any different once I returned home. Would I be strong enough to not turn a blind eye to the poverty I had experienced?

I bobbed up and down in the dive boat. I wondered whether I could truly empathize with understanding the concept of lack. Or if I could fully embrace the meaning of poverty. Or if I could "get" not having choices in life. I struggled with the unfairness of it all.

I don't know really.

I just sat there in the sun, looking up and thinking.

TURN IT AROUND
LEAD WITH EMPATHY

When I started my first nonprofit, my mother claimed that I was crazy since 'normal' people start foundations *after* they become wealthy. After all, Bill Gates did not give away billions of dollars until he had earned billions of dollars. So how would I get to a place where I gave away millions of dollars to those living in extreme poverty while having only a few thousand in savings? How would the connections and networks form that would actualize my philanthropic intentions into something that mattered?

It began with a resolution to act. To build steadily but not necessarily immediately. My conditioning towards purpose began under the guise of recovery in the humidly dank Les Passages hotel. While the loose walls tried to confine my clouded vision, the teeming poverty of Tulear expanded my thinking outward. I could no longer push this inequality aside. My vision opened. A small plot of land with great people that continually struggled to get on their feet became clear in my widening line of sight.

Lack.

Scarcity.

Hunger.

Frustration.

Resolve.

Determination.

Loss of dignity.

More lack, more frustration.

Repeat.

My recovery in Tulear immersed me in the challenging waters of economic poverty. Here, hunger gave rotting meat in the sun monetary value and dark kerosene burned light and lungs simultaneously. This was a place that robbed the dignity of noble people faced with choices that only decreased their opportunities in life. Cast away and isolated by a severe power outage, my vision expanded as I observed people struggling in the context of their lives. They endured a daily struggle for clean water, the endless queues for basic healthcare, and the saintly patience of getting what they needed just so they could get by.

Everything happens for a reason, the universe unfolds exactly as it should. Thrust into darkness and entirely disconnected from the world, I had countless hours of solitude to dwell on the 'why' behind my accident and my long recovery. In those reflective moments, the hours were hard and minutes dripped like beads of sweat. Darkness prevailed. The worst part was the guilt of asymmetric information. I knew I would be okay. I could literally *see* my progress. Yet that information remained trapped within the walls, as I could not relay my recovery to those who loved me. Only faint details of my evacuation had reached my friends and family. Imagine it from my parents' perspective: your son had an accident, he's been evacuated, and due to severe weather, we cannot figure out where he is. Sorry.

In my head, I figured no one actually knew where I was in the world. Thinking of my parents, I suffered both mental and physical pain. I struggled. Eventually, I learned to give the struggle meaning and defined a purpose within the experience. No doubt, my physical recovery stimulated this train of thought and helped cast light into the darkness of my mind. I knew I would eventually find somewhere with power to send the quick and powerful email of, "I'm okay mom". Slowly, I began to strip away the 'me' from the 'why me' that persisted in my selfish lamentations. I realized my time there was temporary and this was not the case for the rest of Tulear. I saw all those other damaged eyes waiting for treatment at Doctor Moray's clinic. I knew their prognosis was of a more permanent nature. Their suffering was not temporary. It was cyclical. I could leave and move beyond. They could not.

Millions of these moments permeated my brain. They cast a deeper sense of empathy within my being. It compelled me to act even though I only had intentions, not even ideas, on what to do. Eventually, I figured out how to catalyze those millions of moments into millions of dollars and channel that energy to make a dent in the global international development sector. The most effective lever I could find were local leaders like Doctor Moray, those embedded social entrepreneurs living in marginalized communities who would cease at *nothing* to improve their community. Then came getting them the resources they needed to thrive. Then things grew like wildfire. Then somehow things went wrong.

But that all comes later. First came empathy, the act of observing and engaging myself into the experiences of others who lost the ovarian lottery. Poverty that I poorly conceptualized in my brain became a reality I could not turn away from. My vision physically and metaphysically grew during this time of healing and solace. The solution to all of life's great challenges and problems began with this step. If one masters the vital yet profoundly complex skill of building empathy, any challenge is surmountable.

Fortunately, a framework exists wherein nearly anyone can learn the mechanics of empathy and wield that power to change the course of their lives and of the communities around them. This framework is called human-centered design (HCD), a design and management framework that develops solutions to problems by involving the human perspective in all steps of the problem-solving process.

Unwittingly, my recovery set me on the HCD path to start tackling the immense challenge of extreme poverty. Made popular by global design companies like IDEO (who designed many of Steve Jobs' creations including the mouse, the iPhone, and other game-changing applications) and the Stanford dschool, this framework is a vital method of building great products, projects, and companies. HCD is a creative approach to solving the world's most difficult problems by putting people first and empathizing with their needs to help deliver value. First proven in the commercial sector (IDEO has over a 1,000 patents that are used by billions of people), the framework has demonstrative impact to the social sector.

Visually, the framework looks like this:

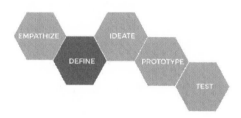

The foundation is empathy, a place where we immerse ourselves with users, the people who need our product or service. It continues with defining the problems that afflict their lives and then ideating a solution or product that could help improve their wellbeing. Rather than taking lots of time to develop this product or service, just get it out there. Make a rapid prototype and get it in the hands of your users. Start, fail, learn, and repeat. Test and iterate over and over and keep adding features that make your impact greater and greater.

My foray into empathize mode was forced upon me. Stripped of books and the infinite content catered by the Internet, I absorbed the daily lives of people who lived in extreme poverty. Before Tulear, I hauled my backpack to over 50 countries across five continents. Yet I moved at such speeds that I often neglected the wonders of immersion. I listened to music on bus rides to wane out the noise of choked up diesel engines, crying children, and squealing livestock. I buried my nose in books while waiting in lines. Like most backpackers, I witnessed selfishly. I experienced selfishly. And when things became challenging because of delays, I escaped to the comforts of home by reading, hearing, or watching something, anything, that could take me away.

In Tulear, a town with no power, all outside content removed itself from the equation. Batteries could not be charged and films could not be screened. There were no books in languages I could understand. The only story to watch was reality and the only song to hear was the din and jabber of the streets.

The most remarkable discoveries of this empathy journey were the unremarkable acts of humanity and goodwill. Every day I witnessed selfless and circular sharing of resources directly caused by the scarcity within their communities. Both at the dive site in Madagascar, where we only ate beans, rice and fish every day for every meal, and in Tulear, where people struggled daily to make ends meet, I realized how much of our true nature as human beings depends on sharing. How our humility to help others makes us all thrive. Ironically, this selfless giving occurred most frequently in the communities that had so little to give. From the glasses the clinic crafted gratis during my recovery to the French grammar book given to me by a sympathetic nun, there was something more grandiose than mere hospitality in those gestures of kindness. Sharing is no accident. It's how we came to thrive as a species.

Our brains actually became wired to share over eons of evolution. As anthropologists recognize, our nomadic ancestors knew full well their survival depended upon sharing. One day the nomadic family had plenty; their pastures were vivid and green. Travelers came and in their spirit of plenty, the family opened their doors and shared their resources. Soon the family's resources dwindled as the pasture faded so they pulled up their stakes and sought out greener lands further down the plain. They moved in steadfast faith that doors would become open to them as they traversed the road to better wellbeing.

I witnessed this hidden miracle of evolutionary empathy firsthand. Upon my journey home from Tulear, I took the long way home with my new friend Kyle Miller. We first headed north to Poland and then made our way east to San Francisco, passing through Mongolia. There, we witnessed evolution's gift of sharing in action by living with a nomadic family. Like their ancestors had done for centuries, their extended family built yurts in the vast plains to raise animals and grow crops.

Kyle and I had commissioned a guide in the capital city of Ulanbataar to find a family that would willingly take in strangers for a few days. In exchange for housing us, we would work alongside them. After hours of driving off road in our Isuzu Forerunner, we found a family that would take us into their daily lives. After perfunctory introductions were translated through our guide, the hardy looking family patriarch welcomed us. He stood alongside his wife, his three curious children, and various members of their extended family. They walked us towards three brightly colored yurts, each one being the size of a single car garage. After a brief exchange with his wife, they decided Kyle and I would sleep in their yurt and they offered up *their own bed*. They would not hear of any other arrangement and they refused money with a hearty laugh. The patriarch and his wife slept on the floor in their eldest sons' tent during our stay.

Upon our departure, their hospitality made me want to reciprocate. As a token of my gratitude, I gave the patriarch my prized knife. I will never forget his shy grin with a snappy shake of his head upon receiving my meager gift. I remember how utterly sensational it felt to give something away and I reveled in that privilege. It felt *so good* to give and in this moment, I began to understand.

This nomadic father, like his close ancestors, knew that one-day scarcity would return. Weather would change, pastures would fade, and times would get tough. And so his family would travel onwards while seeking shelter and food. Pay it forward, whenever and wherever you can, so a bed will always be made available when your time of need appears. This pattern of sharing has been the global bedrock of human development for the past 100,000 years of Homo Sapiens' existence. Why? Because that *so good* feeling is no accident. We are biologically engineered to share as Mother Nature gives us a vitally important dose of Oxytocin—the same chemical in the brain that bonds a mother to her child—each time we do so.

This biological phenomena was formulated in our brains so we could thrive as a species. Giving and sharing feels naturally good because a community can achieve more than an individual. This is the reason we have thrived as a species: our ability to cooperate with others in tandem with a neocortex that empowers us with critical thinking is our supreme advantage on Earth.

Yet we in the developed world, steeped in excess, perversely build bigger fences and sophisticate our security to drive *Others* away. We are less inclined to share. The other primal instinct of our brain—fear of the unknown—hampers our ability to thrive as a community. We push empathy down and fail to understand the root causes of inequity.

For me, no more of that. Madagascar changed me and life hammered home a point upon my return. A new addiction formed. I have taken a lot of drugs in my life to relax, escape, and to explore, but mostly for selfish pleasure. It was fun though that fun fades. Yet here was the powerful drug of giving that continually grew in impact and reciprocated its gifts in an upward spiral of growth. Giving is *by far* the *best drug* that I have ever taken. It's a beautiful addiction that reinforces the greater bonds of community and helps us thrive.

With that seed of empathy planted in my brain, I returned to San Francisco to enter a new phase of life, one that would bring a state of wellbeing I had never thought possible. I left as a traveler and returned with a mission.

CHAPTER 6

STARTING SOMETHING GOOD

The expedition in Madagascar draws to a close, a new journey begins. I travel through Uganda, Rwanda, Cambodia, and Mongolia, continue seeing things in a new and austere light. Ideas slowly take hold as moments of inspiration wedge themselves into my being. Eventually, I stretch my travel budget far beyond its means. It's time to start something and become someone who doesn't glide above responsibility. I crash land in San Francisco on a foggy winter morning. It's Tuesday. No plans, no job, and no place to live. Just a dreamer with a backpack, walking down the gray streets with a new vision in life. It's a situation that could use a few favors and having been a nomad before, I am comfortable with the challenges.

I email J.J., a close friend that I met in my Accenture days and ask for a couch to crash on while I sort out life, work, housing, etc. As a fellow traveler, he knows the patterns of acclimatizing back to the real world and generously offer his couch in his tiny apartment. Still, I need to move fast and waste no time. My savings are dwindling and I am thousands of dollars in debt.

I need to figure out any means necessary to make life work again. I am determined to simply 'make it happen'. The only thing is that I am not quite sure what 'it' is, how that would exactly 'happen', and how long that may take. It's time to shake my networks like a can of soda, and start a chain reaction that bubbles ferociously and then see what fizzes up to the top.

I venture out into the fog and start shaking with anxious determination.

With no time to plan, the only course I had left was to get up and move, form a story, meet people, and get the word out. I needed to move fast, make motion, and unleash confidence while stifling panic. I figured I had slightly less than two weeks to find a job and a place to live. My ignorance of San Francisco's real estate market kept me in a positive mindset. I held fast to unbridled optimism and determination.

That Wednesday, I started emailing friends from my bed-couch, hoping to get myself invited to holiday parties so I could build out a network while enjoying the festive December season. On Thursday, I got word that a few Accenture friends were having a holiday party in the Marina the next evening. I instantly accepted and began a Craigslist hunt to find a place to live. I found a few places and then spent the rest of the day scheduling appointments while getting my credit report ready. I gave no concern to the stories of waiting hours before the appointment to be the first in line, having thousands of dollars in cash on your person for the first month's rent, or other insane acts that one had to perform while finding an apartment in San Francisco. I just focused on executing appointments.

The party on Friday felt like a warm hug; my relationships from my Accenture days remained intact and vibrant. The atmosphere was charged with the cheer of the season and the variety of supplements that fueled ambitious yuppie metro youth. While a bit stoned and mildly drunk, I met a recruiter starting a new consulting branch of a company called Slalom Consulting and loosely gabbed my way into an interview on Monday. I woke up Saturday with a mild headache and headed to the beach to clear my thoughts. While gazing on the water, I got a text from my couch-landlord J.J. that the next-door neighbor was moving out in January. A one-bedroom for $1,100 a month, way under market rate, across the hall from a dear friend, was going to be available precisely when I needed it.

I snapped my phone closed and scratched my head with both hands. I had been in San Francisco four days, had found a place to live, and had a solid lead on a great job that would have me earning six figures. I stared at the sand.

It didn't feel fair.

I felt bothered.

~

Two weeks later, I jiggled the keys into my barren apartment. I secured the job without hesitation or negotiation. I had planned for none of this. The situation simply occurred as I created action around me. I planned so little for this settlement process that on my first night, I did not know where to sleep. I opened my suitcase and rumpled dirty clothes together to craft a makeshift bed on top of the hardwood floor. The next morning, I ate yogurt with my fingers. After seven years of being on the road oscillating between being a traveler and management consultant, I owned very few things. I had no bed and no spoon.

The thought of establishing roots somewhere thrilled me yet I spent a lot of time alone. I stared out the window where I had a full view of the largest car wash operation in the city. I watched hundreds of immigrants washing new cars all day long. I listened to the BBC World Report from my laptop, and fixated on a series called *Living on a Dollar Per Day*. The stories of the daily struggles with poverty now only flowed into my ivory tower via a shiny new laptop that I got gratis from work. The memories of life lived in severe austerity kept burning and the light refused to fade.

I had grown up listening to these stories on the news though now they felt different. They resonated deeper and I carried their words with me as thoughts of guilt weighed my steps forward heavily. While billions endlessly toiled for scraps, I landed a six-figure job in one day of mini-marathon interviews and secured a great apartment.

And I had a loving circle of friends and family that formed a core support network around my life. Yet anxious doubt lingered, sitting like a hungry ghost in my mind. I felt odd about sharing my growing feelings of uncertainty with the ambitious, successful, and pretty youth that pervaded my professional life. I had every measure of success beaming from the exterior, yet the interior felt empty and sad. I had the *what* and *how* of life all sorted out, but the *why* was entirely missing.

I felt unhappy.

So I emailed Kyle, the only person who I thought would understand. Despite not having seen each other for months, he responded instantly and we booked a date that would forever change our lives.

~

We met over coffee around 10am, early for the Berkeley crowd. After reminiscing about our various global adventures, our discussion pivoted to people that had profoundly affected our lives. I kept coming back to Doctor Moray. I was astounded by the miracle of it all and the long odds of finding such a talented leader in such a remote region.

Kyle relayed thoughts about a journey he made while studying abroad in South Africa. While in Cape Town, Kyle began a lively exchange of emails with a man named Peter Luswata, who he had met on an Ugandan internet messaging board focusing on nonprofit work. Their conversation lit a fire and Kyle took a step most people would consider unthinkable: he went to learn more. He longed to hear this man's stories directly, and to listen to his thoughts and embrace his vision. So he bought a plane ticket and flew to Kampala. Just like that. It was a seemingly random decision that would alter the course of his life for the better.

Kyle spent six weeks in a small apartment with Peter's wife and two daughters sharing heaping plates of banana mush, roasted pork, and many cups of tea. Peter shared a vision with Kyle about everything that was wrong with international development and everything that could be made right. At the time, Peter was working for Mercy Corps, an international charity whose mission was to alleviate poverty by helping people build productive communities. He was the second employee of their Kampala office and grew it to a two hundred-person workforce. His entrepreneurial spirit made him eager to break off on his own and start his own model development farm. This farm would be a living and breathing farming laboratory where farmers could tangibly learn sustainable farming methods to grow healthy and organic food and earn more money.

Our wild discussions spilled out to the street. We were intoxicated by our prospective thoughts of giving. Even *thinking* about the act of philanthropy made me feel good again, the addiction ran that deep. And like any drug, we wanted to take more and more so we could give back more and more. As Kyle was on winter break from Claremont

McKenna College and I had yet to start actual client work at Slalom, we had the time.

We listened to more episodes of *Living on a Dollar Per Day* to derive clues from the people who were suffering from poverty first-hand. We blindly grasped to find some lever we could pull that could help out. We learned how small holder farmers, individuals who own very small plots of land and grow subsistence crops, relying almost exclusively on family labor, in Kenya received donated seeds from Monsanto to start their farms yet had no fertilizer to grow them. We learned how one Cambodian considered the purchase of mosquito nets to be the greatest investment he made for his family. With the nets, his family did not succumb to malaria or dengue, which in turn, gave them precious time to work more, learn more, and increase their opportunities in life. The stories covered a wide array of societal ills: lack of food, no access to healthcare, no schools, and unsafe communities that were breeding grounds for violent factions. Though lacking proper structure and guidance, we embarked upon a path of the human centered design process from afar. Not ideal but we had to start somewhere.

Our ability to truly delve into observing, questioning, and designing about why affected individuals suffer and how they perceive poverty were obviously limited. You cannot interact with a radio show. Exacerbating this fundamental fault, we heard these distant radio voices from the bubble of Northern California, an area exorbitantly bountiful in many regards. Still, we felt that we needed to try *something*.

No first step is perfect. We all wobble. Whether it's the first actual step we take as a toddler, pushing our wonky weight away from our mother's fingers, to metaphorical steps we take as an entrepreneur, the result is the same. The movements are clumsy, full of bobbles, gropes, and the wind milling of the arms as we fight forces that are fully incomprehensible to our ignorant minds. The first step is just about staying up and getting the foot down. The next is simply falling over. Then you repeat, failing forward, over and over until you begin to walk.

With no idea where to start, we took our first step and decided to start our own organization to help people in struggling communities.

Historically sealed in our opening clause to attain our tax-deductible status from the IRS we wrote the following:

> *"The planned purpose of Groundwork Opportunities (GO) is to provide direct and immediate relief to Third World countries on a small operational scale. GO will provide goods, services, and funds to individuals and organizations as part of each project. A given project will operate out of a certain Third World country that is in desperate need of food, medical supplies, and aid."*

Today, these sentences read opaque and offensive. The term 'Third World' is demeaning; a Cold War era term to categorize capitalists from communists. Such words carry a weighted stereotype of being universally 'undeveloped' from a strict economic and political circumstance. Additionally, this mission gave no voice to the local leaders that would become foundational in our work. A decade later, these intentions offer no value outside of a definition of intention: a thing intended, an aim or plan. They mark a place where we acted. Like our first, then second, then third, and then fourth iteration of our mission or our logo or our website, we had to begin somewhere. Then we continually redesigned our approach as we grew.

With a documented purpose in hand at the onset of 2007, Kyle and I each cut a check for $1,000 and started filing forms and submitting signatures. We wrote articles of incorporation, chartered by-laws for management, figured out a name, and formed a board of directors. The board was comprised of just the two of us since we had no idea what we were doing.

Most startups use lawyers to draft all of this yet we did not have the cash for such services. The application fee for the IRS alone was $750, about one-third of our entire investment. The only thing we had was our determination so whenever we got lost in the shadows of administration, we leveraged our stories to find help. Tara Navarro, the wife of my December couch-landlord J.J., worked as a paralegal at a law firm and generously donated all the templates with a concise one-pager on how and where to file. Megan Vesely, a friend at Accenture donated her time by doing what management consultants do best: finding existing templates that worked for others, scrubbing out their names and ideas and then replacing them with the client's name. Six months later, we received this terse announcement from the United States government:

"We are pleased to inform you that upon review of application for tax-exempt status we have determined that you are exempt from Federal income tax under section 501(c)3 of the Internal Revenue Code."

When Kyle and I met over that fateful coffee, I had no idea what the alphanumeric code of 501(c)3 even meant. And in less than six months' time, I found myself cofounding and owning one.

With a formal seal of approval, we moved on to our next challenge: raising money. Even with our scrappy approach, we had a little less than $1,000 left to actually begin the process of creating the remaining infrastructure of an organization. Spending time between university classes, Kyle learned how to code and publish a website. I spent nights and weekends wrangling people to help design logos, teach me how to raise money, and then ultimately invest those dollars to have a meaningful impact. We debated over phone calls regarding where to start, and weaned down our choices to places where we knew people, or to those who could help us identify local leaders that needed resources to implement their own projects.

In the end, we selected Ghana. Long celebrated as the model for African progress and development she was among the first African nations to gain independence in March of 1957. Ghana is also among the rare African nation states steeped in the values of true democracy. Though her initial independence was rocky, pockmarked by coups and the grabbing of power, she found an extraordinary leader in the early 1980s in Jerry John "J.J." Rawlings. Though Rawlings attained power by a coup d'état, he went on to legalize political parties and organized presidential and parliamentary elections. And once that was all in place, J.J. Rawlings took the ultimate act of leadership and stepped down.

Though popular during his final second term as president, he took the rare African leader's path of allowing democracy to flourish by stepping aside from power.

Through personal connections, we found an early supporter in Dr. Valerie Yankey-Wayne, a Ghanaian residing in Canada who worked for the United Nations. She navigated us towards internet posting boards where various community-based organizations (CBOs) posted their ideas and needs. We looked over their proposals and modest websites from afar. The sheer number of locally based organizations were staggering and our first step to organize all this information began with the principles of management consulting. First, we created a score-carding system (a matrix of metrics to evaluate projects) and ranked the top 20 organizations we were most interested in learning about. To that list, we sent each candidate a naïve email that, in essence, stated the following:

Hello,
If we gave you $1,000 to help your community, how would you invest it?
Thanks,
Bart and Kyle

Nearly everyone responded and we reviewed his or her detailed proposals and plans. We were wary of sites that appeared to be too slick as this indicated that they were already functioning to some degree. We also avoided any indication of religious proselytizing. We wanted to help provide food, water, and education, not Bibles. We debated the merits of each respondent and ranked their responses on our matrix. Those with detailed financial budgets were given high marks and those that responded with fawning notes praising our nobility were given low marks.

We scrutinized ideas by looking for something that would create opportunities for people to work on the ground and that took the long-term view of sustainable development. Skype calls were made and email chains grew. Things had begun. Ideas churned and were inspired. We needed to get out there. Nothing could ever supplant the ability to work directly with the local leaders so dedicated to improving their communities. Yet we were both broke, with no money for the projects and no money for our flights.

So we threw a party.

~

A public forum is a vital method to get *that* idea out of your head and into the discerning fray of society. Whether a meeting, party, lecture, or just a conference call, getting a specific date and time where you can face people directly forces you to get things buttoned up. While people are more scared of public speaking than death, it is, by far, the best way to test an idea. To connect. To inspire. To give the idea wobbly legs, potentially even crooked wings. You may be afraid to fall though, my dear, what happens if you fly?

Once we concluded that we needed to visit the four best contenders from our ad hoc email campaign and then award them money that we did not have, it became clear we needed help from others. We had a mere two hundred dollars left from our initial investment. Promises had been made and promises needed to be kept so we committed to a date for our trip to Ghana, and then began to reverse engineer everything that needed to happen to make that worthwhile. Hence, a party.

From that point forward, all my conversations at work and at play were about this event and our trip. I made the story infectious; underlining its purpose, as I had little idea, and virtually no budget, how to actually stage an event. I spoke about it to my colleagues at Charles Schwab and Slalom Consulting. I managed to slip it into every conversation I had. I added a link to the event page on every email I sent. My cubicle neighbor offered his jazz band to play live music. Slalom encouraged clients to donate products or gift certificates for our silent auction. Another co-worker at Schwab offered to match the first $1,000 raised. A new friend and excellent photographer named Peter Prato offered to shoot the event and donate exclusive prints of his work. Kyle and I drove to Napa, posing as tourists on tasting tours to negotiate donated cases of wine in person with any vintner that would listen. I hit the pavement on the weekends by visiting every restaurant in my neighborhood of NoPa, a neighborhood where any given square block can house up to sixteen restaurants. Hours were spent pitching, failing, re-pitching, and then learning the art of the close.

I went to every business with pre-written letters, signed by me, the Executive Director of a non-existent yet an up-and-coming organization. I designed the letterhead myself and printed out 250 copies. While utterly meaningless in any official capacity, the physical letter bolstered my authority, as it became a makeshift badge certifying what was otherwise just an idea in our heads. Letters can also get passed around. And it worked. Eventually, I went to enough businesses that the NoPa neighborhood association called me and offered me the opportunity to speak at their next meeting with NoPa business owners. Whether the word had gotten out or the local business owners were tired of seeing this demanding Polack loitering at their doorstep, I didn't care. I spoke. The gift certificates came in and we got about $10,000 worth of goods to auction off.

Another Accenture friend by the name of Ojay Malonzo donated his community space in a flashy high-rise in San Francisco that came stocked with a full kitchen and glassware for up to 100 people. This was a huge donation since large event spaces in San Francisco usually start around $1,500. Everything began to click.

Eighty people came to 'Black Star Shining', our first ever GO event. Nearly one-quarter of the guests were volunteers of the fundraiser, making the gathering more of a potluck. We cooked the food ourselves, poured the wine, shot the photos, played the music, and people gave what they could, which turned out to be a lot.

Amazingly, this first family of supporters helped us raise nearly $15,000 that evening for a series of promises and pledges of what me *might* do with those funds. In reality, all we had was a geographical point on where to begin and a few leads that we hoped would pan out. Yet we had purpose, drive, and tenacity. This crucial first group of supporters resonated in that purpose by trusting us as people dedicated to their beliefs, not in our depth of experience or strength in rigorous development methodologies. A remarkable lesson had been planted, one that would not sprout fully until years to come: people give to people, not organizations.

Though future GO events would evolve to raising ten-times this amount in a single evening, their meaning flutters in comparison to the virginal experience of our first event. From the bottom of my heart, thank you to Kyle Miller, Megan Vesely (you found my socks!), Peter Prato, Alex Chassy, Pat Meade, Marius Zaugg, Charmane Crain, Ojay Malonzo, Jeff Ellis, Kate Richardson, and Cynthia Miller for helping build this first crucial stage for GO.

All we had to do now was demonstrate impact and transform this money into tangible achievement.

And so off to Ghana we went.

TURN IT AROUND
BIAS TOWARDS ACTION

I penned a lot of this book on planes and in particular, the sleek interiors of Virgin Airlines. Legendary entrepreneur Richard Branson founded Virgin Airlines, now owned by Alaska Airlines. As he tells the story, it all began with a cancelled flight. There's Richard, already successful and wealthy beyond comparison, when he is told that his flight from Puerto Rico to Miami was cancelled. Richard being Richard did not accept the status quo and simply chartered a plane to take him home.

And then he did something extraordinary. He turned around and saw all the other stranded passengers in the terminal. Those who did not possess the ability or finances to simply summon a plane. He empathized with their plight. And so Richard grabbed a pen, jotted down the words "Virgin Airlines" on a piece of paper and started selling tickets at cost to the remaining passengers. The elated group cheered him on their flight back home. The next day, he ordered a used 757 and a $2.7 billion dollar company was born.

Richard did what all entrepreneurs do: he had a *bias towards action*. Start. Act. Fail. Learn. Repeat. The benefit of having nothing in the beginning is that little can be lost. Set aside pride, beef up on humility, and jump in. Start small and grow it bigger. If you are passionate about a subject, start writing a blog about it. Figure out the minimum effective level to get something out there into the world and *just do it.*

While these words sound painfully obvious, it's one of the biggest hurdles that any entrepreneur can encounter, as there is huge societal pressure to "get it right the first time" or "show when complete". While prudence is necessary to convey competence, it should not stop you from acting. Nothing will ever be "complete". The sheer definition of that word prevents so much true action from occurring when it comes to launching a product, service, or game-changing nonprofit idea. Nothing will ever be "done" since the only thing everything can be is better. Just get it out there.

Undoubtedly, Kyle and I did things that were painfully naïve when we first started. We made promises that we could not immediately fulfill. We duplicated efforts that already existed in the nonprofit market. We hovered towards white man savior complex, a self-serving rationale that made us arrogant and patronizing in our belief that we had all the answers. We made mistakes. Yet we *did* and so we *learned.* Where we lacked in ability, we made up for with grit and determination to back-fill areas of responsibility.

By having a bias towards action, you are able to immediately start testing out your ideas with a lean startup concept called a minimum viable product (MVP). In Sir Richard's case, all he needed was a plane to rent, a pen, and a sheet of paper to launch an entire airline. In our case, we had a three-page website with a scrappy and unclear mission statement. We sent vague emails to offer money we did not have. We staged an event to raise money for half-baked ideas. We started, got things moving, and those actions led to reactions, which kept things growing.

By distilling an idea down to a MVP, you move towards action that will generate failure. And failure is the gold mine of learning lessons that will help strengthen your product or service. If you want to become a chef or own a restaurant, start by hosting dinner parties at your home. Home too small? Offer to cook at a friend's place or offer your dinner parties as gifts to friends or family. Work in the evenings? Volunteer to cook breakfast at a homeless shelter. Make it a habit and figure out the most distilled version of what you wish to create. Then fail and iterate.

If your curiosity piques on something or if there is a certain idea that fascinates you to no end, take a bias towards action and get your ass off the couch. Whether you desire to start your own event-planning company, become a baker, or launch the next big thing, here is a list of ideas to get the ball rolling:

Visualize the idea. If you want to make sure that other people understand what you intend to do, you need to visualize the ideas to drive the point home. By visualizing your ideas with drawings, icons, and a few words, you will instantly distill an idea into a MVP. This will not be easy as any fool can make a simple idea complex and only true genius can make the complex idea simple.

Write the idea down. Get the thoughts out of your head and onto paper. Now.

Simplify your idea by visually drawing it on a napkin. A picture is worth a thousand words and people are visually oriented. If you are stuck on how to make a word into an image, use Google Image search to see what images are returned with your words. Here is the napkin drawing for the concept of our nonprofit:

Design a potential logo and share it with friends for feedback. If you don't have design skills, ask a friend that loves doodling or is into graphic design to help.

Share your work. One of the most daunting aspects of entrepreneurship is determining how you will actually physically make things happen. But it's important to know that you don't have to do everything by yourself. Perhaps in the design section you already jumped ahead and enlisted a friend to help you design a logo. If not, it's time to get others involved by sharing your ideas and passions. Here's how:

- Start writing a blog about your idea or area of curiosity.
- Tell stories about your idea to friends and family.
- Share pictures on Instagram and Facebook.
- Go to events and meet-ups to meet others with similar interests.
- Offer your time and volunteer.

Learn and iterate from everything above. Here's how:

- Take classes to learn more about the subject. Ask questions so folks in the class are aware of your purpose.
- Finished that class? Now start teaching others to push you even further toward your goal of mastering your craft and purpose.
- Speak at a conference about your failures so that others can learn from you. It's never too early to share.
- Find a mentor in your field of purpose and ask if he/she can guide you.
- Join on-line forums and actively post with thoughts and insightful questions. Get your opinion out there.
- Embrace failure. Be entirely open to the lessons, as they will teach you far more than any successes.
- Nothing reverberating? Go back to the top and start again.

The quicker you put this book down and start the above, the better. The list of next steps will begin to flow naturally through your work and you will be amazed at how quickly reactions will start to occur. In other "words":

CHAPTER 7

THE HUMMINGBIRDS

The first six months clicked by quickly. We received our accreditation and turned $2,000 into $15,000. And here we were, lulled into a self-satisfied stupor, sitting in San Francisco Airport on a crisp Friday morning, calmly eating a sausage and egg breakfast before our flight to Accra, Ghana.

We sip coffee and lazily thumb through emails. With a sigh and a stretch, we pay the bill and stroll to board our plane. As we draw closer to the gate, I wonder why the boarding area appears so empty.

We approach the desk to verify we are in the right place.

The gate agent stares at us in disbelief.

He's been calling our names for the past hour.

Our bags are en route to Ghana.

We are not.

Our first official GO trip and somehow we missed the damn flight.

And so, our inaugural voyage began with pleading for another way to get halfway around the world. The weary agent routed us through New York to intercept another flight heading to Accra. The catch was that our connection time would be only fifteen minutes and they would not hold the plane. We had no choice and took the flight to get 3,000 miles closer.

We arrived into a massive thunderstorm that grounded every flight leaving from JFK. Though Kyle miraculously confirmed us on the next connection to Accra, nothing would fly out that evening. Bodies of weary travelers were piled on top of chairs, cushions, and tucked into dark corners to get rest. Stranded for the evening, we asked about hotel room rates near the airport. Delta handed out nice informational cards to all passengers stating that they could not control the weather and would not pay for our rooms. They did, however, offer a "distress" rate for all passengers with a listing of hotels and phone numbers to call.

I called the hotel and was quoted our "special distress rate" of $795 for a double room. I concurred that the rate was indeed 'distressing'. She failed to find the humor in my remark and hung up.

The airport was stifling from the humidity of the storm and the off gassing of thousands of delayed human bodies strewn about the terminal. Rejecting this sauna of humanity, we decided to sleep under the stars since no more rain was in the forecast. We purchased eight *New York Posts*, a stapler, some snacks, and headed outside. We made the newspapers into bedding, stapled the rest into makeshift sleeping bags, and settled under a large bush near the airport car park. Newspapers make for great insulation should you ever need to sleep on the street. We awoke at dawn to the sound of a man pissing next to our heads and headed back to the throng of passengers. We boarded the flight and 16 hours later, landed into Accra.

Eric Annan, the first local leader we were to visit, greeted us at the airport and immediately intuited our sense of well-intentioned ignorance. I immediately sensed I was meeting a friend for life. We were both right. The first thing I noticed about Eric was his cracker-jack smile and infectious raspy laughter. He engaged each of us in a chest level hand-slap, evolved the grasp into an interlocking finger-pinch, and then snapped his fingers back with an audible *snick* as our fingers departed their once interwoven air. At his side stood Charlie Perkins, our first ever GO volunteer, who had flown in from England for this virginal adventure. She had beat us by a day given our delay.

"Welcome to Accra!" they bellowed.

Hugs were quickly exchanged and Eric immediately proceeded to give us a crash course about the slum life of the capital city, Accra. Our bags were tossed into the backseat of his Jeep, and we immediately headed for a jet-lagged tour of life at the bottom of the ladder. No rest for the weary. With newspaper smudges still marking our faces, we headed to Sodom and Gomorrah.

Sodom and Gomorrah is the biggest slum in Ghana, located right in the heart of Accra. Its frontier economy sprouted shantytowns like nobody's business as people from the impoverished countryside flocked in droves to the city for its perceived benefits and opportunities. About eighty thousand residents were crammed onto less than half a square mile in the capital city. People that lived there had space equal to a bathroom stall as their private space, sometimes less and definitely no more. Fitting to its biblical name, Sodom and Gomorrah was surrounded by a toxic lagoon and a channel of raw sewage. To enter, you had to cross a river of shit and garbage. Nearly everything here was unplanned.

This lack of any central planning led to a rickety outdoor billiards table sitting adjacent to an occupied barber's chair. That chair was next to a shop that sold tiny bottles of soaps and shampoos crammed into unbelievably colored straw baskets. The store was surrounded by endless tiny homes with corrugated tin roofs, shelter that must have been deafening during any heavy rainstorm. Barefooted children ran everywhere and playfully tugged at our everything including my shorts, Charlie's hair, and Kyle's backpack.

I saw Charlie lightly quarrel with a girl who appeared to be about twelve years old. She tried to convince Charlie she was a mother. Charlie shook her head, laughed and stated that this was impossible for such a young girl. The girl lacked the English skills to win an argument against a cheerful English university student. Instead, she pulled out her breast and squirted Charlie in the face with "mother's milk", effectively ending the debate. The entire slum burst out in laughter, Charlie included. We continued onwards as an ever-growing stream of curious children followed our every move. Their nervous giggles echoed against the narrow pathways and trailed behind us as we went deeper into the slum.

The bones of these slums were strong in pride despite both the physical and emotional wounds created by the immense poverty around us. A sense of safety and community seemed inherent here. Everyone worked hard to make a living and proved that the distinguishing line between entrepreneur and survivor was razor thin. If you could make it here, you could make it anywhere.

Eric came here every week. He greeted mothers by name, purchased things from nearly every shop, and expertly navigated the byzantine labyrinth that reeked of wood-smoke, fried bread, garbage, and human sweat. Eric made his living as the preacher of a dedicated congregation who supported various immediate aid programs to the street children of the slums. He leveraged whatever he could collect at the church and bolstered the money raised with his personal income. Eric arrived here every Sunday with his family to provide food, water, and life lessons to the horde of street children.

Eric led us to a defunct railroad station in the heart of the slum. Its vast and open courtyard provided spatial relief from the suffocating narrow paths and powerful sunlight streamed across the dirty grass. It was in this courtyard that he, his wife Felicia and their two teenage children hosted a weekly feeding program that was served with a side of English lessons and moral guidance. Eric's little truck stood in the center, packed to the brim with Styrofoam boxes loaded with fried rice and bananas. We looked around the dusty yard, dwarfed by a tin-roofed maroon building that once served as the main station. Its clock tower had permanently frozen in time. Deathly silence settled into our ears. The dense heat sidled against our skin.

The Annan family had the silent and cheerful resonance of a team that often worked together as they started the perfunctory stages of setting up. Everyone knew his or her role and they worked in silence. In less than ten minutes, a feeding station that could feed hundreds had been setup. I looked around the barren courtyard and wondered why we had brought so much food as only a few children had followed us this far.

Then a resonance gnarled in the dirt. I turned the corner and saw swarms of little black bodies that pierced my ears with joyful cries. They poured in and we became engulfed in a tidal wave of children. They jumped. They laughed. They screamed. They fought. They were ecstatic, some from giddiness and some from desperation. The frenzy teetered from joy to fear as the children resorted to survivalist tactics of pushing and climbing over one another. One smaller boy fell under the crowd and rose up a minute later with a deep gash over his eye. I took out my first aid kit, put on gloves and addressed his wound. My mind entered into a childlike state where time played only a supporting role. I recollect little about that moment of time and only fragments of memory exist. I remember the smiles, the laughing, the crying and the blood. Each was suffocated together in what could have been a minute, or perhaps ten.

The Annan family deftly established order with booming voices, and used both metaphorical carrots and literal sticks as their tools to establish order in chaos. They organized the children into groups and calmed their starving emotions. In minutes, orderly yet quivering queues formed. I found myself in charge of fifty rowdy children and hopelessly tried to contain order of the desperately thirsty.

There was a blazing fire of need.

We were armed with so little water to help.

~

Reality sank in the next day. We felt powerless. How could $2,000 even make a dent here? Eric met us early at our meager hotel (bucket showers, intermittent electricity, and one bed for three people), and over breakfast, we openly expressed our concerns about sustainable development programs and the hazardous intermixing of aid work and religious beliefs. We sympathized with his feeding program and expressed our thoughts that while we found it well intentioned and endearing, we did not see any end game. This point on sustainability was under-scored the previous evening as when we left the train station, Eric hit his truck against a pole. He had no means to fix his broken taillight as repairs meant giving up the feeding program for a month.

Eric suspended his smile. He lamented about how much damage religious institutions had made in the field of international development work. He complained about how the proliferation of Western aid dollars in his country deteriorated his government's ability to be transparent. Billions of aid dollars had streamed into Ghana and nearly every Minister of Parliament (MP) had a plan on how best to leverage those funds. The first priority was for the MP to secure projects for his district, the second priority was to hire independent contractors from major companies to conceive a plan to build something, and the third priority was to ensure everyone got a cut. An MP just needed to build the schools, the wells, and the roads; he never needed to think about how to keep them running in the long-term. The Ghanaian government became so inundated with misuse of aid dollars that they started to outright ban the building and operating of orphanages, a business that was greatly abused by both local and international organizations. Eric's diatribe ended with an explanation of why he formed his organization, Sovereign Global Mission (SGM), as a non-denominational and non-governmental organization. With the government reeling in corruption scandals, they shifted their burden to Community Based Organizations (CBOs) and church groups to direct aid and welfare programs. Reverend Eric had found his calling. Though funds were lacking, he created a vision and accepted the position of being a leader of the community. He had no money and no resources. Yet he had a very powerful voice, one that transcended continents.

The immediate vision was simple: build a private school away from the slums and on the outskirts of the city, a place of peaceful solidarity. Once the school was built, Eric had devised a financial plan where eighty-percent of the neighboring population (a relatively wealthier area) would pay school fees to cover the costs of teachers, cooks, a janitor, and a bus driver. The remaining twenty-percent of students would be selected from the slums of Accra, and would attend for free.

The conversation continued in Eric's dented truck as we drove to the site of the school. I expected to see a meager plot of land accompanied by a request to visualize the spot where the library would stand next to the fictitious school building that did not exist.

Instead, we arrived to a clear plot of land. The library and the administrative office had already been built, and the foundation for a five-room, 120-child school had been laid down among a field of bricks.

"Eric, you've started something good here," I said.

"Yes. Seven years ago," he responded.

"Where did you get the money?" I asked.

"I saved my own. I bought each brick and paid people when I could. I started with the library," he said.

"And this has all been built with your own savings?" I asked.

"He-he-he. Well, at first, yes. Then I met Randi from Peacework about two years ago. He flew me out to Virginia and his university gave me some funding," he said.

Eric pointed at the library.

"You see this? Thanks to Peacework, it is complete. The kids here can read. For this, we are so very grateful," he said, looking past us.

Eric had been building this school long before we came. And if we had left that day with only exchanging a consolatory handshake over the words, 'Best of luck to you', it would not have changed a damn thing. Eric would have continued building his school, and brick-by-brick he would have continued to grow the foundation of his dream.

While Eric's germination of success was mired in tenacity, he had only started with his own scant resources. He then built a partnership with Peacework, a nonprofit founded in Virginia in the early 1980s. They had supported Eric's work for nearly a decade. With an established and diverse Board of Directors, valuable university partnerships, and volunteers that visited Eric's school annually, Peacework provided that much needed important guarantee that Eric's diatribe was more than just empty words to woo an ignorant donor.

In that moment, we decided to give Eric $2,000 to literally help him with shit: the school needed a large septic tank enclosed in a cement shelter.

We shook hands to seal the deal.

"Let us start building!" Eric exclaimed.

"Now?" we asked.

"Yes. Now. *Today*," Eric responded.

"Okay!" we replied.

We high-fived. Then awkward silence fell, accompanied by sidelong glances.

"So, uh, Eric, how do we give you the money?" we asked.

He gave us a look of baffled incredulity, as if someone had just told him that a truck full of carrots hit a clown on the street.

Silence.

"Let us go to the bank," Eric said.

~

Like much of the developing world, Ghana is a cash-based economy. Nearly all transactions, even those well into the thousands of dollars, are handled in cash. This came as no surprise, which is why GO opened its inaugural business account with Citibank, which has 1,000,000 automated teller machines (ATMs) worldwide. Armed with our trusty ATM card from Citibank, we hit the city to finance our investment and promptly entered into a liquidity crisis.

Coming from an economics background, I academically understood the macro-level impact when a country's access to liquid capital is deprived. Generally speaking, countries with access to liquid capital steeped in contractual and emotional trust have a significant socio-economic advantage over countries that do not. Cash presents an on-demand availability that empowers people to get things done. Liquidity attracts investment, savings, consumption, and other factors that increase productivity.

And there we were with none, illiquid like a desert. All we had to do was get $2,000 in local currency (the Ghanaian Cedi) by day's end. Simple to write but in Accra, difficult to execute. Our steep learning curve of the micro-level reality of getting that much cash in a frontier economy began that morning.

First, there were no Citibanks. Their office in Accra had no tellers and no machines to withdraw any actual money. Then we learned that our daily withdrawal limit was $200 so other banks' ATMs were out of the question. A cash advance on our debit card was another simple solution yet the banks we visited did not even accept cards from foreign banks. So a cash advance on our personal credit cards would work, right? We only had Mastercard and then quickly learned that Ghanaian banks only accept Visa. Fail, fail, fail.

Dismayed, we sat down for lunch in the town center and Eric gave us that same surprised look. I could see in his eyes he was beginning to question our competence. Clearly we had not thought through the vital link of financing his project whatsoever.

We had one option left: Barclay's bank. Though other banks stated Mastercard is not accepted anywhere in Ghana, this international banking beacon surely had some means to navigate the illiquid waters of finance. So we stood in a byzantine queue, hoping against hope. After a few hours of waiting in line, we were informed that such a withdrawal on Mastercard indeed was possible. Success came only with a $25 bank fee. We gave our credit cards and passports and were told to wait.

And wait.

And wait.

After an hour, the teller who held our passports and cards decided to close out his drawer for the day instead of processing our transaction. He handed our stuff over to another teller who was sipping Guinness on the sly. That teller placed the transaction aside and started counting a large pile of bills.

My mobile phone rang and I could see it was Eric, who wanted an update as to why Kyle and I had spent over two hours waiting in the bank. He could find no place to park. As I tried to ask Eric about how to speed things up, a security guard carrying a rifle slung across his back jabbed a commanding finger at a frayed, "No Cell Phones" sign behind us. He snatched the phone while clicking his tongue. He put it with our documents and paper work.

Keep calling Eric, I thought, in hopes that the incessant braying of the mobile phone would annoy them into doing something.

Time clicked by. Customers lurked in lines and chairs, all waiting to simply get access to their hard earned cash. I watched the clock as the doors to the bank were locked. Barclay's closes at 1630 and at 1650, we had no status on our withdrawal. Each minute clicked by with the painful realization that we probably were not going to be getting our money.

Guards paced. Beers were finished. Drawers closed. Windows shut.

And then through the corner of my eye I saw the teller arrive with our cash. We jumped to the counter and watched the cash counting begin. Two thousand U.S. dollars equals $20,00,000 in the local Cedi so thousands of notes had to be counted *by hand*. We watched a growingly irate teller, his fingers slowly sliding down the notes like wet cement; count his way through a barrel sized pile of cash. Kyle noticed an electronic "How did we do?" survey monitor at the teller's desk to rank the service. He picked up the pen to rate our "service".

"Don't fill that in!" yelled the teller "We don't use those!"

He glared and then yelled again that he had lost count. He unplugged the machine, preventing us from rating this customer "experience", and began the counting process anew. Finally, after hours of waiting, the money was handed over and I realized that we had nothing to carry this suitcase-sized bundle of cash. We stuffed every possible pocket with thick gobs of cash and waddled out into the darkening streets of Accra. People looked at us incredulously, literally stopping in their tracks to understand this farcical scene. Two young white idiots had just walked out of a bank at night, their pants clearly bursting with cash. Were we a joke being filmed? A clever trap set by the police?

I called Eric frantically. No answer. We flattened our backs against the doors. Endless minutes went by.

Finally, Eric pulled up in his busted up Jeep and we hustled into the car like robbers fleeing the scene.

Again, a "WTF?" look flashed over his face as he roared with laughter. *You guys are crazy!*

~

We began work before dawn the following day on a single lane road on the outskirts of Accra. The sun had not yet baked the boil and the morning breeze was still acute. Our band of three lay tucked in the back seat of Eric's truck. We were ready to get the blocks, cement and piping, the essential goods and materials needed to make progress.

Eric advised us to lie low so sellers did not see he had *Mzungu's* (white people) with him. A savvy move. Once sellers see white skin, the price of their goods magically leaps thirty-percent higher. The white man's burden brings a heavy tax.

Eric pulled his Jeep over. He moved himself away from us and stood in the middle of the road. I watched with earnest curiosity. We were surrounded by tiny storefronts laying claim to their religious nature. Nearly every small business here was steeped in Christianity. There was the, "God is Love Hair Salon", the "Jesus Love Me Forex Bureau", and over yonder lied the catchy, "Christ Resurrection Enterprise and Shopping Centre". Yet nothing said anything remotely close to "blocks, cement, or construction materials."

We sat puzzled as cars and trucks whizzed by while Eric's eyes darted and scanned each one. Finally, he waved his hand to pull over a medium sized truck while shooting us a look to stay out of sight. Eric and the driver exchanged a few words and Eric unrolled our donkey-sized wad of cash. He doled out a few thousand Cedis, and the truck rolled off. Eric proceeded to do this again and again, truck after truck. After several repetitions, Eric totted over, gave us the receipts for everything and without a word, we rolled off. Neither Kyle nor I knew exactly what Eric was doing though we wordlessly understood and trusted.

We pulled into the work-site where a few workers were clearing the fields. We waited for the next step to happen. I observed quietly, didn't ask any questions, and occupied myself by helping to clear the field. After about forty minutes, the first truck that Eric had flagged down (just an hour prior) appeared and dropped off cement. Soon another drove in carrying large stone blocks. Then sand, iron rods, loose rocks, and some basic tools arrived. Before noon, Eric not only managed to assemble a team, he had gotten materials purchased and delivered to the work-site. Once empowered, cash starved micro-economies in frontier cities like Accra can charge ahead at magnificent speeds.

Imagine this situation playing out anywhere else. For example: You are in Dayton, Ohio and you drive to Lowe's Hardware to get your supplies. You request delivery of everything to your work-site outside the city in about an hour. You explain that there is no address. You explain that you'll pass a tree here, then turn at the hill there, and beyond the tall grass you will find the foundation of a school. "Don't worry," you explain, "all your drivers will find this location and no GPS is necessary." You then plop down $5,000 in cash.

Hard to fathom?

Let's take the lunacy even further. Imagine that "Lowe's" is not even a physical store. It's just a bunch of trucks driving down a road, and you have to drive to a neighborhood where they *might* be passing by. Then you have to flag them down with a wave of your hand, and negotiate while traffic zips by. Same delivery process, same time-line, same donkey wad of cash. Same result?

No way.

Yet there in Accra, people were hungry for work and with the right leadership, projects moved at a pace liberated from the administrative burden of a coddled welfare state. Once investment capital was secured things got done very fast. The roads and infrastructure, to be sure, did their damnedest to slow things down. So did corrupt politicians and sleazy police officers that would pull over delivery trucks for various "custom" duties. But the people zipped and the pride of work energized their veins like a noble cocaine.

We built the septic tank with rudimentary tools grasped by determined arms. We mixed cement into concrete with shovels. There was no concrete mixer. It was old school muscle grease. Large blocks were carried and laid by hand. The local contractor relied on the oldest and most basic of hand tools to ensure everything was level: the string line, to create a straight line between two reference points. Modern tools were lacking yet the magic ingredient that we found in ample supply was human labor. Both professional contractors and volunteer community members pitched in to carry, fasten, push, load, mix, shovel, and create. In four day's time, a functional septic tank that would ensure the cleanliness of hundreds of school children was complete.

Eric hired a bus for nearly fifty street children to come celebrate at the work-site on Sunday, the day of rest. The children read in the library while others played football in the open grassy fields. My first aid kit needed no action that day. Removed from the cramped alleys that smelled of rot and fed the frenzy of fear, those lucky few children played in fresh air under the open skies.

They acted like they should.

Like children.

They were happy.

TURN IT AROUND
BE THE CHANGE

Imagine a raging fire burning down the jungle. It's such an overwhelming disaster that all the animals are in a state of shock as they watch their homes burn and their community fray into ash.

A hummingbird says, "I'm going to do something about the fire."

She flies to the nearest stream and takes a drop of water. One, solitary drop. It's all she can hold.

She races back to the fire where she drops the water onto the flames. Back and forth she zips, over and over, while the larger animals — like the elephant whose trunk could deliver so much more water — stand watching.

Dumbfounded, the elephant cries to the hummingbird, "What do you think you can do? You are so little!"

Without pausing, the hummingbird answers: "I'm doing the best I can."

This fable from Kenya is one I learned from an amazing community leader named Abdul Kassim. Like Eric, Abdul was determined to improve his community. Specifically, he focused on improving the education and confidence of girls through an organization he founded called Kibera Girls Soccer Academy (KGSA). He started with little, just teaching girls football in his hometown of Kibera, an area in Nairobi, which is similar to Sodom and Gomorrah, so they could play the sport and compete against the boys. Eventually, his lessons became a program. Then the program got a building. Then the building became a school and then evolved into a boarding center for hundreds of young Kenyan girls. Like Eric, Abdul's physical stature was impressive though it did little to mask that he was nothing but a hummingbird. He fluttered and zipped, teaching hundreds of girls to compete, and beat, the boys in a sport. These were small and worthy acts of grace in the fire of Kibera, the largest slum in all of Africa and home to over 170,000 residents.

So why does the hummingbird even *bother to try?*

None of our actions truly matter in the wider scope of the universe. Like the hummingbird, I am so little and so are you. But I must do something. While we cannot change the universe, we can and must change the world around us to lead purposeful and happy lives. Yes, some people have access to more resources than others. They are bigger and stronger or faster and smarter. But do not let your mind be trampled by the perceived might of the elephant.

I reside near Silicon Valley and am surrounded by people that are absolute "elephants." It is staggering what my neighbors have achieved and I'm thankful for their guidance in the growth of my endeavors. But despite the titans of industry and philanthropy that I have met, it's the hummingbirds like Eric and Abdul that leave me in utter awe. They are the noble leaders who inspire action in their communities and drive things forward with absolute conviction.

Working with Eric in Ghana, a weight of doubt drearily weighed me down. The raging fire of poverty in Sodom and Gomorrah seemed absolutely out of control. I felt impotent standing in front of this blazing wall of heat with only a few buckets of water. At times, it felt senseless being there. And I felt entirely ignorant of what was happening around me and how I could help, a point underscored by that ridiculous encounter at the bank. I couldn't even inject money, which I possessed, into the equation!

Alongside other determined hummingbirds like Eric, Felicia, his children, Kyle, and Charlie, I continued to move forward and did the best that I could. The mere effort of trying to do something, taking the bias towards action, and holding onto the steadfast perseverance that eventually something will turn towards our favor never left my mind.

Eventually, my drops of water became buckets. Then the buckets began to multiply, first linearly, then exponentially.

As this tidal wave grew, I found myself reporting to individuals who had decades of experience in their fields. What on earth could I offer them? How could I even consider *leading* them? The more I compared myself to their achievements, the less I believed in my own accomplishments.

I became impotent, drearily dwelling in a headspace I refer to as "imposter syndrome." This is a mental block marked by an inability to internalize your accomplishments, which leads to a persistent fear of being exposed as a 'fraud'. I know it all too well as with any encountered success, my mind quickly dismisses that achieved win as luck or timing. I disregard my efforts and avoid displaying the erstwhile confidence that is required in positions of leadership.

As my early success grew, so did the pain. Success begets praise, which in turn, perpetuates the impostor feelings and fears of being 'found out.' The 'impostor' then felt it was necessary to work two or three times as hard to over-prepare, tinker, and obsess over details. He embellished to appear more successful externally while the internal pain of perceived failure gnawed ever deeper into his hollowing core. This process led to burn out and sleep deprivation as I returned from Ghana and did what I could to grow GO. Like Abdul and Eric, who seemingly never rested, we were tireless in our efforts and internalized our own pain. Slowly things began to click with our burgeoning organization. We grew in size, and others with far more experience took notice. Yet the thought persisted that others would realize we were only mindless birds that had no idea how to fight fires.

As I struggled, I reached out to a mentor by the name of Chip Conley for advice and counsel. An elephant in his own right, Chip is a veteran hospitality entrepreneur, *New York Times* bestselling author, and speaker. His calling began at 26 years of age when he launched the world-renowned Phoenix hotel, a legendary San Francisco hotel that catered to the likes of David Bowie, Linda Ronstadt, and Nirvana. Chip never looked back, opening boutique hotel after hotel until a private equity firm bought a majority stake in his business. Over a dinner with friends at Chip's home, I explained my situation and asked him how he dealt with imposter syndrome. Surely he must have also suffered from this malady?

He grew quiet.

And thought.

Then he looked at me and said, "Go out into nature."

The conversation moved on while I sat perplexed. Yet the next weekend I took Chip's advice and hiked out into the Marin Headlands. I stood amongst immense redwood trees, my being dwarfed by these native "elephants" of the forest. Redwood trees are massive in stature and emanate a hardened sense of quiet power. These giants can live to be 2,000 years old and have graced the planet for more than 240 million years. Once mature, even the hottest of fires will not destroy them. Walking amongst their quiet, stoic power, I realized how insignificant everything around me could be. I marveled at their indifference to everything around them.

Upon my return, I spent months reworking my brain by drawing upon the spiritual power that I encountered during my hike. I refused to stop trying. This inspired me to have others do the same. Out of this mindset, GO launched a fundraising and awareness building program called GO Champions, wherein we inspired people from all walks of life to become engaged philanthropists by raising the seed capital and visibility that people like Eric and Abdul needed to thrive. These local leaders needed resources to rebuild their communities and our humble crew at GO inspired thousands of "hummingbirds" to fetch water against the raging fire of poverty. While we explore this in more detail later, here are but a few of their stories:

> Apurva and Carly were classmates at Orinda Middle School. Inspired by a school-giving program, they ran a half marathon to raise funds and awareness for a school we supported in Rwanda. Together, they raised nearly $2,000 so 60 children in Muhanga, Rwanda, could have safe drinking water in their classrooms.

Two best friends (JoAnna Wulffenstein and Michelle Bratt) wanted to make a difference in the world so they found and reached out to GO on Facebook. Together, they threw a "Battle of the Sexes" themed party in Juneau, Alaska where men and women competed in trivia, sumo wrestling, and karaoke. They raised $10,000 for an entrepreneur named Peter Luswata to start a pig farm in Uganda that would provide a sustainable source of food and income for thousands of rural farmers.

Margo Mayes was the Director of Business Development at the Salesforce.org when she heard me give a speech at her company off-site. Inspired, she decided to become a GO Champion and informed her colleagues that she was raising money for bio-sand water filters that would provide Cambodian families with safe drinking water. She did this again for her 40th birthday. Given that the Salesforce.org matched all the donations, she raised over $5,645 so 165 families would have their lives changed forever.

These GO Champions acted. We gave them a chance to help, and presented them with an opportunity to give what they could to help those in need. They didn't wither when considering that billions of people around the world lacked access to clean water, or worry that their actions might be rendered inconsequential in "the grand scheme of things". They did the best they could, and they did not consider themselves imposters in the byzantine world of international development.

Our time on this planet is limited, so let's not waste it comparing ourselves to elephants and throwing our heads into the sand. These are but mere examples meant to inspire and empower you to make a difference in our world. These stories are as extraordinary as they are ordinary. I come across them all the time and if you ever begin to doubt that you, a committed citizen who can change the world, cannot compete with the elephants that are lauded in our press and media, then do these three things:

- Make a list of your accomplishments. **Write them down.** If you feel you have none, think of three things you can do this week that will change the life of another person. Call your mother and tell her "I love you." Visit a friend and say you value their companionship.

- Get or inspire feedback from your actions. If you tell a true friend you love them, they will respond in kind. If you volunteer, you will get a thank you. Impact drives success, not the other way around. Even on the darkest of days, when all my projects seemed to be failing and I was meeting more with my lawyers than my friends, I found that nothing more radically helped course correct my thinking than a simple "Thank you" from a GO Champion like Margo or a partner like Eric. These seemingly slight success stories can manage impostor syndrome and despair like none other; they make you take the next step forward.

- Develop a strong support system that provides feedback on performance and has discussions on a regular basis. This is imperative. I've noticed that the most successful people around me ask earnestly and honestly, "What can I do better?" They want feedback regarding what they are doing well and what they can improve upon.

Act. Now. Don't get trapped by dogma, which is living your life as a result of other people's thinking. Be a consequence and make others think differently. Don't be afraid to act or look like an idiot. Be that moron walking out of a bank into the darkness of night with bulging pockets full of money. Do the best you can and don't let the noise of other opinions drown out your own inner voice. Most importantly, have the courage to follow your heart and intuition, as they will guide you to purpose.

Everything else is secondary.

The fire is raging.

CHAPTER 8

UNSUSTAINABLE DEVELOPMENT

Evans Tasiame is a white-collar professional living in Ghana. His eyes flicker with deep thought and he talks rapidly with ideas that come bursting out like scampering birds escaping the cage. Which is odd since he was raised in Kome, a sleepy fishing village in the far north of the country. Kome is a tiny speck of land where time moves by in heavy lethargic waves. Its people are welcoming and always stop to learn more about you, even if it's already the third time you've spoken to each other that day. It's a place that thousands call home yet few can find reasons to stay.

Like many young people, Evans left Kome to seek better opportunities in Accra. He's among the lucky ones as he comes from an educated and supportive family. His father is the village teacher, a capable fisherman, and a noble provider who gave nourishment to Evans' mind and belly. And in Evans, he found a child with a bottomless hunger for both knowledge and fish. Evans was a child of conviction, determination, and duty. Even at an early age, he fished alongside his father late into the night to help his family earn more money. He never let this get in the way of schooling and excelled in his studies. He got home when today became tomorrow and listened to midnight broadcasts of the BBC to learn English. Tireless and focused, Evans shined. His British flecked English rolled off his tongue fluidly; he loved mathematics, and could catch even the tiniest Tilapia with his bare hands. The only thing Evans couldn't do was find a job.

So he left Kome to make it in a big city.

He earned a degree in electrical engineering while working two jobs simultaneously to make ends meet. He graduated and prospered in a variety of technical fields working at companies big and small. Yet he never forgot his rural roots and his family's sacrifices that enabled him to follow this path of learning and opportunity. He found solace in his father's lessons of hard work and perseverance.

So Evans never stopped planning his return to Kome and fumbled towards an idea that would bring hope to a place he once called home. He yearned to show his father that he could teach others to fish and grasp commercial opportunities in their lives, and to find something that would empower a future generation of leaders from Kome.

I could sense his conviction. I knew he would roll up his sleeves to get the work done himself. I loved everything about him as we corresponded from afar via Skype. I loved him more when we met in person.

And so it broke my heart when I told him, "No, I cannot help you."

~

We met Evans outside a classroom one early morning before another day of building the septic tank. He taught a free computer class for young adults. Dressed in a spotless button down shirt neatly tucked into professional blue slacks, he commanded the attention of faces that glowed against the blue light of their computer monitors. As the fire of poverty raged around him in Ghana, this hummingbird of a man volunteered at a local computer lab to teach people the basics of Microsoft Office despite his taxing work schedule. He had only one goal in mind: to help his fellow neighbor by teaching vital technology skills.

Evans and I met in person after he finished teaching. From his wide smile to kinetic energy, Evans radiated the same boundless enthusiasm for life that came across so vibrantly in his emails. Over many cups of tea, we dove into more detail about his mission to build a fish-farming project in Kome. He had framed a vision of economic prosperity and sold the idea to us over emails and Skype calls before our trip. And despite the long travel required to reach the Ghanaian countryside, we grew more and more excited with every unfolding detail. Evans even volunteered to help at Eric's school and worked alongside us building the septic tank on the weekends. Once that project launched, we set a course for Kome to explore our second potential investment.

Kome lies one thousand miles north of Accra. No highways exist and planes do not fly there. Despite Evans' cheery email that his work was, "a short journey", our team quickly realized that the word 'short' is quite relative to the eye of the beholder.

We had no travel budget so we mapped out a journey of primitive buses and a ferry ride over Lake Volta, one of the world's largest manmade lakes. Lake Volta is home to the *Yapei Queen*, a popular ferry for the local population to traverse from the south to the north. We expected a no-frills ride though imagined sipping cold Ghanaian beers over Africa-orange sunsets that bled into the lake.

We were to forge this journey alone as Evans had left in advance to prepare for our arrival. His directions sent via email for crossing half the country using a complex web of buses, boats, and taxis totaled a mere 38 words. Google Maps couldn't even find the village, so we printed out his Spartan email and cast ourselves into the fray of Accra's main bus station. The first step from Evans' email read, "Take the bus to Yapei Queen".

We blindly navigated Accra bus station at the break of dawn and discovered, well, there is no bus to the *Yapei Queen*. Apparently, only a series of local *tro-tros* would be able to make that journey. Tro-tros are battered, carcinogenic versions of school minibuses that leave to and from designated areas. They have no schedule and leave once at capacity. They are wobbly and crowded, with 'at capacity' really meaning 'packed to the brim'. Adults, wailing babies, plastic bags full of smoked fish, odd livestock sitting on laps, and countless bags occupied every square inch of space. Each tro-tro carried inspiringly vivid phrases painted on its front, rear or sides. Some were mesmerizing (*Does God Change?*), some curious (*Observers Are Worried*), and some truly thought provoking (*If 7 + 2 = 11 then WHO CARES*). Ultimately, we found a near full tro-tro bound for the rough direction of the *Yapei Queen* and settled in for the cramped three-hour ride.

We arrived to a mosh pit of people at the ticket office. Contradictory to the information from the bus station information desk, seats on the ferry were sold out for the day. Yet we knew how this process worked, so we asked the ticket office for the 'extra' seats by offering 'extra' cash for their troubles. After some good-hearted banter, we haggled our way into getting second-class seats on the top deck.

We moved towards an iron gate underneath a starkly honest sign detailing the trip ahead:

WARNING: It is possible to travel on board a cargo and supply boat, which covers more than half the distance of the country. This boat stops at an unknown number of villages.

My eyes drifted from the sign and I witnessed a rusting behemoth inherited from Germany shortly after World War II. There stood the *Yapei Queen*, our home for at least the next thirty hours. While she did not look like a BMW, she looked sturdy beneath her thick coat of rust.

We waited. And waited. Then, a foghorn pierced the air. Like some eccentric Olympic sprint, everyone just crushed it towards the dock. Tiny children charging down the hill were quickly surpassed and outpaced by women with entire kitchen sets on their heads. The surge of people propelled us forward so quickly that my breath yelped out of my lungs. We ran forward to keep up with the melee. We had heard we would be sleeping on tables and they were first come, first served. We were at the front of the pack so we were able to secure a wooden table big enough for six people in the second-class deck to call our own. A few minutes later, a family of six and a military officer joined in. Our table for six quickly became a table for ten. The cabin temperature rose to a sweltering level and our shirts clung wetly to our backs.

We forfeited the table as the teeming mass of people continued to swell inside the cabin. Nothing inside seemed remotely safe. We grabbed our packs and decided to find room on the top deck. We secured a corner with a good view and claimed it by heaving our backpacks down on the ground. The *Yapei Queen* cast off. The two-day trip seemed to spread out idyllically before us, as the sun set over the lake and new single-serving traveler friends from Germany placed cold beers in our hands. A cool breeze hung over the lake and we had plenty of room to stretch out our legs in the twilight. We were too exhausted and comfortable to wonder why no locals had joined us on the top deck. The reasons became quite clear as night set and we unrolled our sleeping bags for the evening's rest.

Three simple choices faced our team. We could sleep by:

A. The exhaust pipe that could cause, at best, hallucinations from the fumes and, at worst, death by asphyxiation.

B. The blocked and overflowing toilet, complete with a steady trickle of urine under the door.

C. The bare metal floor in front of the captain's bridge.

Lack of comfort trumped suffocation or nausea so we chose to sleep on the iron casting of the deck. We unrolled one hiker's sleeping pad between the three of us and settled in for the evening. The lake was quiet as the dull throttle of the plump ferry chugged along underneath a starry night sky. The captain's door opened to capture the cool evening breeze and we got our first glimpse of our captain. He stood stolidly at the helm, wearing nothing but a torn t-shirt and bright white underpants that contrasted magnificently against his dark, bare legs. He wore no pants, no shoes, and no socks. He steered the ship and kept himself awake through the night by singing American pop songs.

Killing Me Softly filled our ears under a moonlit sky.

I closed my eyes, found something that resembled sleep.

~

Morning came and we rose and wiped off the night's grime. We lumbered sleepily off the *Yapei Queen*. We were specks of white in a sea of black. Evans found us in no time and took us the rest of the way to his hometown of Kome. Bathed in the fire of the Ghanaian sun, this tiny and sleepy fishermen's village possessed the great ability to slow the progress of time.

No one rushed here.

A simple walk to the village store was slowed with the obligatory hello to every passerby. Their response, spoken soft and timelessly, was one of sincere welcome. Everyone listened to one another, and when you expressed an opinion, you were given time to fully finish your thought. Coming from the attention deficit disordered village we call Silicon Valley, where every other sentence is quickly intercepted with,

"Yeah, and" to move onto the next matter, this cadence of speech and thought was both refreshing and inspiring.

Despite the patience of time, our stay in Kome adopted the schedule of the local fishermen with our days beginning at four in the morning. We visited the proposed site of Evans' fish farm, and met with local elders, including Evans' infectiously joyful father, to get a better understanding of the project specifics. We sat in an open circle and the community welcomed us with locally caught tilapia, fried whole and served upon a fermented rice cake. Bone, jaw, head, tail, and the little body of meat all went down the gullet. This crunchy 'delicacy' was washed down with fermented rice, which tasted just like it sounds. As we quickly chewed it all down, the elders welcomed us and conveyed their devotion to beginning a much-needed economic development project in their village.

They were ready to act at that precise moment.

To underline this point, they arose and we were joined by dozens of villagers tangibly ready to demonstrate their devotion to work. We spent the remainder of the day clearing and marking the land for the fish farm with machetes, sticks, and strings. Their economic and survivalist drive for *any* sort of work was clearly prevalent, and since Kome stood on the beautiful flood plains of the Volta region, the availability of Tilapia would be great.

We realized we needed more convincing the next day. We jumped straight into the *how* of the project (clear the land!) and forgot to ask about the *what* (project plan!), and the crucial *why* (the vision!) that would enable a successful project. Unlike Eric's NGO, Evans' organization was new and had no third party support like Peacework to bolster its ambitions into demonstrable progress.

Additionally, Evans was not based in this community and only visited in between breaks from his work in Accra. These were significant hurdles and given our preciously small amount of gathered funds, we knew these were significant risks. Evans acknowledged these risks though confidently stated how successful a fish farming enterprise could be in these parts. Evans asked us to recall the statements we'd heard earlier wherein many of the local villagers stated how much fewer fish they caught in the wild.

"If so few fish could be caught in the lake, then the profits of raising them in farms would be huge!" Evans exclaimed.

Yet the more questions we asked about the cost of operations, the clearer it became that Evans and his team were guessing at figures. They had an answer for everything, which was not a good sign. It's nearly impossible to know everything about a given subject, and if you never hear the words *"good question"* and *"let me get back to you on that,"* then you must be wary. Constant prodding is a common managerial consulting technique to distinguish risky bullshit from prudent projects.

We vetted further by visiting other fish farms in the area. We wanted to get a better picture of the opportunity, and get an idea or two so we visited a fish farm of comparable size the next day. The owner had been in the fish farm industry for thirty years and was a noted speaker on sustainable fish farm development in Africa, Europe, and the USA. We interviewed him for about four hours, and asked him questions about fish farm sizes, fish to area ratios, waste disposal, water filtration techniques in developing world environments, and the like. Everything that had a figure became a metric in a financial model Kyle and I drafted in Excel. We visited local markets to determine the wholesale price of Tilapia and the market price of individual sales. We played with figures for raw, smoked, and fried tilapia. We visited feed centers to compare the price of mixing locally grown cassava instead of hormone-induced bio feeds to reduce costs. We figured the cost of gas to get the feed to the farm. Ultimately, we determined that fish farming is a very low margin industry and one that could rarely profit. We saw figures losing money all over the place.

Confounded, we returned to the large-scale fish farm and were convinced that we had missed something. How can an operation that loses money be perceived as a replicable model? The owner, surprisingly transparent, told us how he had "diversified his revenues" to make his business successful. He charged other NGOs consulting fees on how to run a fish farm like his. He rarely worried about creating competition since he knew most would fail. He also got paid to travel abroad to speak to foundations and grant-makers about running fish farms. Those speeches were met with much fanfare so he then got grants from foundations to help him expand his operations. In other words, people paid him money to enlighten others on how to successfully run a failing business. The owner shrugged with open hands, and gave us a self-satisfied *works-for-me* smile. International aid dollars and a burning need for success stories had created an economic opportunity that, much like a Ponzi scheme, only benefitted the early entries at the top of the pyramid.

We left dismayed. Given the local challenges of operations, the low price of fish in the markets, and the high cost of feeds, we could not make the numbers work. Though a profit could have feasibly been attained for Evans' fish farming venture, we would have needed far more than $5,000 to start it properly. Even then, its returns would have been very low assuming nearly everything went right. The risks were high and our funding pool was small. We told Evans that we could not fund his project while in his father's living room on our last evening. He left the room and sat on the stoop as the sun went down.

After awhile, he came back in. The room was flooded in darkness. We could only see the whites of his eyes and teeth.

"I will find another way," he said.

We said our goodbyes the next morning.

We never saw or heard from Evans again.

TURN IT AROUND
THE POWER OF NO

When you start something good and traction takes hold, you say yes to every partnership offered, every client request demanded, and every idea shared. People *love* to say, "yes" and avoid saying "no" which quickly becomes a big problem. I also make this mistake as I have this perceived notion that by simply being agreeable to everyone then I will be universally liked and admired. That path of vanity and unbounded scope of purpose would surely lead only to good fortune, right?

Wrong.

In reality, this is an awful way of not only conducting business, it's also a slippery slope that prevents you from finding satisfaction in life. So I work constantly and mindfully to remind myself of the power of these three rules:

1. Yes gives LITTLE value.
2. No gives GREAT value.
3. Maybe has NO value.

Let's start with reviewing why I have an aversion to the affirmative:

- YES drains resources and burns people out.
- YES begets another YES and that leads to becoming overwhelmed.
- YES provokes no argument and no substantiation of a claim.
- With no substantiation, YES encourages ideas that simply do not work.

Whatever unit of measurement we use—be it hours in the day or dollars in the bank—resources are limited. And while it is incredibly tempting to want to be agreeable or affable, we cannot be everything for everyone. We cannot provide value with infinite scope. It will either cost us more time, more money, or provide less value. Visually, this thought is captured thusly:

Your ability to serve—whether as an adviser on a project or as a loving partner in marriage—is the *quality* you bring captured within the triangle. Do you want me to increase my quality to this relationship or to this project? I can though I must realize that *if* I am to increase the scope of my quality, then I will need more time or to spend more money. Simply responding with a "yes" to each and every request will inevitably decrease the quality since cost and time are fixed values. And while you can borrow money, you can never borrow time. It's temporary not infinite.

So learn to say no, a word of clarity and profound depth.

- NO begets a *why*, especially when the project or relationship is vital in the eye of the beholder. This *why* forces the party to clarify your reasoning on the matter.
- NO forces analysis to determine time and cost.
- NO focuses your resources (time, money, people) only on critical items.
- NO encourages ideas to find another way to work.
- NO provokes arguments that better shape the perception of the idea itself.

My favorite thing about "no" is that it separates those who never take that word as a final answer from the people who simply give up. "No" forces the strong to try harder, improve, and then through some change prove that the original negative judgment was incorrect. The idea may pivot, the model may improve, or an entirely new idea is launched. Whatever the change is that drives a "no" to a "yes", those who start something good should never take no for an answer.

I have trained my mind to embrace the terse candor of "no". Whenever I hear the word "no" from a potential donor, investor, client, or vital stakeholder, I always frame it in my mind as, "I have not provided enough information". "No" means that either my argument is not convincing enough, the data is incomplete, or I missed their heart by aiming for their head.

I then go back and reassess what I perceive to be the "why" behind the "no". I replay the engagement in my mind, putting myself in the mind of the listener(s), visualizing their body language or tenor of tone, so I can simultaneously empathize with them while 'seeing' how my communicated thoughts were being perceived. Sometimes I find that I did not tell the right story in the right way. Other times I find that I am simply wrong. And so I pivot and turn the idea around in my head (more on this later).

Which finally brings us to the most vilified of words: "maybe". I *loathe* that empty word. I cannot execute on "maybe" and can only wait until it is better defined. That prevents my efforts to help. "Maybe" also masks intention and whenever I hear the word, I try to clarify what is being covered behind its foggy letters. Do you really want to say "no" and are just waiting for a better moment? Do you need more time to get to "yes" or "no"? Do you not know all the facts? If that is the case, say so and only then will you quickly earn my trust.

One of the least heard phrases in the English language is, 'I don't know'. In the modern Western world, we are obsessed with 'knowing' and can spur all sorts of data or facts in milliseconds. And so we feel shame in not knowing something and we shy away from these remarkably useful words, ones that are more meaningful than hazy "maybe".

I greatly respect people when they tell me, "I don't know" since I bond with their raw honesty. It displays a level of trust by showing a vulnerability in thought. Most importantly, it means I can help by providing my thoughts or connecting them to someone who does know. During my consulting career, I would purposefully barrage clients or colleagues with questions to solely elicit this statement. I did not care about the subject matter though I kept asking questions until these magical words came out. And if "I don't know" never arose, I grew suspicious about their claims.

Embrace the power of "no", especially when you hear it yourself. This word is a challenge to be better. Once you grasp the conviction that what you are doing is vital for the world, the word "no" will never be a wall. It will only be a speed bump. Even if you hear the word "no" ad infinitum, it only means that your *current* idea is either not viable or perhaps your ability to explain its purpose needs more crafting. Either way, the result is pivoting on one or the other, story or method, to turn a "no" into a "yes".

Once you discover your calling in life, you will find a way to make it viable. I have done this over and over in my own life, and have coached others to do the same. Perhaps that craft or method may not be in the form once anticipated in your mind's eye. Sometimes our preconceived notions of how we think things are going to pan out are misguided or misinformed. Yet once you find that great talent that only you can provide to the world, an identity forms around that. Once that identity is established and the mind is focused on it, a method forms, or is perhaps discovered, that enables you to fulfill that purpose. This is the mindset great leaders leverage to make "no" into "yes".

CHAPTER 9

ARRESTED DEVELOPMENT

"Your passports please," he says.

I freeze. We're only a hundred feet from the gate. The plane is boarding and there's no reason why these men with fake smiles need to see our passports.

"Please gentleman. We need to see your documents," says another.

We look at each other, surrounded by three plainclothes cops. We give them our passports.

"Do you like drugs, Bart?" the first one asks.

"No," I respond cautiously.

"Did you buy drugs here Bart?" the other asks.

"No."

The first flips through my passport slowly. The second looks at Kyle.

"You can go," says the second cop.

"I'll wait for my friend", responds Kyle.

"You will go," he commands. There is no smile, only a stern point towards the gate.

Kyle looks at me.

"It's okay. I'll be right there," I say.

"Mr. Bart, you will need to have a drug test. Are you ready"?

I'm being setup and I cannot say no. I know this search cannot be chance and there is no way I will pass this test.

And I was so close to escaping Ghana.

~

Your first "no" is powerful. International development work, even at a naïve shoot from the hip stage, is inherently high risk as you make investments in countries with high political, economic, and epidemiological risk. You have to navigate trails of anxiety as you learn to accept failure. Though unpleasant, our decision not to fund the fish farm evaded risk of a failed investment and hopefully bore no ill will. Sometimes, the best and only action is not to act, a lesson we were quickly about to learn. For many reasons, the names of organizations and individuals in this chapter have been changed.

After our visit to the unrealized fish farm project, we inspected one more organization before our trip home. On paper, the Inspirational Orphanage Center (IOC) run by Kwase appeared to be our finest candidate. Kwase's emails were professional and prompt. He answered questions thoughtfully and with exquisite detail. His project proposal, to build a new school at the existing orphanage, was well written and provided detailed financial plans. He offered recommendations from other partners, both local and international. His work scored the highest marks from our external reviews. As such, we decided to save the best for last.

While visiting with Eric, we called Kwase about twice a week to figure out our ever-shifting schedule. As travel difficulties arose on our end, he put us in touch with two Belgian volunteers working at his orphanage to assist with our trip planning. They had been volunteering for four weeks and were sad to leave. Kwase, though not always around, had been a wonderful host and their validation of his work and hospitality piqued our excitement.

After the long days of building the septic tank at Eric's school, Kyle, Charlie, and I spent our evenings pleasantly fatigued, drinking beers on dusty roads. Kyle thumbed through his emails on an ancient smart phone. All of a sudden, he jumped up, spilling his warm beer onto the hot dirt.

"Oh shit," he said. "Read this."

He jabbed the phone into my face. I recognized the writing even before seeing whom the email was from. Dropping their formal and creepily good English, the two Belgians, Jérémy and Emma, wrote a flow of unpunctuated and incredulous sentences:

there are no orphans here
he brings in children from the community to pretend to be homeless and orphans
he just wants money
this is all just lie
we are in danger
someone helped us run away
be careful of kwase
do not come here

I stared blankly at the phone.

"Call them," said Kyle.

I hit the green phone icon and Jérémy answered the phone immediately on the first ring. Kyle put the phone on speaker mode so we could all hear their story. Jérémy and Emma were classmates and they had found the IOC through their university's volunteer program. They wanted to spend their summer volunteering and traveling through Africa. The IOC was thoughtful and prompt in their responses so it became their clear favorite. They would be able to volunteer and live at the IOC shelter for a fixed rate of two thousand Euros each for six weeks. Room, board, and volunteer activities included.

Though expensive, Kwase's quick responses and his good standing with the university led them to accept his offer. Their first three weeks went great. They were the only volunteers and became quickly embedded in the community. Though lacking a set curriculum, the IOC had a good library. Jérémy and Emma taught English in reading, writing, and speaking. Kwase was there at the beginning to greet and welcome them and then left them in the hands of Kwaku, a young and local villager that volunteered at the IOC. Kwaku hit it off quite well with both Jérémy and Emma and they became close. Kwaku attended to Emma in particular, helping her with any task with his strong arms and love struck eyes. As their volunteering drew to a close, a young orphan girl asked Emma if she could go home. Puzzled, Emma asked her to elaborate. The girl said she missed her family. She said she liked the IOC though she wanted to go home now. Emma asked the other children about this and they expressed the same sentiment. They missed their families and home-cooked food.

These were not orphans and this was no shelter. They were children from the area that came here when volunteers were present to present the facade of an orphanage. As volunteers only came for a few weeks at a time and given that so many people in the West would pay a premium for "voluntourism," Kwase had discovered quite the economic opportunity. The ruse was simple. Parents sent their children to the orphanage when international volunteers came to "voluntour". The children were fed and housed during the visit and they also learned English in the process. Additionally, Kwase made investments into the community with the earnings gleaned from well-intentioned though ignorant do-gooders. He had built an Internet cafe and had the local government install better power lines to provide a constant source of electricity.

For years, this situation labored onwards as a counterfeit win-win on both sides of the ailing international development equation. The volunteers posted Facebook photos of themselves hugging little black children, the declared orphans spoke better English, and the village got Internet and electricity. Kwase took his cut as the entrepreneur behind the business fueled by a supply of white guilt and sentiment. Everyone was happy until the merry-go-round of false expectations came to a screeching halt when Jérémy and Emma realized they had just bought a sham product that robbed them of their trust. Worse, they became jaded against aid-work in general. And the cycle of poverty continued to spin.

Fearing for their safety, they fled to another village where a legitimate and accredited orphanage existed.

We said we would help and hung up.

"What do we do next, Team America?," asked Kyle.

I laughed and then called Valerie, our Canadian-Ghanaian friend who worked at the UN. I thought I could help make things right.

Yet 'thought' had nothing to do with it. The call was an arrogant reaction.

And like many naïve first steps taken with good intentions, things got worse.

~

Valerie reacted in a mortified and intrigued manner. She was a director in the United Nations and had general awareness of corruption occurring in international aid through statistics she read in various briefings. Yet here we presented her with a tangible occurrence, a face and a real story that could be directly acted upon. I heard wounded anger in her voice as we spoke. She regretted how opportunists like Kwase perpetuated a false narrative that all aid is sallow and corrupt. We debated whether Kwase was technically doing anything illegal. The community seemed complicit in his actions and though falsehoods drove the narrative, they were producing a benefit to a community otherwise ignored. And all of our information came only from one source: two young European students who were on their first trip to an African nation.

Valerie identified another orphanage in the area operated by Caritas, the international development arm of the Catholic Church. We contacted them directly and they corroborated a near identical version of Jérémy and Emma's story. They were thrilled someone had finally begun to take notice as their honest work had been suffering for years. They then relayed out a compilation of facts they had collected over many years. To the consternation of the Caritas orphanage, Kwase was a savvy marketer. He became successful at roping in hundreds of volunteers from around the world by aligning himself with various church groups. Rather than targeting individual "voluntourists" like us, which is quite time-consuming, Kwase had built an efficient network of churches in the United States and Europe that supported his work. He carefully maintained these relationships and helped organize Christian mission visits to his orphanage. The groups that would visit for brief intervals left happy with their experience of sharing their love of Jesus with "orphans" in Ghana.

Despite the brevity of their trips, a crucial factor in keeping Kwase's counterfeit business model humming, they donated quite generously. Though the community did benefit from the corruption, the distribution of the funds was not equal. Generous allotments fell along tribal and political lines with certain community members being left out entirely. Worst of all, the actual orphans at the Caritas orphanage suffered as the IOC grew in stature. Success begets success and the relatively better-off children that acted as orphans at the IOC perversely received more aid in terms of better food, housing, and education than the actual orphans.

While shameful, this all makes financial sense. The profitable economics of for-profit "voluntourism" companies are exploding due to the worlds growing fascination with cultural immersion. The repercussion of sending so many unqualified, un-vetted volunteers into frontier economies like Ghana artificially creates a large 'demand' for the tourist attraction of orphaned children. According to Tourism Concern, a UK organization that promotes ethical and fair tourism, ninety percent of children in Ghanaian orphanages have at least one parent. This scheme had become so prolific in Ghana that the government announced an outright ban on all orphanages in 2007. Despite loud protests of this damaging ham-fisted approach, the government pursued this effort by jacking up the annual licensing fees of all orphanages. More fees means less orphans get the proper care and attention they deserve. Much of this is accountable to doe-eyed Westerners who "generously" spare a few days of their time to "voluntour".

Valerie had heard enough and asked about my relationship to Kwase. I replied that it was still in good standing and that he had even emailed us twice during these exchanges. Valerie was personal friends with the chief of police in Accra and contacted him about this affair. He had no jurisdiction in affairs outside the city and referred us to the Criminal Investigation Department (CID), which like the FBI, acts on a more federal level. The CID seemed quite earnest in handling the case and various CID officers rang my mobile multiple times per day.

After a few conference calls, the CID requested that Kyle and I extract as much information as possible about Kwase's international network of church and university groups so they could notify them of their actions. This seemed to be a plausible course of attack since we still had a good relationship with Kwase and could leverage our potential donation as bait to request as many references as possible. Over an hour-long phone call, Kwase relayed to me information about the many churches and universities that directly supported his work. He had well over 20 partnerships, nearly all with American faith-based charities since their evaluation criteria for efficacy and impact were so low. As we ended our phone call, Kwase asked again when we were coming to visit.

"Soon Kwase. We are coming very soon," I responded.

"Good, Bart. Good. We are waiting for you. Bless you in Jesus' name for all that you are doing," he said.

I hung up and immediately called CID to relay back everything I had scrawled down.

Two days later, we received a phone call from Valerie over breakfast.

"It's done! The local police arrested Kwase this morning!" she exclaimed.

And that's when all the troubles began.

~

With only a few days left in our trip, we felt that this bit of news gave us reason to celebrate with a night out. We had traveled over the entire country, began a great project and helped to stop a fake one. We drank cold beers and watched the sun dip below the ocean's horizon with undue self-satisfaction. I remember laughing loudly as the night darkened. The moment was interrupted by the piercing sound of my cell ringing. I saw Valerie's name flash on the screen.

"Hey there. We are at the sunset bar at the beach. Want to join us?" I asked.

"We have a complication," she said. "Kwase is not who we thought he was."

The words hung in the air for a bit.

"What do you mean?" I asked.

"Kwase is not just any scam artist. He is an MP in the government. His wife is quite influential in politics and has friends in high places. He is out. And he is very angry."

Unwittingly, we had helped arrest a minister of parliament. Even while I was painfully naïve of the inner workings of international development, no one needed to explain to me the gravity of this situation.

~

Kwase spent perhaps a few hours in jail. He made phone calls and flexed his political muscle to get himself out and exact retribution. He immediately drew the conclusion that the recent disappearance of Jérémy and Emma must be related, and arrested members of his own community that had friendly relations to those volunteers. Valerie and CID assured us that we were not under suspicion though advised us to not leave our hotel. For the last three days of our trip, we spent every hour locked in our hotel room watching pirated DVDs from China when the power was on (the minority of the time), and staring at the wall when the power was off (the majority of the time). We would walk out together to the quickest fried chicken joint for meals and immediately walk back after ordering take-out. We did not send emails and we did not make any phone calls. Kwase's frequent emails ceased and paranoia sank in.

The day for our departure arrived on a gray, cool morning. We stuffed our packs and Eric drove us to Kotoka airport. Despite our recent profound stupidity, the one sensible judgment we did make was to not involve Eric in our current dilemma. In the small 'good ole boys' network of African politics, it was best to keep one's head down in ignorance. Eric cracked jokes and we responded with cracked, nervous laughter. He dropped us off curbside and we took in the scene. Police and security sat stolidly in front of every door. Men in fatigues held large rifles and stared hard. Everything about this was completely normal yet given our current state, it felt anything but normal.

We stuttered through the ticket queue with paranoid thoughts in mind. We had no problems with the tickets. We arrived over three hours early since this was one flight we were not going to miss. We held our breath at the sole security inspection line, which took an unfathomably long time. The machine broke and our three-hour window dwindled down to 40 minutes as all bags were searched by hand. We hurried through and on to customs, the final hurdle of our exit. We went into separate lines, constantly exchanging glances as we inched towards the front. I relished hearing the square echo of the *ka-chunk!* from the customs officer's stamp. The dull sound officially released me from Ghana and I stepped past the rickety wood frame of the customs shack. Kyle did the same, and we hugged.

"Let's get out of here", he said.

I nodded and we strode down the terminal. We bought trinkets with our remaining Ghanaian cedis and I hopped into the bathroom. I had not gone all day, as nerves had choked my bladder. I stepped out, we laughed at each other in the hallway, shaking our heads in relief, and started to walk towards the gate.

I turned towards home and the path got blocked.

A plain-clothes police officer stood before us, his right hand raised like he was taking an oath.

"Your passports please," he said.

Thoughts raced through my brain at breakneck speed. I tried to control my breathing and kept myself as still as possible to prevent hyperventilating. I must have looked like the guiltiest person alive. For a brief moment, I lost composure and just entered a state of near panic as Cortisol and Testosterone coursed through my veins. I took a breath. I knew that my mind was entering fight or flight mode. I knew the reactions to expect and tried my best to control them. I explored every avenue and possibility of my situation at high speed with clarity of mind. I looked haggard. I had not slept in days, I hadn't shaved in two weeks. My clothes were all dirty. I looked like a bum. I had to submit to the drug test and keep my options open.

"Mr. Bart, you will need to take a drug test. Are you ready?" asked the officer.

"Yes," I replied.

"Perfect. Let us go to the loo," He said.

Okay, this was happening. I was walking with a plain-clothes officer into a bathroom at an airport to submit myself to a drug test. This was payback. There was no way I would pass this drug test despite the fact that I was completely clean. Something would be found and I would be arrested.

We arrived at the stall and I stared at the standing urinal as the officer handed me a plastic bottle cap from a Pepsi bottle. I squeezed it with my thumb and forefinger.

"You want me to pee in this?", I asked

"Yes," he replied.

"This? You don't have a cup or bottle?", I quipped.

"Into the cap," he said.

His eyes shifted left and right, and then he glanced back at his partners he could no longer see. I started to calm down and I got the scam. I unzipped and waited.

"So, um, I cannot go. Remember? You caught me leaving the bathroom?" I said.

He paused.

"Try *harder*," he commanded.

"I can't! There's nothing left!" I blurted.

He bit his lip.

"Let us get some water," he suggested.

"Me daa si. Too se adamfo."

He smiled as he noted my broken Twi of thanks. We left the bathroom and he rattled off orders to the expectant duo waiting outside the bathroom. One gave a grimace with a fatigued roll of the eyes, as the other went to fetch a bottled water. They pointed to a table in the hallway and pulled out four chairs. Three went on their side and one on mine. I sat down in an arrogant, louche manner—body open, leaning back in my chair, neck exposed, and legs open—and a bottled water was placed in front of me.

"Drink," the officer instructed.

I started to drink the water and glanced at the gate using peripheral vision. The line was down to about ten people. Kyle hovered at the back and glanced in my direction. Strength in negotiations is all about timing and I had no leverage in this department. They knew I had about fifteen minutes to resolve this matter and they had all the time in the world. They sat and smiled. I had few moves left.

"Am I being detained?" I asked.

Laughter ensued.

"Of course not! You are not being detained at all," the officer responded.

"But you have my passport. Can I have it back?" I asked.

Fake smiles, a shaking of the head.

"Then you are detaining me against my will." I challenged.

Silence. Sidelong glances. An opening.

I pulled out a notebook and opened it to a blank page. I uncapped my pen.

"Gentleman, I know you are trying to do the right thing. I know you need to ensure that people are treated fairly while preventing any drugs from coming into your country. You have a fine order of law here. A good sense of justice. This is true of you and your country yes?" I asked.

"Yes," they said with pride and determination as they slowly walked into my last gambit.

I took a breath, ensured my voice would not shake, and turned the game around.

"Excellent. My friend (I dropped the full name of the chief of police) has always shown me the greatest courtesies when I visit. He would be happy to know how well you have behaved. Additionally, (I dropped the names of everyone I knew at CID) would equally like to know of your efforts. And to ensure you are given due notice in your work, could each of you please give me your full names and badge numbers? I am sure they would like to know who you are and commend you for your efforts." I declared.

They stared at me incredulously.

My passport slid across the table.

"Leave here and do not come back," the officer replied.

I took my bag and walked briskly to Kyle awaiting at the gate.

"Let's get the fuck out of here," I said.

We boarded the plane and were the last ones to take our seats. I looked at the window and realized the full weight of my lesson. Focus only on the good that you can do and not on the bad you can stop.

TURN IT AROUND
THE ART OF NEGOTIATION

The airport arrest was a scam, completely unrelated to the Kwase affair. The moment the Pepsi bottle cap was handed over to me, I knew this was a shakedown for cash. I looked incredibly guilty and I started off on the wrong foot. Nervous and shaking, dirty and haggard, I realized I looked like an easy target, an ignorant "voluntourist" who would gladly pay, say, a $50 fine for failing a "drug test" to not miss his flight. Despite all my mistakes that got me to that point, my competitive spirit forced me to double-down on principle.

I didn't want to take the easy route. I wanted to negotiate my way out.

Negotiation and compromise is at the heart of nearly everything I have attained or accomplished in life. Rarely is anything given outright. Once you leave the womb of the home, the world is malleable to those that know how to ask and negotiate for what they want, whether on behalf of themselves or their communities. Not all negotiations are pleasant experiences though all are incredibly valuable as a learning exercise. From dodging scams at foreign airports to getting millions of dollars invested in projects, here are some general lessons of negotiation:

Speak to the Heart

Nelson Mandela spent 27 years in jail in South Africa. During this time, he taught himself Afrikaans, the language of his colonialist oppressors. And he leveraged that power of language as a tool against the brutal regime of apartheid. He knew a simple yet incredibly powerful notion: If you speak to a man in a language he understands, you speak to his head. If you speak to a man in his own language, you speak to his heart.

In the above story of my brief arrest, I leveraged a brief opening by saying a basic phrase of "Thank you and I'm sorry" in the native language of the police. I knew that this would register to his subconscious and start to establish rapport, which I define as the process of getting the attention and trust of the unconscious mind. Trust, however minimal, is the foundation of every negotiation and rapport must be established at some level.

Controlling Time Controls Everything

Time is the most finite resource on the planet. It can never be borrowed, and is therefore the most important factor in any negotiation. I had everything against me in this regard when I walked into that airport scam. The guards knew that there was only one flight per day and that if I did not get on that plane, it would leave without me, causing me distress and financial woe. They intercepted me at the perfect time, right during the boarding process where humans become anxious lemmings desperately awaiting entry to a mechanical bird. The strongest position you can have in a negotiation is *all the time in the world*, which necessitates a Buddhist mindset that removes desire from the mind. If you can remove the desire—even if just superficially—for the car or home you are negotiating for, you have created space to make a wise decision and greatly increased your position in the dialogue. I knew I could not control the plane's departure. Yet I could control my demeanor and hence that is why I sat with a rather arrogant pose that read, "I don't care about this flight". I tried my best to not glance at the dwindling line. Yet the odds were against me.

If you control the clock, you control everything.

Expect the Unexpected

Once I made the great mistake of getting entrenched in dirty Ghanaian politics, I thrust my team and myself into a whirlwind of distracting and disheartening activities. I had failed on many levels and the greatest of them all was not being prepared. Sun Tzu, the great Chinese general and military strategist once said, "If you know the enemy and know yourself, you need not fear the results of a hundred battles," capturing the essence of being adequately ready to engage in negotiation. You must think of all possible outcomes of the current state and then be prepared to face them all. I have been sued a few times though never have I been unprepared for litigation. When things started going remotely south, I'd tap the counsel of experienced individuals and legal professionals to better understand all my options and remove all of the unknowns. Together, we mentally explore each path and become prepared to trudge down each and every one. Yet it took epic failures like my encounter with Kwase to learn how to be prepared and to understand how to act.

Third Party Parry

The cleverest move of the scam was to separate me from Kyle. Negotiating with one individual as opposed to many has countless obvious benefits. The Japanese, who are excellent negotiators, were very wise to this notion and at a negotiation table, would wear identical suits and would purposefully—through words, lack of titles and hand actions—mystify whom the decision maker(s) was/were in the group. In the world of business sales, delineating executive sponsors from decision makers to influencers is vital in getting the upper hand. This same principle works when buying a car. If I am meeting a car salesman and express interest in a car, we will inevitably enter into a bidding tussle. If I find the terms not to my liking, I sidestep with my third party: "Thank you for the information but I need to speak to my wife about this." I have now rendered his arguments useless against me as my wife is not present and he cannot directly negotiate with her. I have also then increased the time we need to make the decision. (Note: this is a highly fictitious scenario as my wife is a far greater negotiator than I am.)

Always Act, Never React

All of us have buttons that can be pushed and we cannot allow that to happen when seeking common ground between parties. Controlling the mind, steadying the breathing, and realizing when your emotions trump logic are vital negotiation skills. An impassive Zen-like state of solidity is the most masterful way to handle any negotiation. Like all great poker players know, finding a 'tell', a change in a player's behavior or demeanor that gives clues to that player's assessment of their hand, is an incredibly useful tool in controlling the game within the negotiation.

Once my makeshift captors realized I could not urinate, I was asked to sit at the table. Their backs were to the gate and I faced them, where I could directly see the dwindling line of passengers getting on board. Perhaps this was unintentional though it would be remarkably effective in eliciting panic from a person who is desperate to get on a plane. Once I stalled to buy more time, they did their best to push my buttons. I tried to maintain my calm and then questioned their authority.

Badge of Authority

A powerful tool in negotiations is showing a badge of authority such as a document, title, certification, or a shiny metallic object to convey that one party has dominance over another. I am rarely impressed with badges of authority. While I respect the mastery of craft in receiving a certification or badge, I am also aware of the myopic views this same focused path can create. Many people and companies also dilute the value of many certifications that exist not for compliance to excellence (such as an Olympic gold medal or a PhD in a given field) but instead for profit generating purposes (such as an MBA from an online 'university' or Salesman of the Year statues on a car dealer's desk). Badges are important though they are prolific so their value is questionable and are politically corruptible (let's not forget Adolf Hitler was nominated for a Nobel Peace Prize), and can be leveraged for mere advantage. So question authority.

Sitting at that table, a whirlwind of thoughts entered my mind as I stared at my opponents. First of all, I was beyond customs and therefore in international territory. What on earth were local policeman even doing there? It was no longer Ghana. These badges were useless outside of the fact that they existed to merely prove their dominance. And hence my next thought was that I should counter with my own badge of authority. If they were going to play the cop card, I would trump it with the, "I know your boss" card. They misread me as a clueless tourist who could be shaken down for a $100 bribe. The names I knew disrupted their illusion of power and my own badge trumped theirs. I took the risk and poked the bear. They turned over and howled.

Be Kind to the People, Be Tough to the Cause

I am not upset at the officers as people. They have tough jobs and are paid little. Corruption is systemic in all parts of the world and while I may hate the game, I respect the player. That "player" is a human being, a living soul that is trying to increase his or her choices in life. Who am I to judge them without fully understanding their why? Fundamentally, I believe nearly all people are trying to do good in the world. So I am kind to the people and stay tough on the cause. What those officers were doing was clearly wrong. They were abusing their power for quick gain and lurked upon two shaggy looking dudes who looked like an easy score. I may not have been fully ready in my mind to miss that flight though I did not want to convey this weakness. Instead, I revealed my risky ace card: I know your bosses and are they cool with this? And throughout that entire ordeal with Kwase, I had been very kind and gracious to the officers at CID and the chief of police, offering them compliments and notes of, "I'm here to help." I knew that by being gracious, someone there would have my back. Always be kind to people as you never know when you might need their help.

CHAPTER 10

THIS IS RURAL STYLE

This is farming rural style!
Thwack!
This is how we eat rural style!
Thwack!
This is what we do best!
Thwack!
I watch Peter Luswata hack off pieces of fresh pineapple as he explains Ugandan farming practices. We stand in a field of pineapples, all grown locally and organically. I cannot help but notice how closely his machete deftly chops away at the succulent pineapple grasped in his hand.

His giggles are infectious. Despite being nearly 40 years of age, he laughs like a child full of wonder.

His stroke is deft and the pineapple is ready for eating in less than a minute. He used nothing more than a machete, a stump of a tree as a cutting board, and his dexterous hands. Replace my hand with his and this prep would have taken about seven minutes longer and resulted in three less fingers.

He hands our volunteers the literal fruit of his labor.

Without a doubt, it is the best pineapple I have ever eaten.

I can taste the power.

~

The African soil felt natural, as if my home had shifted 15,000 miles from underneath me. It felt wonderful being back in the field after a year of working in San Francisco. Transforming our side hustle GO into a full-fledged company moved slowly in the first two years. Kyle was still finishing university and I was working at Slalom Consulting. Though we were challenged in our pursuits, nothing compared to the thrill of discovery as we grappled with the complex issue of global poverty. We came back energized and wiser after our trip to Ghana though with little direction on how to proceed. Kyle spent his free time teaching himself how to code, and took course work on design so people would be visually attracted to our work. I spent time seeking a unique idea to grasp as our own by reading books on international development and speaking with other people in the field. We called and emailed with our partners on the ground in Ghana weekly.

I spoke to people about our experiences with Eric and what we had learned. While people were interested, my immigrant background made me timid on asking for help. I came from humble origins and was a descendant of hardworking people that did not ask for help when one's own effort could do the work. So we languished those first few years as we tried to do everything ourselves.

Inherently, I wanted to inspire people to do something yet when it came time to ask for help, I didn't how to properly do it. We were drawing a map while driving the car and though things were moving, it was more drift than direction. We needed a spark to zoom us forward and it came from a lightning bolt of a man that would evolve into a trusted partner, a wonderful friend, and mentor. That man was Peter Francis Luswata.

Peter was literally born on a farm. His mother gave birth to her boy in the banana plantations of Uganda as access to a hospital was not possible in their community. His first breaths of air in life were toxic with the rich smell of farming. His passion for agriculture came from his first moments of life. He worked hard, and earned himself a scholarship to attend St. Mary's University in Virginia for his bachelor's degree. He studied theology with the conviction of a man destined to be a priest. He then completed a Master's in Philosophy at the University of Maryland. Most importantly, he discovered a world of pristine roads, liberal democracy, and endless food-shops; a land of freedom, justice, and opportunity. He saw the world as it could be if the right leadership was in place. And at a certain moment in his life, inspired by this vision of the "could be", he knew that his life's purpose was steeped in humanitarian efforts.

Peter returned to Uganda a changed man. He left the path of becoming a priest, and sought a higher calling in community development and activism. He started working at Mercy Corps and worked tirelessly, his entrepreneurial efforts shined, and he became known as a peak performer. Despite his talents, he always reported to a white foreign "expert" that supposedly knew more about Uganda than he did. He grew determined to start his own organization. He just needed the resources to start and his lucky break came in the form of an email sent by a college kid who wanted to see the world.

Shortly before Kyle and I met in Madagascar, he had flown out to Uganda after randomly exchanging a few emails with Peter on a nonprofit bulletin board. They spent hours over countless plates of steamed matoke (a green banana mush) with rich peanut sauce while Peter shared his vision of launching a model development farm—a hands-on training center that would help farmers learn sustainable methods of farming. The farm would act as a living laboratory where farmers could learn from each other and form into cooperatives to grow and sell their food at scale.

"Farming is what we do best. With a little help, we can go a long way on our own," Peter shared.

Peter comprehended Uganda's rural agricultural development sector like the back of his hand. He was politically savvy and understood the varying needs of the local farmers, the distributors, and the politicians. He knew the local practices, the players, the markets, and which crops thrived. And his time spent abroad presented him the mental images of a successful farming future for his native land.

He had a vision and a plan. He just needed a small investment to make it happen. Kyle provided the seed capital Peter needed by obtaining a grant from a family foundation called Morning Glory. Morning Glory funded $10,000 for Peter to launch the model farm and three years later, we were standing in the fertile earth of Peter's creation, our hands sticky from pineapple juice. Our second round of project investments had begun and we came to Uganda with high hopes of expanding our impact.

And like all sequels, we had bigger budgets and bigger ambitions so we shot for the stars and landed on Peter's moon.

~

Together with a close friend named Ryan Gilpin, Kyle and I returned back to Africa to find more disruptive social entrepreneurs like Peter who were establishing their own organizations to end poverty. We had a better formation in our minds of who we were looking for and developed an itinerary that would take us across Kenya, Uganda, Tanzania, and Rwanda. We exchanged many cups of tea with community leaders and social entrepreneurs that wanted to create a better and more just world. While some had shady elements to their character, the vast majority had the passion and determination to move things forward. However, few had the impact of Peter. While some of my African brothers and sisters that I met on this trip equally deserved their own chapters (James Nathaniel and Costa Nzaramba, I miss you dearly), it was Peter who demonstrated the power of this equation:

IMPACT   INCOME

If you really want to launch an organization that will scale, you must create impact and make yourself irreplaceable. Always. This impact will drive more income, whether for your project, your services, or your organization. It drives me insane when people tell me all the impact they could have given the right amount of income. No. You must lead with impact. You must demonstrate impact with your own resources before seeking outside support. In doing so, the previous accomplishments and reputation you have created will then manifest into the income you need to see that idea or venture grow.

Peter knew this and it was clear he had leveraged every penny from his first $10,000 investment. From the original funding, Peter built the following farming ventures and infrastructure:

- A multi-tiered livestock complex that housed over 100 goats, four cows, 20 chickens, three guinea fowl, and a perturbed looking duck
- A brick farm house used as an office for the workers
- A water cooling system powered by rain fall
- A seed distribution system for local farmers to try new crops
- A meeting area with chairs, tables, and a generator for town hall meetings
- A village banking cooperative for farmers that provided seed or livestock loans
- Volunteer quarters with a catered kitchen and an open air living space for up to 15 individuals
- Farming plots that grew tomatoes, peppers, coffee, pineapples, bananas, papaya, cabbage, avocados, maize, corn, and other various greens

Peter squeezed out every penny of his first investment. Local farmers made bricks by hand and gave scraps to help the animals grow. Seed companies donated time and seeds to encourage the development of the farms. These acts gave people a hand-up while also providing the company with future customers. Crucially, Peter did not give anything away at the farm. As he put it,

"This farm is a bank. The goats are a bank. The seeds are a bank."

"The lessons are a bank. Nothing here is free."

"You want something? Give me something so I know you are serious."

Farmers in this area have tiny plots of land and most live off less than a dollar per day. To Peter, that still didn't mean that those farmers didn't have something to give. He did not give out charity or pity, he demanded that people give first, no matter how dire the situation.

"Give me your food scraps so our farm can make compost or feed our animals. We will then provide you with lessons on how to grow food."

"When you are trained, we will loan you a kilo of seed. When your crop grows, you will pay us back two kilos of seed."

"Then you will get an animal, perhaps a goat or a pig. And when that animal gives birth, you give us the young one back. And the cycle continues."

In Peter's view, the worst thing about the current state of international development was that poor people were given things outright. If you give something to somebody, they do not value it. There has to be a token of exchange to realize the inherent worth of an object or service. When they invest something of value, they will treat the return with due respect. They are vested stakeholders in the future benefits and opportunities. And even in rural Masaka, an early epicenter of the AIDS epidemic and one of the world's poorest areas, everyone had something that could be given.

Pondering, I looked around the farm and realized something was missing.

"Peter, where are the gates? How do you prevent stealing?" I asked.

Peter gave a hearty giggle.

"Ah child! People do not steal from their own cupboard! This farm is owned by the community!", Peter replied.

A focus of this farm was instructing local farmers how to grow various crops and also act as a central point of seed and livestock distribution. The "farm" itself was not really owned by anyone. It was a cooperative of the community. As farmers were trained, they were put into cooperatives since their individual tiny plots of land gave them no bargaining power. Once the cooperatives reached 20 to 30 members, they all planned growth together of a common crop and then with the model farm's assistance, negotiated contracts for sale. The farm was building capacity of all the members of the community by teaching them how to grow food and then leverage business and economic acumen so they could earn more money from their harvest.

No one stole. No one solitary person gained from this farm. The community was building a better future for themselves. It worked because the biggest investment Peter made laid in the hearts and minds of the people. In his words:

"People need healthy food to grow and learn. They need food for their families and to sell on the market. They just need instruction on how to get started and that's what we provide."

TURN IT AROUND
THINKING IN SYSTEMS

The more I spoke with Peter, the more I realized his approach was rooted in systems thinking. This field of thought was pioneered by Donella Meadows in her book *Thinking in Systems,* and the basic tenet is that the problems facing our world—war, hunger, poverty, global warming—cannot be solved by fixing one piece in isolation. Fixing one piece of the puzzle cannot solve vast problems because even seemingly minor details may have enormous influence. Too often, neglected details have the biggest impacts as they reverberate throughout the system.

Many forces that are acting altogether to reach a given state govern systems, and systems-thinking is the process of understanding how forces influence one another. It's an approach to problem solving by viewing "problems" as parts of an overall system rather than reacting to specific parts, outcomes, or events. If one reacts to only a specific event (people have no clean water) by a single act (let's build a well), they could potentially contribute to an event's further development of unintended and negative consequences (the well breaks since no one maintains it, people lose faith in nonprofit work, stop donating, and the cycle of poverty spirals even further downwards). There is no silver bullet, no one solitary "thing" that will alleviate poverty in a community. To the best of his ability, Peter understood the many factors that caused his community of Masaka to struggle under the heavy weight of poverty. He ensured his ventures would have a holistic approach and steered the impact of his work to have positive transformative development in both economic and cultural terms. This goes way beyond teaching a person to fish rather than giving him or her food.

Think about the cooperatives. They are a group of farmers that grow food. The economic benefit is obvious as the more the farmers sell in bulk, the more bargaining power they hold. Yet the economics are only a part of the system and Peter's vision ran deeper than that as economics influence politics, and politics diffuse through the community in various ways. That is another system we must focus on.

The model farm is careful in the organization of its cooperatives so that men work with women, Christians work with Muslims, and people that are HIV positive work with those that are healthy. This is crucial as it greatly reduces the stigma attached with thinking of people different from you as being *Others* by haphazardly categorizing them based on their religion, gender, race, or even their health. This leads not only to economic opportunity, but also drives people to feel safer in their communities, and growth patterns of the system become self-reinforcing.

Now let's look at a counter example in Peter's community of Masaka to show what happens when organizations do not think in systems. It's well noted that Antiretroviral drugs (ARVs) are effective in preventing the spread of HIV. As the costs of ARVs tumbled in the late nineties, many governments and international aid organizations in Africa began the distribution of free pills. A simple plan that was simply ineffective. ARVs are very difficult for the human body to digest and require to be consumed with food. If only drugs are provided for free and no availability of healthy foods exists, then the medicine doesn't help. In Peter's approach, he focused not only on helping farmers sell food for profit, he focused on selling healthy, organic foods that also benefited the community. These foods made the ARVs potable for the body. These healthy foods also helped rebuild the organism physically and sociologically. By having food grown in a network of cooperatives, Peter's program simultaneously reduced the stigma of the people that suffered from HIV while also increasing the supply of good foods. As of this writing, Peter's model farm—a vastly inter-connected ecosystem of people, animals, and plants— has over 60 cooperatives that encompass

1,800 farmers who are now growing tons of food per month. They grow so much food that they export for profit and contracts have been signed with fruit and juice companies. Goats' urine is made into fertilizer, rainwater is used for irrigation, pig feces are processed into biogas, solar power pumps water, and nothing is wasted.

Remember how I mentioned the volunteer quarters in the bulleted list? That was a crucial early investment as it made Peter's work resonate around the world. With volunteer quarters, you can host international guests that pay good money to see work like this in action. Peter created an authentic experience for backpacking Europeans, university study-abroad programs, and various organized "voluntourist" groups. These people were able to view his work while also creating valuable jobs for locals to cook their food and clean their beds. This experience has value and provided multiple streams of income for the farm. First, volunteers paid $50 per day to live and work at the farm. Most were so inspired by their experiences that they would raise money for new needs at the farm. One such visit led to a strategic alliance with the University of Illinois, who would send hundreds of professors and graduate students to provide technical support for a swath of Peter's agricultural ventures. Additionally, various consultants are helping him scale this model across East Africa.

In short, the members of Peter's community can now afford to save money, live healthier lives, and feel safe. Peter's entrepreneurial vision and passion for helping others has vastly increased the number of opportunities for himself, for his family, and for his community. And he thought out and executed his plan by leveraging both local and international systems.

The causes of poverty are vastly complex and there is no one given solution that will magically fix everything. Yet social entrepreneurs like Peter who think systemically about how they impact their communities are the most effective resources that one can invest in. They make mistakes and they may not always be fully aware of the limitations of their own thinking, yet they learn quickly from failure and pivot as necessary. As Peter continued to speak about how the cooperatives were weaving torn fabrics of the community back together, I wondered about the impact this would have over the coming generations of both local and international communities. The brilliance behind Peter's vision was not in the physical manifestation of this system; it was the emotional creation of hope that reverberated through his community.

Yet back in 2009, before any of this was realized, we simply marveled at what Peter had accomplished with only a $10,000 investment. What could he do with $100,000? Our next question was obvious:

"What's next and how can we help?"

I have come to learn to have a pen ready in advance when asking Peter this question. The man rattles off ideas with the cadence of a teenager who drank their first triple espresso. The ideas and the reasoning behind them splatter and scramble, and the pace is faster than my hands can write. Some of his desires included a grain mill to process the food for higher profit margins, a pig farm to expand pork production, a community center, a library, a drill rig to access water, a radio tower to broadcast grain prices, a much larger training facility to keep up with growth, and on and on and on.

Our team looked at one other. A lot more money had to be raised. Immediately.

Like hummingbirds in the burning jungle, we zipped.

We had a mountain to climb.

Never Finished. *My grandfather, Henryk Skorupa, on his 90th birthday. He followed his calling to build onwards and empowered our family with the privilege of giving back.*

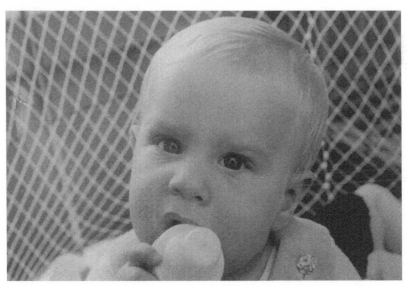

Born in Poland, Made in America. *The dim prospects of life in Poland in the early 1980s compelled my parents to move our family to central Illinois. We would travel back and forth frequently, giving me a global perspective during my formative years.*

Evacuate. *A final parting shot before my medical evacuation from Madagascar. Thanks to an extraordinary local doctor, my vision returns and expands.*

The Hummingbirds. *GO's first foray into international development begins in Ghana when we meet a powerful and noble community leader named Eric. From left: Charlie Perkins, Kyle Miller, Eric Annan, and Bart Skorupa.*

On The Road. *We begin with little and spend frugally. GO staff and volunteers take the Yapei Queen, a 30-hour commuter ferry, that traverses the world's largest man-made lake to inspect potential projects on a shoestring budget.*

Leadership Development. *GO Co-founder Kyle Miller meets Costa Ndayisabye at his home in Kigali, Rwanda to discuss community development via local leaders.*

Trailblazers. *By climbing Mount Kilimanjaro, Clare Cottle (left) and Sarah Sowden (right) would raise $11,000 by climbing Mount Kilimanjaro for our first cadre of projects in Rwanda, Tanzania, and Uganda.*

Transformative Development. *GO Champion Michelle Ewoldt (left) visits Uganda to see the well she raised funds for via friends and family in San Francisco, a project envisioned by local leader Peter Francis Luswata (right).*

Delegation Trips. *To inspire more Champions, GO organized trips to visit projects so volunteers could learn about the needs of various communities. Katlyn Torgerson visits ClearWater, a movement to provide clean water in the oil-ravaged Ecuadorian Amazon.*

Do What You Can. *Kenyan community leader Abdul Kassim tells the Kenyan fable about the bravery of the hummingbird at the 2015 GO Gala in San Francisco.*

We Are One. *GO brings Heather Grabowski into my life, which leads to our wedding in Zanzibar. I am united with my soul mate via the humble guidance of our officiant and trusted local leader Peter Francis Luswata.*

Unsustainable Development. *The spotlight begins to burn too bright. As our stature grows, we find ourselves steering a large ship at unsustainable speed.*

What's Our Endgame? *As projects grow in complexity and scope, monitoring and evaluation of their impact becomes an ever-increasing challenge to manage. In Kampong Speu, Cambodia, Bora Im demonstrates how biosand water filters purify contaminated water.*

Turn It Around. *Ryan Gilpin (upper left), Jeanne (center, top), and Bosco (far right), witness the power of Costa Ndayisabye's (center) leadership. Costa's tutelage of "The Work" methodology helps survivors and perpetrators of the Rwandan genocide to reconcile.*

Pay It Forward. *We don't learn from experience, we learn from reflecting upon experience. And then we pass those lessons on to future generations of change-makers.*

Leadership. *Impossible is what you won't do. Thanks to John Dau, these words of steadfast perseverance to overcome the greatest of life's challenges are forever etched into my mind and heart.*

CHAPTER 11

THE CLIMB

*Ryan, Kyle, and I have a simple plan. Climb a mountain and raise the
capital Peter needs to launch his next social venture. He's taken his first round
of funding and squeezed every bit of impact from that original $10,000. He has
vision—oh so many visions—on how to expand and scale. He wants to build a
middle class in rural Uganda. And like any entrepreneur, he needs more capital
and resources to grow. Money for staff, machines, trucks, and tools. Yet since Peter
works in Uganda, a frontier economy, investment capital is scarce and expensive.*

*So here we stand, a means to an end, looking up from the base camp.
Commonalities bond our motley crew together: a passion for hiking, a dislike for
comfort, and the ability to raise money so people like Peter can do good better. Ryan
and Kyle grew up together in Northern California as avid hikers traversing the
aptly named Desolation Wilderness. I'm an avid runner and hiker who had already
summited Kilimanjaro a few years back. We come from affluent backgrounds
and want to do our part to share our blessings. We gaze at the summit of Mount
Kilimanjaro and prepare with purpose.*

*Dawn is breaking. It's only the first day and I'm already dreading day six.
My experience from previously hiking up this mountain is something that makes
this second hike harder. While thousands of people summit Kilimanjaro every
year, it is not easy by any stretch of the imagination. People have climbed and
died in the process. Additionally, as a runner and cyclist whose body understands
exhaustion, I hold a profound fear of altitude sickness as it blurs the mind's ability
to distinguish being tired from being dangerously exhausted.*

*I remember vividly how difficult altitude sickness impacted my climb many
years back. I doubt my capabilities as I'm the oldest person in our group of
sixteen. The porters carrying our kit look like kids, and Kyle and Ryan are five*

years healthier. A rush of Cortisol comes in. It's that hormone our bodies release when facing stress or grave danger. It surges through my veins as I contemplate the unknown.

You cannot fully trust your mind when climbing to such great heights. Oxygen depletion clouds your mind's ability to reason up there in the darkness. Your pace on the final summit is slow and methodical. The final six-hour trek to the summit begins at midnight. At that point, you've only slept three or four hours. The path is mostly sand so it's two steps forward, one step back. It's pitch black and with each step you lose progress as sand sidles out beneath your boots. This frustrates you. And then the sickness hits. Nausea. Headache. Drunkenness. You have little idea what is really happening while climbing at altitude as a novice. This worries you, causes you to over-think and over-analyze, and you feel doubt creep in.

Your local guide is essential. He leads the way and speaks to keep the group motivated.

He keeps a slow pace.

"Pole, pole," he says.

(Swahili for slowly, slowly).

He keeps spirits up.

"This is all normal," he reminds us.

You nod and keep walking up.

"You are doing fine," he encourages.

One step forward, half a step back.

Repeat.

"You are doing fine. Keep going," he instructs.

One step forward, half a step back.

Four hours down. Two remaining.

It's so dark and you're so tired.

First you hear it, then you see it.

Kyle is throwing up. Fluids of fluorescent yellow stream out of his mouth. The groups' headlamps converge to bring light.

You look down. You've never seen vomit that shade of bright yellow.

His eyes are drunk.

"Are you doing fine?" the guide asks.

No response. The guide repeats the question, now louder.

"ARE YOU FINE?" the guide demands.
Who knows?

~

Peter ignited a spark that compelled us to act. After a few days surveying his work, we wanted to help. With his determined vision, a methodical approach, and a strong team of master farmers to back his efforts, he didn't need us to pick up shovels or stack cement blocks. We acted like fools a year ago in Ghana when we jumped right into the construction. While rolling up the sleeves may be symbolically helpful, such actions do little outside of framing vanity selfie shots of shirtless white guys in medium physical condition lamely shoveling cement. Worse, volunteer efforts like those merely slow things down. By jumping in shovels first, you neglect to consider just how bad you are at shoveling. While you may get better at it by the third day, you also probably are unaware that you took the job of a local community member that could have really used that money.

We ditched the metaphorical shovels and huddled under a large thatched canopy of banana leaves that served as the open-air training center. The "training center" was built with a modest budget, had no walls, and sported a thatched roof made of banana leaves. It housed 200 plastic chairs, a small stage, and a generator to power a small microphone. The farm surrounded us and the sky hovered with expectations. We looked around to take in the scope and impact of Peter's farm. As previously stated, if $10,000 created so much impact, what would $100,000 do? How about $1 million? These simple questions caused ideas to roar out of Peter like a waterfall. We jotted down expansion ideas with pen and paper and made drawings in the dirt with our feet. A swirl of ideas catapulted out:

"Let's build an eco-friendly lodge for tourists!"

"Water! We must have clean water!"

"We need an industrial-sized grain processing facility. Processed food earns us more money."

At that moment, the skies opened and huge rain pounded on the thatched hut. Water dripped on our plans and smudged our ideas. The surge of thought continued:

"We need a *real* training facility with a proper roof! And walls!"

"Yes, and a library!"

"We must build a pig farm since the price of pork is so high!"

"Yes, and we can harvest biogas from the pig shit! We need power!"

We moved the pig farm made of rocks here, the training facility made of leaves there, and Peter poked holes in the dirt. Idea after idea stormed out.

"Yes and *this*."

"Yes and *that*."

The sky was the limit and each idea begot another until our dirt floor was littered with potential investments. Some were crazy and some seemed obvious. I plugged my laptop into the diesel generator and fired up Excel to bring focus, and then prioritized one idea after another. Our limited funding formed a plan.

Once we collected all the ideas from Peter and his team, we focused on what we could achieve *now*. Unlike the fish farm we reviewed in Ghana, the numbers looked much better on the potential investments Peter sought to make. We focused on how much each would cost and what the potential return on investment would be. While GO was now more financially ambitious with more funding, resources were still tight. We were all still volunteers, so our scarcity bred cautious investment.

Peter ultimately made the executive decision that the first logical step was to fund a maize mill. Certain farmers who were now growing acres of maize wanted to move up the food chain by processing their food at a higher profit margin. However, while milling is profitable, it should be done at scale to be market competitive. We did not have $100,000 for an industrial-sized grain processing facility, so Peter envisioned a small prototype mill that would cost $10,000 or less. Once up and running it could establish a proof of concept by eking out a small profit. He also planned it to be modular. By making the building big enough for three grain mills, we could add more and expand if the first became successful. We would start small and think big.

To get started, we needed to prove that if the farmers here could process their maize at the model farm, they would then earn more money, and literally and figuratively move up the food chain. To be sure this bet was worth the gamble, we scoped out the competition.

We toured other mills in the area and talked to farmers about why the existing processing facilities were not good enough. We empathized with their needs. We did not guess *what* the problem was. Instead, we wanted to figure out the challenges of what was preventing the farmers trained at the model farm from achieving wellbeing in their lives. We saw first-hand how certain farmers were growing acre upon acre of maize. We saw how the farmers with the most amount of land were scaling their work faster, and were hiring laborers in the community and providing precious jobs.

One Muslim farmer named Hajj introduced me to his daughter. Like any father, Hajj wanted only the best for her. She wanted to get her degree in law, which requires heavy investment costs. Yet Hajj, a farmer working in a rural community, had little chance of affording her university education. He had land and through the development farm, had made efficient use of his limited space by growing 7,000 kilos of maize per harvest. Yet even with three maize harvests per year, he saved little money. He wanted more profit, for his farm, for his daughter, and for the workers he could hire. By processing the maize into flour, his margin would double. We heard this same story repeated over and over from more and more farmers.

"Peter, why are there no maize mills in this area? Surely with this much demand there must be something here?" I asked.

"Of course. There are quite a few in Masaka," Peter responded.

That made sense as the only mills in the area were in the central town and close to the motorways. The model farm was about a twenty-minute drive from the Masaka city center, yet no farmer here owned a car. Peter was the only one with a truck in the entire area and that was strictly for usage at the farm. Most farmers had Phoenix bicycles, which were cheap, rickety frames from Shanghai. Rarely did we see anything that resembled a complete bike. Some had missing pedals, some had makeshift handlebars from wood, and nearly all had patched tires. A ride to Masaka on a bike in one direction with 50 to 100 kilos of maize (and consider the size of whole maize versus processed flour) strapped to your back would take at least two hours.

We opted not to get the full experience of the "maize-ladened" bike ride and instead hopped into Peter's truck to visit the maize mills in Masaka. We arrived at the first mill in central Masaka and observed a monstrous machine that could theoretically process 100,000 kilos per day. The queue outside numbered around 40 people, which meant about an hour's wait. We visited another mill to check out another line. And then, like nearly every other day in this area, the power browned out. The roaring hum of the mill belched to a halt. The farmers waiting in line sat down.

"Now what happens?" I asked Peter.

"Ah, now you see! These mills are electric!"

He pointed excitedly at the cord, his face lighting up like a child finding a long lost toy.

"You see? You see? Electric! Can you imagine? These guys, these guys here, are running an electric mill. Now they will just wait. How long? How long? An hour. Two hours. Some will just go home and return tomorrow. You see? You see?" Peter lamented.

Peter stood as a man possessed with simultaneous passion and frustration. We spoke to the farmers who confirmed the same. Hours were being wasted.

"Peter, how would you fix this?" I asked.

Peter rambled excitedly.

"Our mill will be diesel powered. We cannot rely on the power here. Diesel will power us all day and every day. Then, we will build a pig farm. Pigs multiply quickly. We can give birth to 64 pigs each gestation period with eight pigs and one breeder. There are three gestation periods per year for a pig. That means 200 pigs per year. Do you know what 200 pigs produce? Poop! So much poop Bart! So much! Can you imagine 200 pigs pooping?"

I hadn't thought about that. Ever.

Peter went on.

"That's A LOT of poop. And do you know what poop is? Poop is power. Poop is p-o-we-r. We can build a bio-digester at the farm. We can use that poop to sequester methane gas. We can use that gas to support the maize mill and run off our own power. And the power that is left over or the gas we cannot use can be bottled and then we can..."

This went on and on. We drew the conversation back to its origin, a tactic I would learn to employ with nearly every conversation I would ever have with Peter. I had one last question.

"How much for the mill?"

~

Peter's $10,000 quote hung in our minds, steeping purpose into our climb as we stood in Mount Kilimanjaro's base camp. We're here to climb Africa's tallest peak to raise the funds to buy a grain mill. We told our friends, family, and colleagues, and asked them to donate to our website in advance of the trip. Kyle built a crude fundraising page on GO's website to track both our fundraising progress and the six-day climb. We carried a GPS unit that transmitted a signal every time we checked into one of the various camps up to the summit.

Our team enlisted the support of Team Kilimanjaro to facilitate the logistics. They are an outfit known for providing its guides and porters with fair wages, and who emphasized safety for all. This approach resulted in a surprisingly large team. Our crew of three climbers apparently required a crew of thirteen porters, one cook, and two guides to haul our food, water, and equipment up the mountain. This seemed overkill though we found solace knowing that we had created 16 temporary jobs. Our team of twenty converged at the Rongai route, a rarer path that avoided most tourists.

The familiar first two days of hiking were easy and rather short affairs. Many hours were spent acclimatizing to the high mountain air, an act of patience that prepares the body for the final summit push. Kyle, Ryan, and I spoke as old friends sharing stories of new futures we wanted to build for our lives. Often, we were quiet and comfortable in each other's presence. We felt no need to fill the thin air with thick chatter.

Patrick our guide led us both mentally and physically. Built like a bull, the soft-spoken Patrick ensured our pace was right, our minds were prepared, and that we did not push unnecessarily. He checked in daily each morning to give the hike briefings for the day and then returned in the evening to check on our mental condition. The first days' hikes were incredibly and deceptively light. We wanted to cover more ground and hike longer stretches than originally planned by Patrick's squad.

"Pole, pole," he responded.

Pronounced "poh-lay", these Swahili words literally meaning "slowly, slowly" cautioned our novice minds from moving too fast for our own good. Climbing a mountain is a system that takes time and patience. Many forces are acting upon the body and there is no way to fast forward. Your body will not be able to handle the pressure. Your brain will swell, fluids will build up in your lungs, and then if you push through, you may die. Like anything great, you must put in tenacious effort and acclimatize to the ever-higher levels of success. Mountains are not climbed in a day, and empires are not built in a week.

We moved slowly upwards over six days. We were anxious yet determined on summit night. Collectively, we had raised $9,000 of our $10,000 goal. I knew that summiting would tip us over the edge. We were at that crucial stage of crowd funding (the practice of funding a project or venture by raising small amounts of money from a large number of people) called the tipping point. The tipping point happens when a crowd funding campaign reaches around eighty-five percent of their goal. It is that moment when the organizers and their tribe of supporters can sense victory. The people you have involved get emotionally motivated to see the campaign succeed at this crucial juncture of raising money. The ones that have been waiting to donate, had flagged it in their emails, or just set it aside for any given reason will come out and will act. Often, an existing donor will give again to get the entire effort across the finish line.

Summit night was our tipping point. Donations kept ticking in as we sent our supporters daily GPS updates during the climb. Yet the closeness to the goal carried the risk that we would push ourselves too far. Historically, the odds of summiting via Rongai were only slightly in our favor with a sixty-five percent success rate. The pressure to summit was acute and I worried we would fail at both goals. Outside of the mental wrangling of not finishing the climb, we would also not have enough money to fund Peter's next great venture.

These thoughts fought against sleep in the frigid air of summit night. The night was so cold that I wore my winter coat, snow pants, and two pairs of hiking socks in my sleeping bag. Our tent shook at midnight as Patrick woke us for the final haul. We began the summit ascent. I had never seen so many stars. The black night glowed with vivid sparkles of white points. A winding trail of bobbing headlamps worn by other climbers dotted the faint outline of the road ahead. *Pole, pole* we went. Two steps forward, one step back. I remembered the grueling thin sand the moment it began, and that vicious robbed progress that ate away at each of our precious footsteps. We thought of Peter, we thought of family, and we pressed on.

The faint feeling of being drunk enveloped my brain. I felt like I had just slid into that second martini. My vision blurred and my thoughts became incoherent. I felt breathless while walking our slow pace. My head started to pound.

Then I heard the vomiting. Turning around, I saw fluids of fluorescent yellow streaming out of Kyle's mouth. Patrick rushed past me.

"Are you doing fine?" asked the guide.

No response. Patrick repeated the question louder.

"Are you doing fine?" the guide demanded.

Kyle's eyes were glazed over though I could see his determination.

"It's just Red Bull," Kyle responded.

"Have you been drinking water?" asked Patrick.

"I can't," Kyle replied.

Kyle's eyes bulged while he sipped on his straw like a kid with a milkshake that was too thick for its vessel. Patrick gripped Kyle's back where the straw connected to its plastic pouch nestled within the lining of his backpack. The pouch of his Camelback was frozen solid. The summit air of -20C had frozen the thin layer of water in his plastic pouch.

"Should we descend?" asked Patrick.

"No, " said Kyle.

Ryan and I split our remaining water between the three of us. With gloved hands, we carefully poured out our water bottles so the metal wouldn't freeze onto our hands. We all took big gulps.

Patrick nodded.

So we pressed on to Africa's ceiling.

The sun rose over the summit at 6:30am as our feet stood at the top of Africa. We embraced, stood with sore feet, bad knees, and clear hearts.

We had raised nearly $11,000.

A new method to support future social entrepreneurs was born.

TURN IT AROUND
DESIGN THINKING

Peter innately understood that many simultaneous forces caused his community to struggle. Yet he also derived hope by believing that many levers also existed to tip the system towards sustainability. Perhaps enacting force on one lever or another could propel the most systemic change. Perhaps many at once needed to be pushed. So how does one quickly identify the most effective levers within the system?

By design thinking, a passionate process of creating meaningful innovations by listening to people and caring about their lives:

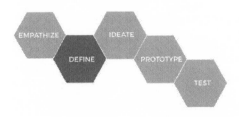

Its fundamental principles revolve around human centered design, a process that starts with the people you're designing for and ends with solutions that are tailored to meet their needs.

This all begins with empathy, an ability to authentically connect with other human beings. The ability to walk in the shoes of others while sharing a moment of their reality is the surest path towards starting something good.

During my recovery in Madagascar, empathy drew me to understand what life in an impoverished community feels like. This situation repeated itself in Masaka where we learned about the difficulties of local farmers. We listened to their stories and rode their shabby bicycles. We waited alongside them in endless queues to mill their maize. Those experiences began to define the scope of the problem. Peter naturally thought as a design thinker. He ideated endlessly, asking "What if?" questions to help fuel a storm of ideas that could help his community thrive.

Eventually, one must focus and cease the blue-sky thinking of various "What If" scenarios. Otherwise, nothing gets accomplished or measured. And what doesn't get measured, doesn't get done. The process to drive "What If" to a tangible idea in "design thinking" is called "flare and focus." You spend an allotted amount of time "flaring" out any and all ideas that can help the product or service. There is no such thing as "this won't work" thinking at this stage. It's helpful to employ the words, "Yes, and…" to begin your thoughts in a group setting where many people are involved. These simple yet powerful words help build off the ideas of others and propagate the flow of thought into a consistent and vibrant stream. "Yes and *this*." "Yes and *that*." Ideas flow freely, from the novel to the bizarre.

You will then insert a "rule" or a focal point to help narrow down the ideas once the pool of ideas are exhausted or have become too unruly to manage. You then flare ideas again with the new rule in place, and a newly refined parameter. Keep repeating the process until you land on an idea that the team agrees could be a feasible prototype.

Visually, the process looks like this:

After flaring ideas with Peter, our first rule to establish focus came from our $10,000 budget. Then we flared ideas on everything $10,000 or less could do. The drill rig was out. Pigs were possible and biogas could work. We iterated those ideas. Then we added a new rule: immediate impact. What one thing could we introduce to the system *now* to effect change so we could get data and test our theory as quickly as possible? We helped facilitate Peter's thinking towards the maize mill by asking that question. While he had grander plans of industrial-sized mills that ran well north of a $150,000 investment, we stuck with a smaller $10,000 version so we could test out a prototype.

The tests came back with definitive results a few years later. Demand and revenue spurred the purchase of a second milling machine, which Peter bought from the earnings of the first mill. Farmers earned even more money, and they grew even more crops. Two mills then became three. These mills currently run 24/7 while Peter shops around a vast expansion to move his operations to Kampala to turbo charge growth. He has a proven model, data to back up his claims, and funders considering his proposal.

Herein lies the beautiful intersection of systems thinking and design thinking; a marriage of the macro and the micro view of designing and implementing groundbreaking ideas that can change the fate of our world. So why doesn't everything and everyone just magically succeed if this blueprint is so simple? After all, Ideo.org publishes the detailed methodology of human centered design for free on their website and anyone can read *Thinking in Systems* by Donella Meadows. While Peter's innate approach to design thinking positioned him for success, nearly everything else in his life set the odds against him. He wasn't born rich and didn't have access to many resources. So what made him successful?

My conclusion is grit and determination. No matter what calamities Peter faced in his life, he persevered with those two core values. In our decade long relationship, I have seen him retain hope and dogged determination against all odds. Peter is a fighter. Over his life, he has seen projects fail, friends and family attacked, a close friend beheaded, a relative shot in cold blood, colleagues arrested, riots that set Kampala afire, and countless other calamities. Yet he always gets up again and rises to the task at hand. He is a loving father and husband, and an incredible social entrepreneur whose mere giggle has won over so many hearts. He's the first person I call when tragedy strikes since he always seems to have the right answer.

This is not merely an anecdotal notion. This idea is backed up by the work of Dr. Angela Lee Duckworth, a professor of psychology and a MacArthur Fellow. She specializes in non-IQ competencies, which predict success. Over her career, she studied children and adults in challenging environments, including West Point military cadets, national spelling bee contestants, and rookie teachers in difficult schools. In each study, her research team asked essentially the same question: "Who is successful here and why?" Across numerous contexts and varied fields, one characteristic emerged as a significant predictor of success: grit.

Grit is the quality that allows an individual to work hard and maintain focus – not for weeks or months, but for years. Grit is what makes the honor student study late into the evening and pushes the elite athlete to do "just one more" set. It's the pulsating lifeblood of the design process as prototyping always leads to the same destination: failure. Like the scientific method, design thinking is a grueling exercise of trap doors and brick walls that impede progress. As you get further along, momentum starts to build, and success begins to trickle in. And that success is only a higher stage for failures epic in scope since more is at stake.

It's the grand failures that test the determination of true leaders. Those enlightened with the knowledge of grit can rightfully assume that their power is limitless. Anything can be achieved, any mountain can be climbed.

This is the lesson Peter bestowed onto me. No words exist in any language I know to convey how meaningful this gift has been in my life.

CHAPTER 12

STORY MATTERS

PART I

She and I would never be the same after this.

I like to think we both knew that.

I walk into Vesuvio on a blustery Saturday afternoon. It's loud in that jovial pub sort of way. Literary energy crackles over fermented drinks. I am looking for someone I do not know. She is English and traveling solo, so I scan the room for the smaller tables. I see a bright smile under a stylish hat. She waves me over.

I am nervous and frail from being so tired all the time. Days and nights are intense as I endlessly stir things up about GO. I hope my state of difference will keep her engaged. The curiosity continues upon this man who spends summers traveling through Africa. I hear a lot of, 'You need to meet Bart'. The problem is that GO gets anything out of these dates. I need money for our local leaders, not frivolous chat. Yet here I am again.

We share pints and Pimms. Her name is Sarah, better known as "Glitter Girl". We reminisce on the one person we both know. Vanessa Sloan. She's doing great, we agree on that. We move on to travel. She travels frequently, has seen a lot of the world. But not Africa. She hasn't seen that magnificent orange sun that burns a daily hole in my heart.

I tell her about my immigrant background. I explain how my family made me realize the power of hard work and sacrifice. I elaborate about how management consulting burned me out. I share my eye story. My vision changed, I say.

I tell her about my past summer building homes in Rwanda. I worked alongside perpetrators and survivors of the genocide. I explain what it felt like to build a home for Jeanne, a woman whose husband was butchered and her home burned by a man named Bosco during this dark time. I share pictures. I point to our team standing outside the completed house. Jeanne is shyly smiling from the entrance of her new home.

I point to a man standing by her.

"This is Bosco."

Her eyes widen.

"Yes, he helped build the home. They work together in peace," I continue.

I point to another man standing in between them.

"This is Costa. He brought them together," I share.

Her eyes soften.

I tell her the story of Costa Ndayisabye, our newest partner at GO. Costa has known more war than peace in his life. Yet he transformed beyond atrocity and is now a community healer.

"Would you like to meet Costa?" I ask.

"He is waiting for you in Rwanda," I explain.

I tell her the story of Peter, a man born into a banana plantation. I tell about his journey across many lands, and how he found himself back home as a leader who propels the common unity in his community.

"Would you like to meet Peter?" I ask.

"He is waiting for you in Uganda," I explain.

Two stories. Two leaders. One reflection of their power.

It is all there for her to envision.

I stop talking.

Her mind is already made.

~

The adventures on African soil stirred something within me. I had a package delivered to me with no return address from a sender named "fate". Once Pandora's box saw the light of day, the entirety of the contents spilled out everywhere. I had no idea what needed to be done, in what order I should begin, or how to start assembling things together. I had a start-down on my hands, not a start-up.

No one has prepared for, nor can anyone prepare for, the necessities of everything that needs to be done when starting your own organization.

No single outline or instruction manual exists that will plot your steps. I hoped that empathizing with people's problems and then ideating solutions with local leaders would make a viable business model magically appear. A shearing white light of doubt continually burned in my brain. I hesitated with every step. I longed for the certainty that I was following the right path as our humble crew blazed the trails of GO. That certainty never appeared though failure often did. She always presented herself as a wise teacher.

We learned quickly, things began to move, and we got traction. Impact happened. Eric finished his school and Peter bought his grain mill. Funding and interest began to flow in. Suddenly, we had five projects in five countries. While our 'staff' was still all volunteers with day jobs (myself included), we were still raising around $200,000 per year for our ever-growing portfolio of social entrepreneurs. It was 2011, and we needed to scale funding to keep their ventures growing.

A moment of truth—a time in life when, for better or worse, everything changes—was coming. It's that moment when a change of perspective on life happens. It makes the world around us appear different such as a huge investment of money, a thought provoking idea, a divorce, a winning of the lottery, the birth of your first child, or a loss of a parent. Things will never be the same after that moment, we think. We worry whether we are prepared for what the new frontier holds. Can I be a good father? How can I live without her? Will I be able to lead this movement?

Such moments of truth cast strings of doubt into our minds since we inherently fear change. Yet these purported life-changing moments are merely instances when our *perspective* of the world changes. We have spent years preparing for this moment. We will cope, endure, and find a way. We cannot change reality but we can control the story of reality and shape its perception.

My moment of truth came from two instances which both led to the same conclusion that life is nothing but a story we tell ourselves to make sense of the world around us. More importantly, we can control our stories and use them to influence the thoughts and beliefs of others. The example of my 'fundraising date' with Sarah Sowden will be explored here. The second will be covered in the next chapter. Both are about how the power of story and storytelling changed not only the trajectory of GO, it also radically changed the trajectory of my life and those around me. Once I witnessed the power of story, the curtain veiling the secret of success and wellbeing came crashing down.

When I met Sarah that fateful afternoon, GO was gaining traction. We were grappling towards that next "thing" which would take us to the next level. And like most great things, the next evolution began in the holy church of empathy and discovery: the bar. The place where beers, wines, and liquors free the truth, ideas get set loose, and where vital relationships kindle. The bar was where I met Sarah, ditched the facts, and simply told her stories of GO that inspired her to take unprecedented action. She hosted parties, ran marathons, and even climbed Kilimanjaro herself. Sarah would go on to raise over $50,000, which gave thousands of people in Uganda and Tanzania a chance for a better life.

How did she do it?

She told great stories.

~

Let me ask you a question. Does it bother you that almost half the world lives on less than $2.50 per day? That is over three billion people! Do you care? Perhaps discomfort is arising while your brain is analyzing these words and the concepts behind them. Perhaps you consider yourself an awful person for not feeling bad.

It's not your fault that empathy is failing to form. Imagine three billion people. Try to envision what they look like. Do you see them? Where would they sit? Assuming the average football stadium fits 70,000 people, you would need 42,800 stadiums for each of them to have seats. Can you picture 42,800 stadiums? Really?

The average person cannot *see* this picture in the window of their minds. People are visually oriented and need palpable language to truly have a point sink into their understanding. If you want to start something good, learn to wrap your facts into stories so that they will penetrate deep into the mind of those you wish to inspire.

After our fundraising climb, Kyle and I had a semblance of a story for GO. We could not quite distill it down into a coherent strategy, but we felt the presence of a method growing around us. We zipped along like hummingbirds, kneading rough concepts out of our "dough of thought." Community projects led by strong leaders were sprouting around us. We raised the funds ourselves for the first projects though how could we inspire others to follow? We needed to expand our tribe.

This began with getting attention, something I was good at since I lived a double life, oscillating between effective altruism and management consulting. People at Slalom and many of my clients became curious about their hardworking colleague who would sojourn to Africa or Southeast Asia. People at all levels of the company kept pressing me for stories during lunches and happy hours. I got unparalleled access to executives at large companies. This made me a peak performer since when challenges arose, I could pull strings. After all, solving almost anything is really about *who* you know.

However, I was awful at telling stories that would generate an action for GO. I talked about the poverty I witnessed and what it felt like carrying water for hours. I lamented about the injuries people endured in places with no access to hospital care. Facts, facts, facts. No narrative, no story.

People shook their heads against the impossibility of it all. Their questions ceased against the avalanche of poverty. I watched their shoulders sag with despair. Conversations quickly drifted back to more neutrally friendly topics and I just felt out of place. I walked away.

Then Social Capital (SOCAP) happened. Founded by Kevin Jones and Rosa Lee Harden, SOCAP is a kinetic frenzy of a conference that connects social entrepreneurs to potential investors. I stumbled across my invitation to this global gathering of change makers by being at the right place, at the right time: a Friday happy hour in the Mission. A friend crashing on my couch invited me to meet someone named Jon

Axtell. Despite having work piled up to my eyeballs, I made a fateful "ah, fuck it" decision and joined in. We headed to the Atlas Room and there I clicked instantly with Jon, a like-minded soul seeking to disrupt international development.

After a few drinks, Jon asked if I was attending something that sounded like "snow-cap". I briefly hesitated sharing my ignorance but the powerful IPAs prompted a gut response of:

"What's snow-cap?"

Jon laughed and told me with my background and work, I had to be there. I committed on the spot. The door to SOCAP had been opened and would forever change the course of GO's growth.

Two weeks later, I walked into a hive of energy fueled by social purpose and financial speculation. Hundreds of social entrepreneurs weaved the room. Billions of dollars followed, most of which was sitting around waiting for the right pitch. Silicon Valley's unrivaled passion to change the world swarmed in full effect. Every third person had an idea that would transform this industry or that, or a company that would solve this crisis or that.

I dove in. I blathered facts about poverty and how local leaders like Peter or Eric could solve everything. The responses?

"Perhaps."

"Let's keep in touch."

"Mmm-hmm."

And if I got the response that makes every entrepreneur's heart zing *("How can I help?")*, then I had no clue what to do next. My clumsy execution of "The Ask" always ended in a "no".

Always.

And deservedly so. I hadn't learned the art of the pitch, and was smacking 120 mile per hour fastballs into the dirt.

Woody Allen once said that 80 percent of success is just showing up. He's right though the remaining 20 percent is making that perfect pitch that influences the listener to commit and do something. On SOCAP's last night, I began my pursuit to master this art of influencing others.

The journey began at the after party, which featured an endless bar and rad Bay Area DJs spinning late into the night. I decided I'd had enough of my horrendous pitching so I went out purely to enjoy myself. I played ping-pong with investment bankers. I stood in awe of the electronica blasting from a Rastafarian guitarist playing Radiohead chords while mixing in beats with foot pedals. I made light chat and stumbled towards a table occupied by a dear friend, Eve Blossom.

Eve has been a social entrepreneur in Silicon Valley since the early nineties and is the founder of various social ventures. She introduced me to her friends: Sekou Andrews, a noted speaker, author, and a successful poet, and Nick, a board member of Blue Ventures. My heard turned at the coincidence. When Nick asked why I was here, I relayed my eye story in vivid detail. I shared how Dr. Moray saved my vision, how much trust I had put in that local leader, and how that experience led me to start GO. He stood captivated while I spoke. We shook hands and exchanged cards.

Then Sekou pulled me aside.

"Tell me the story again." He said.

I repeated everything.

"Shorter."

I repeated it quicker. He edited away nonessential details and he stopped me in certain intervals.

"Say it this way. Use this word. Now tie this to that. Again from the top." He declared.

My pitching arm kept getting stronger.

"Now tell me your story in one word." He asked.

I stood quiet.

"I can tell you your story in one word. Ready? Vision. *Vision* is your story, this is your frame." He said. "Now tell it to me again."

"I lost my vision. Dr. Moray saved my vision, and gave me a greater vision on life: there are selfless and talented leaders in communities around the world." I responded.

"Now you have your story, ready for any occasion."

The fastball of my story squarely found the mitt.

I was ready to pitch.

TURN IT AROUND
THE WHY OF STORY

Our minds are biologically engineered to tell, retain, and regurgitate stories. Humans made their first appearance around 200,000 years ago and for nearly our entire existence, our histories, values, and traditions have been passed down through oral history. We only began writing (the physical act of capturing history) these stories in Sumeria around 3,500 BC, while the modern printing press, invented to distribute the Bible, wasn't developed until 1450. Visualizing this historical path in terms of a football field, we had walked nearly the entire field talking about ourselves, our culture, and our history, until we finally got to the one-yard line and someone decided, "Hey, maybe we should start writing some of this stuff down".

Our history of telling stories to pass down all of life's lessons over time looks like this:

THE **WHY** OF **STORY**TELLING

Stories are the wrappers that weave facts and values into a soluble form that our brains absorb. Whether to pass down religious values via the greatest selling book of all time (The Bible) or to sell Coca-Cola, stories are the most powerful conveyor of information. Our brains became wired for stories and you are 22 times more likely to remember something if it is told in the form of a story as compared to a bulleted series of facts. Stories are all around us. They are what move us, make us feel alive, and inspire us. Maya Angelou once said, "People will forget what you said, people will forget what you did, but people will *never* forget how you made them feel."

Once I began to focus on our ability to tell better stories, the success and growth of GO sprouted quickly. After SOCAP, storytelling became a focal point at GO and the organization tripled in size in one year. Like any skill, the ability to tell better stories can be distilled into basic principles that anyone can learn.

First, there needs to be a frame. Like Sekou pointed out, the frame of my story was vision; a dual-purpose definition that captured my physical loss of vision and a vivid mental image of the person I became. To find a frame, it's important to first realize that nearly all stories follow a basic 'Story Spine' that looks like this:

> Once Upon a Time…
> And Every Day…
> Until One Day…
> Because of That…
> Until Finally…
> And Every Day Since…
> And the Moral of the Story is…

Once a upon a time, I was a kid who loved cartoons. Every Saturday morning, I would plop down in front of our television to watch Scooby Doo. The gang is out on a trip. Shaggy and Scooby think up a mischievous prank. Because of that, the gang gets marooned in Spookyville. Because of that, they uncover a mystery and a scary ghost. Until finally they realize it's old Mr. Willers dressed up because he is bored and cranky. And then the following Saturday, it would be the same damn thing. And millions of kids would be chomping away at their cereal, eyes glued to the screen, as if they had never seen it before. The "Story Spine" is a timeless narrative piece that anyone can use to better pitch his or her idea or project.

Yet the spine is merely a backbone structure that shapes your ideas into a digestible narrative. More is needed to spice up your story into something unforgettable. Here are my key elements to tell great stories:

A Feel'd Goal: When telling a story, set a purpose with a 'Feel'd Goal' (a concept I detailed in Chapter 4). What do you want the audience to feel when you are done telling your story? Know that the listener(s) will not remember what you said though they will remember how you made them *feel*. Once a 'Feel'd Goal' is established, reverse-engineer the details, facts, and lessons for your audience to arrive at that goal. You have countless stories from your life to convey any point, so find down the right one to share by setting a feeling you wish to pass onto the audience.

A Hook: Written or verbal, every story needs a hook early in the beginning to grab the attention of the recipient. From a basic claim *('You'll never believe what happened to me today!')* to a more sophisticated allusion *(She and I would never be the same after this...)*, stories need something early to grab attention. A vivid image. An opening that makes them wonder. Begin at a pivotal moment so people want to discover what will happen next.

A Journey: Every great story has an arc. What do the main character(s) go through to reach a goal? All great stories have journeys. Jesus left Nazareth to Jerusalem. Prince Siddhartha departed his palace to find enlightenment as Buddha. Muhammad migrated from Mecca to Medina. Luke Skywalker left Tatooine to become a Jedi. And on and on. Why are journeys so powerful? Because we all eventually leave our homes to make a stake in the world. As humans, we are destined for exploration and admire those who leave, and those who seek.

A Protagonist: Whom are we rooting for on this journey? Identify a protagonist, one who undergoes some change that causes a turn of events. Be cognizant that it often may not be you who should be the hero of the story. In fact, when driving inspiration for your tribe, the hero of the stories should almost *never* be you. The heroes should be the listeners themselves, they must imagine themselves taking part. When I met with Sarah, I did tell her my eye story, which clearly had me as the protagonist. However, I leveraged that merely as my introduction so I could pivot to tell the stories of the true heroes: the Peters, the Erics, and the Costas of the world. I spoke about their lives, their journeys, and their transformations. I then gave her an opportunity to join them in East Africa, and to raise the seed capital and visibility they needed to thrive. It's great to root for a hero, yet it's absolutely magnetic for someone to join their journey and take part in their transformation.

A Challenge: To keep the story engaging, ensure that the hero(s) will encounter a challenge or a conflict. There is nothing engaging about smooth sailing. For example, I introduced many challenges pertaining to my eye story including the hurricane, lack of transport, and a half-paralyzed doctor. The story of Jesus in the Bible had so many challenges to it that the Catholics created a whole concept around them called the Stations of the Cross. These are a series of fourteen carvings representing successive incidents during Jesus' progress from his condemnation by Pilate to his crucifixion. In Star Wars, the highest grossing film of all time, Luke Skywalker traversed across planets, lost his right hand, struggled to become a Jedi knight, and killed his own father. Challenges make us hold our breath as we watch protagonists teeter on the brink of destruction.

Enablement: If your story is shareable, people will spread your ideas broadly. Why would someone want to share your story? Because it enables them to be better people. The Bible and Koran are filled with morals for people to be better citizens. There is no way to learn what is memorable outside of repeatedly telling your story to others and watching for cues when they stop paying attention. If possible, have a listener repeat your story back so you can learn which elements stuck and which ones drifted. Once you know the stickiest elements, distill them down as less is more.

Engage: The shortest distance between two people is laughter. Situations that are ridiculous in nature or impossible to believe will cause people to laugh and shake their heads in disbelief. While being funny is not easy, it's a vital connection mechanism to grab the attention of the audience.

Once an individual, team, project, or company is empowered with storytelling, their growth potential is limitless. Our ability to influence others finds a harmonious medium in this masterful art form of communication. It helps companies thrive, projects soar, and empires to crumble.

CHAPTER 13

STORY MATTERS

PART II

Working in Africa, you become used to a life stripped of comfort. Head torches serve as your light after dark, a bucket of water suffices for a shower, and steamed mashed bananas are dinner. You are grateful and at peace.

Then one Thursday evening an email arrives from work. Work beckons. You need the money.

A game-changing role is offered and you have to act fast. You are in rural Uganda, near the end of your annual site visit to survey impact. Now you need steady access to the Internet and an American phone number so a client in Silicon Valley can interview you. You need a mobile office in a place where people have no access to electricity or running water.

You are a consultant.

You can fix this.

Kyle hacks open your iPhone. He strips away the software that requires the AT&T restriction using a manual downloaded from a hacker's website. You pray it will turn on again. It does. You buy a local Safari-Net SIM card and insert it into the phone. Kyle adjusts the APN settings on the phone to receive the Internet over Safari Net Next network.

Amazingly it works.

You then 'borrow' a Skype number from Kyle's account and have calls forwarded to the iPhone over Skype. You have a friend from California call for a test and are astounded that it works. You now have a local California number in Uganda.

This solution is worthless without electricity. After working out in the goat fields, you attend a party held by a local Ugandan priest. He has powered the music thumping through his home with a diesel-powered generator. Viola! The next day you borrow the generator from the local parish so you can charge your phone and laptop. In the middle of nowhere Uganda, you have an office, a place where you spend evenings reading process diagrams and coordinating interview schedules. A PDF file takes ten minutes to download and costs two dollars per megabyte.

On Sunday, you receive your interview schedule and the expected start date of the gig. Neither are pretty. Two phone interviews over the next two days. Then, if hired, the role will start in one week in England, which is quite far from all your work clothes in San Francisco. The schedule is non-negotiable. You use the hacked iPhone to book a ticket to fly back home from Nairobi's Kenyatta airport on Wednesday afternoon. You are 1,200 kilometers and two countries away from that airport. From Kenyatta International, you will need to travel 15,000 kilometers to San Francisco, which is very inconveniently, 10,000 kilometers from Leeds, England. You book another ticket from San Francisco to Manchester less than 24-hours after you land. The dominos of travel are carefully placed in neat succession. First, you must traverse across Uganda and Kenya in less than 48 hours.

You are a seasoned traveler.

You can do this.

Peter finds a car and a driver. They drive you and your team to Kampala. You arrive in the capital around 4pm after leaving at the break of dawn on Monday. It's just one hour until your first interview. You are still on the outskirts of town and traffic is horrific. You pull over after seeing a sign for a Catholic mission with the words "Internet". You speak to the rector and are shown into an empty room with ancient computers and an ISDN cable.

Hallelujah, the house of God has Internet.

You plug in your laptop and iPhone. You review the required materials and the call happens. You pass the first interview, and are requested to attend a second interview with a very important person at a very important company at the same time tomorrow. With twenty-four hours to go, you hug the GO team goodbye.

It's 6:30 pm and you still have 1,000 kilometers to reach Nairobi. The last bus leaves at 8pm. You cannot miss it. Back outside, traffic is not moving. You hail a taxi and sit in traffic for fifteen minutes. Nothing moves. You get out. You see a man sitting on a motorcycle. He sees you: A white man with a 20 kilogram pack on his back, a 10 kilogram pack on his front, and with one hand holding a cardboard box stuffed with souvenirs and gifts.

This is not a good idea.

Defying logic and safety, you find yourself asking whether he knows where the Kampala Coach Bus is located. He nods and putters his bike over. You flap over the back seat, awkwardly holding on to the back of the bike with your only free hand.

You are sandwiched between your two packs, making you wonder how this will ever work.

He has no helmet and no glasses.

Neither do you.

The motor kicks and the bike speeds of onto the sidewalk. Pedestrians jump out of the way as he beeps past them.

He revs up into third gear and leaps back on to the road.

He is driving on the median between opposing lanes of traffic. The gap between the lanes of traffic is so tight that the shoes hanging off your bag rhythmically thump every car you pass.

You cannot believe you got on this bike.

Ahead of you, you see the lethargic jam of traffic open to a massive roundabout where anything that moves flows in a massive swirling circle of steel and fumes. He guns the bike faster into the madness and you grip tightly with your only free hand to keep from falling off. As he turns into the roundabout, the drag begins to push you off the bike. You close your eyes.

You crunch every fiber of your abdominal muscles to push yourself forward.

You do not see the crash.

You hear it.

Steel grinds on the asphalt and you hear cries of pain. Your eyes open and the horizon is still level.

It's not you that fell.

You look back and see the bike that was once next to you is now on its side, both passengers lying on the road. Your bike goes faster.

The reality of what you feared has just been proven to you.

The bike goes faster.

And then it's over.

You have no idea whether you were on the bike for five minutes or fifteen.

Standing on shaking knees, you pay the motorcycle driver and head towards the bus station. You see by your watch it is 7:30pm, giving you plenty of time to catch the bus.

You push past pushers, hawkers, and other unsavory characters. All say they are your friend.

You know they are not.

You approach the ticket window and put down 50,000 shillings.

"One ticket for Nairobi," you say.

"Sold out," you hear.

A fatal link in your plan has just snapped.

You think. The domino effect of your travel plan is broken. Then you remember the rules of engagement.

You double down and offer 100,000 shillings.

"One ticket for Nairobi. **Please,***" you say.*

The bus manager looks at a week's salary now sitting on top of the bus ticket fare.

He considers.

"Wait here," he says. He returns with a ticket and a foam pad with a steel edge on the bottom.

"Here is your seat. Go to the back of the bus and put this in the corner," he responds.

You want to cry. The bus is fourteen hours and even in a regular seat it's a tough and bumpy ride. Your bags are taken and you enter the bus.

You jam your pad in the back corner on top of a bar where a real seat may have once existed.

Legs akimbo, feet plastered to the floor, you are able to keep balance with your back against the wall. The next fourteen hours are hell.

You arrive in Nairobi at noon the next day with plenty of time for the call.

You check into a cheap hotel on the wrong side of Nairobi.

You open your bag to get out your phone.

Fuck. A ray of light hits your memory. You remember your last phone call at the parish. You remember packing up your laptop. You remember zipping the bag. You do not remember unplugging the phone. The phone is still in Uganda.

You search your entire bag and find your backup, a Nokia "dumb phone." You run out of your hotel and buy a new SIM card and call back to Kampala. The GO team had found the iPhone after we parted ways at the parish. This doesn't solve the problem as the interviewer will be calling you on the wrong line. You go to an Internet cafe and buy another Skype number, configure the new SIM card, and then email the new number back to the client. There is no way to test this setup and you can only pray it will ring.

It's 2:30pm. Three hours left.

You drink coffee and nervously smoke cigarettes at the Internet cafe. At 0.1 kbs per minute, you download a presentation about the project and your colleagues' notes about their interviews. It takes twenty minutes to download the PowerPoint file. You scour the client's website so you can sound smart about something you know little about. Your clouded mind scribbles notes. You haven't eaten or slept in twenty-four hours.

It's 5:00pm and you scarf down two Snickers bars.

You go back to your dark room in the shady bus stop hotel and take out your phone. You place it on the mantle and stare at it.

You mentally run through the interview and hold your hands to keep them from shaking.

You focus on the "now" and try to forget the past two days.

You are a professional.

You can do this.

5:30 ticks.

The phone rings and you answer. The connection is crystal.

"Hello Debbie, it's a pleasure to meet you. My name is Bart Skorupa and I first started working at Slalom Consulting about two years ago..."

~

Many ask how I left the institutional security of Corporate America to run a startup nonprofit. I never left. I oscillated out. And I oscillate back in. No decision is ever final. All you need to find is that moment when things *feel* right and have the courage to act. I began to work full time at GO shortly after the above story, which illustrates how my life teetered between two worlds.

But before that inflection point, it began with a small and dedicated group of volunteers that took a bias towards action. Our small size and tight budgets gave us the gift of frugality. Frugality made us grateful for every dollar raised and wise with every dollar invested. Then we improved upon telling a coherent story of local leaders alleviating poverty in their communities, and growing an army of engaged philanthropists that raised the seed capital and awareness of these leaders. Like the coffee napkin drawing Kyle made a few years back, our model looked like this:

This story of connecting local leaders to champions so their projects could get funding began in Vesuvio. After our first philanthropy date, Sarah and her best friend Claire would go on to visit Costa in Rwanda and Peter in Uganda, climb Kilimanjaro, and raise double the amount Kyle, Ryan, and I achieved on our climb. As Sarah flew to Uganda, Kyle returned to Ghana to attend the opening ceremony for Eric's inaugural class of 30 students in a three-room school. After our inaugural trip, we kept raising funds via a growing circle of friends and family so Eric could finish his school. He started small and kept a bigger picture in mind as funding came in slow. Eric wanted 300 students, not 30. To get there, he knew he had to show immediate impact. While he couldn't build the entire school from our first round of funding, he got the project moving by building enough classrooms for 30 students. Like Peter, he thought modular. The design of his school allowed him to add more classrooms as more funding became available.

Shortly after the opening ceremony, a friend of a friend named Ben Strauss-Malcolm heard the impact of the school first-hand when he met Eric, who was visiting our GO offices (read: my living room) in

San Francisco. When Ben met Eric, he promised to raise $10,000 to double the school's size. He threw an Eighties themed party for his 30th birthday to bring attention to his fundraising goal. Friends and family supported graciously, Ben hit his goal, and Eric's school grew to140 students. After seeing *this* growth and impact, Ben threw *another* party the next year and Eric's school tripled in size. Thanks to Ben, Eric's school now teaches 350 students annually and employs 25 permanent staff.

Erica Swanson, a managing director at Slalom who set me up for the consulting gig in the story above, was an avid runner and dedicated her next marathon to raise funds for a well project in Cambodia. She raised $5,000. The more stories we told of leaders like Eric, Peter, and Costa, the more people enlisted to raise money.

We had tapped a movement and Erica, Ben, and Sarah became our first GO Champions. Hundreds more would follow yet they were the first to start something good through GO. And man, did they have patience with us during this bumpy incubation period.

Like the projects on the ground, we built GO by failing forward. Create a prototype, get it out there, watch it fail, and then make it better. We built our own website and submitted our own legal paperwork. Now we needed a mechanism to empower people like Sarah, Ben, and Erica to raise their funding on a clean website. In 2011, crowd-funding sites like Kickstarter and Indiegogo were in their infancy and they charged a ten percent commission. We thought big and did the math. If we inspired 100 GO Champions to raise $1,000,000, then we would lose $100,000 to fees. That's enough money for Eric to build three schools and so not a scalable solution.

While we were concerned about creating and maintaining our own technology, we had a solution: Silicon Valley was our backyard. So we pounded on the doors of Salesforce and Google, and rang the phones of various startup entrepreneurs. These companies entered our tribe and provided priceless resources of technology, funding, and— most importantly—incredibly talented volunteers to develop our website.

Kyle's beautiful design and adept coding skills had improved and our Kilimanjaro fundraising campaign gave us a good proof of concept.

We leveraged Google Wallet to process credit cards and Google charged zero fees for this service. Of the $11,000 raised, not a penny was lost to fees and all funds raised were invested into Peter's farm.

We then used Salesforce to neatly capture donor data in an organized fashion. Eventually, we would marry these two technologies together but back then, nothing was automated. However, we knew that our nascent crowd-funding site would *never* be ready to launch. We believed that everything is always in beta.

Visually, our approach looked like this:

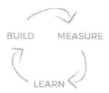

So we launched and came up with creative solutions as Erica, Ben, and Sarah raised money simultaneously. Money came in from around the world. When people donated from the UK, we assumed they were for Sarah. I then sent her emails so she could claim all her donors. Erica and I worked together at Slalom so I ran by her desk when new donations came in. This meant that any donation not claimed by Sarah or Erica were meant for Ben. Throughout the day, I texted Kyle with the amounts for each Champion. Between classes at school, Kyle then changed the amount raised for each Champion by writing over the previous number on the site.

Our website wasn't scalable so we patched the cracks with grit and elbow grease. That mentality raised $30,000 in a few months. Sarah funded a biogas harvester for Peter's model farm so he could run off of a renewable energy source. Ben empowered Eric to expand his school that educated hundreds of children. Erica raised enough money for a well that gave 350 villagers in Cambodia access to clean water.

As the money came in, so did the feedback to improve. Donors and Champions sent their thoughts.

We listened.

We iterated and improved.

And heads began to turn.

~

By early 2011, our misfit band of do-gooders was raising around $600,000 annually. GO Champions began to mushroom as the word spread about our impact. These actualized philanthropists spanned across a diverse range of people, from 7th grade students to church groups to celebrities. Zoë Tryon, a noted activist for the rights of indigenous people in the Ecuadorian Amazon, became a Champion and received a $50,000 donation in one fell swoop. Three of our projects received grant funding in the $50,000 to $150,000 range. Yet while overall revenue surged, most of those dollars couldn't be used for organization capacity building.

Finding funding to operationalize the organization was hard. In the nonprofit sector, funding is strictly delineated between program funding (i.e., products or services meant to directly help beneficiaries) and capacity funding (i.e., management, marketing, and everything else that helps an organization scale). From an organizational management perspective, this entrenched system is debilitating since it forces organizations to spend less money on growth and management. To make ends meet, I essentially had three jobs while figuring out how GO's capacity funding could grow. I worked at Slalom Consulting to pay the bills. I ran GO as Executive Director, which is actually two jobs since not only did I helm the ship of growth, I also had to continually raise money to keep the ship afloat.

Whatever funds were raised for operations went right back into fundraising. We hired a consultant with nonprofit fundraising experience to help GO raise more capacity funding. When finances got tight, I paid the consultant in cash out of my own earnings since I fully believed we were on the right trajectory. We quickly learned various effective strategies to help us grow our organizational base via fundraising galas, direct mail campaigns, and by targeting specific family foundations.

Additionally, this focus on growth raised our profile in the Bay Area nonprofit sector and brought amazing like-minded talent into our tribe.

Among the most influential was Mitch Andersen, who proposed GO fiscally sponsor a project dubbed ClearWater that would bring clean water to the indigenous people of the northern Ecuadorian Amazon. For decades, the rivers of this region have been poisoned by oil contamination. Without access to clean water, the physical and cultural survival of five Amazonian indigenous groups became perilous. With the help of local and international engineers, ClearWater designed and implemented rainwater catchment systems for each family in the region. As the project relied on local leaders and technicians to install and maintain the clean water systems, the project was a natural fit.

Mitch brought tireless perseverance in his endeavor to launch ClearWater. He quit his job and moved to the Ecuadorian Amazon to work alongside the various indigenous tribes. He would end up working for nearly a year without a salary, living off his own means until ClearWater gained traction. Mitch also brought a host of experience from the activist space and taught our rogue crew the art of getting your voice heard. He taught us how to get media to write about our work and was deft at fundraising. Most importantly, Mitch taught me that with conviction and devoted sacrifice towards a purpose in life, anything can be achieved. Through his sacrificial leadership, Clearwater's vision grew fast and eventually became its own 501(c)3 that now raises about $3.5 million annually.

With our focus on strategic growth and networking, we were getting traction in new areas that grew a sustainable foundation. Others started to join our undefined tribe that brought expertise in fundraising and international development. We were locking our fingers around an idea, and forming its sloppy clay into something more concrete and more tangible. It felt like we were driving a car while drawing the map. I saw the tipping point coming and the final few months of getting this venture safely off the ground nearly broke me.

I rarely slept at night. My mind swirled furiously with ideas. Calls from GO partners with 'urgent' updates came night and day. I had

3:30am phone calls with Costa debating cow breeds. Client work for Slalom Consulting began the next day. I went from Melatonin to Ambien as the pressure ratcheted up. But proper rest remained stubbornly elusive during this inflection point. My simple life quickly got complicated as I struggled to balance a dual career.

And right when the trajectory of GO began to surge, I got selected for a monstrously demanding project.

Plucked from Africa, my dead weary body dropped right into the boardroom.

~

The interview went well and Debbie liked me. Once I'd passed the interview, I departed Nairobi and then hopped on a plane. I landed in San Francisco on a Saturday morning. I dumped my field gear, packed a suitcase of suits, attended a wedding, and then skipped the reception to fly to London that same evening. I arrived in London on Sunday night. Six twelve-hour workdays awaited. I had a double Scotch in the hotel bar to end my day. Then Ambien. Then sleep.

I woke up shaking. I knew what awaited: Introductions, strong handshakes, documentation, strong eye contact, questions, fancy shoes, interviews, and more questions. There'd be lunch in a conference room, flashy cuff-links, flow charts, coffee, pleasantly fake smiles, power moves to establish office dominance, diagrams on whiteboards, more coffee, team dinners, and tired eyes.

Rinse and repeat for five days straight.

On Monday morning. I had trouble stopping my hands from shaking. Pressure for the week was steep. The team selected for this project at Slalom was known as the 'Dream Team'. The client, a multi-billion dollar conglomerate, was considered to be a growth account and our team of five were selected for our unique abilities to create opportunities for others. If the project went well, our team of five would grow into thirty. Company "eyes" all the way to the top kept track of our progress.

I was placed among the smartest people I have ever worked with during my consulting career. Their thorough approach and thoughtful mindset to work was breathtaking; the pace and dedication of the team set an unbelievably high bar. I felt distraught, out of place. The previous week I sat around goat herders in the florid green grass under an impossibly bright sun. Now I sat in a conference room with impossibly fluorescent lights that burned my eyes and questioned my abilities. "Imposter Syndrome," the persistent fear of being exposed as a 'fraud', gripped my mind as I tried to keep pace and give a smooth delivery.

Something had to give.

The responsibilities at GO acutely spiked as we were now approaching our first million dollars raised. My health couldn't handle both worlds at once any longer. I had worked myself to exhaustion before and had no interest in another emergency room visit.

The stories GO shared about the impact through our Champions, donors, and volunteers began to expand and diffuse at an ever-accelerating rate. Like a room slowly filling with gas, the atmosphere around us became ready to ignite.

Our rocket stood atop the room, ready to launch.

And if someone ever offers you a seat on a rocket ship, here is what I have learned:

Get on and don't ask any questions.

TURN IT AROUND
STARTING WITH WHY

Before diving deeper into why stories matter, let's explore one foundational element of what set GO apart from other worthy causes.

Benefit From Frugality

Our earliest secret weapon was frugality. GO began with only $2,000 and we were mindful of every penny from the start. Additionally, we made a promise to give 100 percent of public donations directly to the cause. Every penny donated to a Champion would go right to the project of their choice, whether to fund a rainwater catchment system in Ecuador or to start a pig farm in Uganda. The 100 percent giving model instantly built trust with donors. It's also why the average GO Champion raised $4,500—six times the national nonprofit fundraising average—through their crowd funding campaigns. People constantly told me how much they loved knowing that every penny would be leveraged to help people get out of poverty.

How could our model be sustainable? Back in 2008, when we came up with the 100 percent model, we thought it would be game changing. Then Google brought us back to reality. Charity: Water, a nonprofit that brings safe drinking water to people in need, had implemented a 100 percent giving model since 2006 and was then raising nearly $10 million per year. Our bold idea had a model that we could emulate. To learn more, I attended their first San Francisco fundraiser at the home of Michael Birch and met their founder Scott Harrison. Even though Scott needed to greet potential donors, he patiently explained the inner workings of their model. Yes, 100 percent of public donations went directly to clean water projects. However, they had a separate group of donors who only funded their operations. Acting much like "angel investors" in a startup, they recognized the impact of supporting operational funding and received information about how their dollars created more philanthropic dollars in a ratio called the Social Return on Investment (SROI). For example, if an organization's operations needed an annual $1 million budget and could raise $5 million from the public, it had a SROI of 5:1. In other words, for every $1 given to operations, it created $5 of funding for programs.

The key element to properly structuring this group of angel investors is to make it an exclusive. In Charity: Water's second year, they struck gold with a $1,000,000 operational gift from tech entrepreneur and noted philanthropist Michael Birch. While that's obviously a game-changing investment at such an early stage of organizational development, it's also dollars that came from an influential family. Michael and his wife Xochi were well connected and their engagement quickly drew attention from other tech entrepreneurs and celebrities. This initial gift gave Charity:

Water the unparalleled ability to grow quicker than their competition, and also gave the inspiration to follow suit. Scott kindly introduced me to Michael so I could learn more.

As I learned more from Michael, I kept feeling a sting of jealousy. GO had been operating for nearly three years and had no such gift, and no such connections. What I failed to realize leaving Michael's home that evening was that our frugal path helped us build a stronger organization. While it took nearly four years for me to hold GO's first $500,000 check, the precious early years taught us everything about fiscal prudence.

GO's early bootstrapped years became an asset as we grew and money to invest. Rather than lose money paying fees for crowdfunding sites, we chose to build and own our fundraising technology. We knew it would be a longer-term investment and framed it as a *funding rationale* for our angel investor donor base. This funding rationale opened the doors to major donors as nothing attracts more attention in Silicon Valley than the promise of a new technology that could disrupt any given sector. Our idea of connecting local leaders to fundraising Champions via our own technology turned heads and opened up checkbooks.

Once we got the funding to build the platform, we spent frugally and released a website that was truly a minimum viable product. It had no bells or whistles. Yet the prototype worked and after the success of the first fundraising campaigns, Champions gave us many new ideas to build out. They wanted notifications when donations were made, more information about the projects, and the ability to upload videos. We selected Salesforce and Google to develop a more robust platform. Their technologies were scalable and also came with best-of-class corporate giving programs. By doing so, our fundraising platform became an asset that *raised money* rather than one that *cost dollars* to build.

We used Google Wallet to process people's credit cards for donations and given our nonprofit status, Google gave us 100 percent of the transaction. Other payment gateways charge around three percent for this service, so when people made $10,000 donations on our website, that's a huge competitive advantage. Additionally, Google Grants gave us $40,000 per month in free advertising with Google AdWords so we essentially got a $500,000 annual marketing budget for free. News of our partnership spread and through a major supporter and Googler named David Parkinson, our team got to speak at Google's campuses during their annual Giving Week. During this week, hundreds of Googlers heard our stories and made donations, which Google matched in triplicate. The Giving Week talks raised $15,000 in donations.

Like Google, our Salesforce partnership unlocked even more tech dollars. Mandated by their founder and CEO Marc Benioff, Salesforce pioneered the 1/1/1 model which gives one percent of licenses, funding, and time to nonprofits globally. We chose Salesforce to track our donors, volunteers, and their engagement, so we could efficiently forecast our growth.

Once we had Salesforce up and running thanks to Figur8 Cloud Consulting, we leveraged this free cutting-edge tool to grow our operational budget by figuring out novel ways to *raise* money by using it. When customizations needed to be made, Salesforce staff volunteered their time to build solutions. For every 40 hours of time they spent fixing bugs, Salesforce.org (the nonprofit arm of Salesforce) donated a $1,000 check to our operational capacity fund. We started hosting hackathon events where people came to party and code, raising thousands of dollars while we got a better website. By 2015, Salesforce powered our entire organization (from email marketing to donation tracking to financial modeling) for free and streamed an annual $25,000 into our operational coffers.

And guess what happened when these volunteers from Google or Salesforce worked on the site that connected a Peter to a Sarah or a Ben to an Eric? They became GO Champions themselves. GO raised over $100,000 for local leaders through these two corporate sponsors alone. We spurred more Champions so the programs envisioned by social entrepreneurs around the world could thrive. And it all began with us being frugal, our first secret weapon.

Start With Why.

This secret weapon of frugality stood us up on a teetering precipice. Yes, it made us scrappy though it also meant burning the candles at both ends. I couldn't work two jobs forever. Eventually, storytelling broke that exhaustion cycle as speaking in narratives made me a better fundraiser. But at the onset, we struggled to get attention. I lamented to anyone that would listen about the utter poverty that I had witnessed.

Half the world lives on less than $2.50 per day! People have no water! Women are being neglected! Children are starving!

Who wants to be with *that* guy at the party?

As I learned the art of starting with "why", I placed these facts into stories and then people *listened*. The evolution into storytelling had me start my engagements with a *why*, a purpose, rather than a *what* (an idea or project) or a *how* (a method or process). This powerful structuring of thought that captivates people's attention comes from Simon Sinek's book *Start With Why*. The concept is that there is a simple order and predictability in human behavior that revolves around a centric purpose or belief that defines the *why* behind your actions. From the business perspective, people don't buy *what* you do, they buy *why* you do it. From the human perspective, people don't believe *what* you are doing to help, they believe in *why* you are doing it.

What was the why of GO for me? I began with my eye story, a method of conveying my purpose via a life-changing moment: I got the vision, literally and metaphorically, to start something good. Once this "hook" engaged my listener, the story then pivoted towards the leaders on the ground that were launching innovative projects to end poverty. Then, I spoke subsequently about the GO Champions that were raising funds to launch these projects. I told *hopeful* stories of what it felt like for a family to have clean water for the first time in their lives. I told *inspiring* stories of the Champion that raised funds for those water wells and how amazing it felt to give back to the world.

This is the story of what we called *transformative development*. It was the metamorphosis that occurred when leaders like Sarah and Peter engaged with one another. Despite the distance of their homelands or culture, GO Champions and local leaders united under a common purpose to do good better. This, in turn, sparked a life-long quest for betterment on each side of the relationship. This development notion, conceived by the unparalleled intellect of our Director of Partnerships, Sienna Moore, framed the *why* of GO concisely. It became the hallmark of our stories and the core element that tied various weaves of GO's work altogether. We connected leaders to inspire global change.

To put this abstract notion into a story, I remember a repeated sentiment I heard at Kyle's wedding, whose ceremony was officiated by none other than Peter Luswata. Peter and his wife Cissy flew from Uganda to unite my best friend with the beautiful Jessie Curtner in the bonds of love and harmony. There, I heard this sentiment repeated in speech after speech during the reception:

"There was a Kyle *before* his trip to Uganda. There was a Kyle *after* his trip to Uganda. These two people were not the same."

And so it was with Sarah. When she returned from her Africa trip, she got infected with the addiction to do good, to be better. She brought home countless inspirational stories from the field to share with her friends. She leveraged her transformative *why* and inspired her friend Clare Ashmore to join her on a climb of Kilimanjaro to raise funds. Sarah completed her first marathon to bolster her fundraising efforts and prepare herself for the climb. Before this, she had never run more than a few miles. Now, driven by purpose and alongside Clare, Sarah ran 26.2 miles in a few hours. Together, they raised $12,150 in a little over a month. 100 percent of these funds were invested in Peter's farm to build an anaerobic biogas digester to generate a clean source of energy.

This is transformative development, betterment on both sides of philanthropic engagement. Leaders learning from one another and improving their own lives and the communities around them. I saw it in

Kyle, I saw it in myself, and I saw it in Sarah. Hundreds of GO Champions would follow in those footsteps, raising millions for social entrepreneurs like Peter or Eric. Of equal importance, they transformed into globally and locally active civic citizens. They became better conservationists, leaders of their own organizations, and mentors for aspiring social entrepreneurs.

On both sides of these relationships, I witnessed incredible acts of humble leadership. The elimination of impossible begins with a powerful and purpose-driven *why*, the unlimited fuel that can drive forth the *what* or *how* of anything. That's the seed that made everything grow.

CHAPTER 14

INFLECTION POINT

The sun shined and the meat sizzled.

"Get your sausages here while giving back!"

"We've got a Polack at the grill!"

I am standing next to friends volunteering their time to GO. We're hustling meat to a teeming pile of hungry hipsters at Dolores Park. I wade out into the crowd and draw attention to our motley booth. We have brownies, cookies, and beers donated from Lagunitas Brewery to help our young organization raise more cash.

People come up, buy a beer, and chat with our staff. We're hustling and grinding. I took the leap and left Slalom with three months' rent in the bank, no health insurance, and a slew of ideas to raise cash. Start small and think big. Sure, stoners are throwing Frisbees at the sun but Mark Zuckerberg lives just around the block.

You never know.

It may not be a wise investment of time in terms of bang per buck though, hey, I liked to cook.

And those sausages were damned good.

So we have fun and hope to raise around $500 while handing out 250 pamphlets about our work.

Who knows what eyes will see one?

The following Monday was a day of borrowed time focused solely on GO. No more wild pendulums swinging from management consulting to international development. I jumped full time into GO to make it work somehow, some way. We had enough funds for short-term contractor salaries though not quite enough for me, nor the rest of the staff we needed to grow. But pressure makes diamonds so I channeled boundless inner determination to raise our first $1 million. Armed with three months' of savings, I financed my own leap off the cliff. While a strategic development plan existed, anything that could raise immediate cash for our operations was considered.

I refined my pitch and shadowboxed continually. I gave mock pitches while showering, running, and walking to the bus stop. My brain never stopped as I perfected a precise assembly of words, which would make any donor invest. I worked alongside a passionate team and failure to execute on my part would result in their lives caving in. I needed more stages both big and small where I could present the opportunity, meet more people, and extend our network.

After flipping sausages in the park, I started flipping through emails to continue the hustle. While no given day felt like work, there were also no days off. During this development leap, I awoke every morning with an icy fear pulsing through my veins. Every payroll run was a gamble, every bill that arrived got set aside until it was absolutely necessary to pay it off. We planned for ambitious galas, iterated the website during all-nighters, ran half marathons to raise funds for operations, and spent afternoons in the park to scrape up more cash.

The $500 raised in the park bought us nothing in terms of time. Our monthly run rate, the amount of money needed to cover our operational expenses, had grown to $10,000 so $500 only extended out the runway for another day, at best. It took a day to effectively execute, so we were simply treading water. I cursed myself for the poor use of time while entering donor data into Salesforce.

Ping!

A bright notification popped up on my monitor and informed me that someone donated on our site.

$1,000.

Joe Richardson.

I sat confused. I did not recognize the name and no one made random donations this big, at least not yet. I immediately sent this benevolent stranger a thank you email. We earmarked the funds for

Peter's maize mill construction (which was already in progress) and I sent Joe information about the project. He replied:

Bart,

Thanks for sending me the information regarding where the donation will go and pictures of progress so far. I would love to hear about continued progress with the project. I met you guys in Dolores Park and I think the organization is awesome.

Thanks for all the great work you guys are doing.

Sincerely,

Joe

I couldn't believe it. He and I had spoken for five minutes while I ferried sausages up and down the hills of Dolores Park. *That* generated a $1,000 donation? I needed to learn more so we stayed in touch and became friends over our passion for basketball. Over beers and NBA games, I learned that Joe spent the past 13 years managing failing companies and turning them around. He came with a proven track record of managing complex business challenges. I courted him relentlessly as our board of directors desperately needed this type of strategic guidance. Eventually, this benevolent soul would become the chairman of our board and helped us raise twenty times that initial gift.

How did he get so committed to GO? It began with curiosity. Like many people, he was initially puzzled about the 100 percent giving model. How could it work? I explained the vision of differentiating public donations for the projects from our private donations to fund the operations.

In the traditional nonprofit model, donors follow a notoriously flawed yet common 80/20 financial model with their donations. In this model, if an organization gets a $1,000 donation, then the nonprofit earmarks $800 for a program (say, the maize mill Peter was building) and $200 for operational funding (say, an accountant). Coming from the corporate world, I found this model to be asinine. No for-profit company would structure their finances in this manner. Imagine limiting your management budget to 20 percent of revenue. You would never get the right people to lead the organization.

In his Ted Talk, "The way we think about charity is dead wrong", Dan Pallotta, speaker, author, and nonprofit reformer, summarizes why we charities cannot invest in sound management thusly:

"In the for-profit sector, the more value you produce, the more money you can make. But we have a visceral reaction to the idea that anyone would make money helping other people. Interestingly, we don't have a visceral reaction to the notion that people would make a lot of money *not* helping other people," says Pallotta. "You want to make 50 million dollars selling violent video games to kids, go for it. We'll put you on the cover of *Wired* magazine. But you want to make half a million dollars trying to cure kids of malaria, and you're considered a parasite."

With the 100 percent model, we could release the handcuffs of the 80/20 model that constrains the nonprofit sector. There are donors that give to programs, such as building maize mills. And then there are others, our social investors that would give to our operations. Both are considered tax-deductible donations. We send different reporting and measure the growth of each donor group separately.

When Joe first donated, I sent him 'impact reports' from Peter's farm that informed him on the numbers of people using the mill and their higher earnings made possible by processing their maize. This impact kept the conversation going and I knew Joe would likely donate again. As we gained trust, I knew Joe would be a great candidate to become a social investor in GO. So I then presented information about the wider GO model and our SROI. I explained that our SROI hovered around six to one. In other words, for every dollar given to our operations, we created six dollars of funding for our projects. If we raised $250,000 for our operational budget, then we would raise $1,500,000 for our programs. That's enough to build 50 schools, which could educate 350 students per year. The opportunity clicked and Joe became a social investor in GO.

More people like Joe followed. We hit an inflection point in our growth as word and impact spread. I joined various philanthropic groups like Full Circle Fund and World Economic Forum to expand our growing tribe. We set up more and more events so we could build our own stage and keep pitching. I spoke at conferences like SOCAP, Dreamforce, and Opportunity Collaboration. I refused attending events where I didn't get a speaking engagement. Online webinars or in person workshops filled my days as I sang out our gospel of change to the social impact world.

Heads began to turn as more social investors like Joe began to see our value. Early stage employees of Facebook, Google, and Airbnb joined the fold. We appreciated their generous supply of tech dollars though their crucial strategic advice on how to grow fast and bold made the biggest impact. Money came in for meager salaries, rent, trips to the field, press managers, accountants, and a growing team of freelance professional services. Suddenly, our nascent team was responsible for people, processes, federal and state reporting, insurance, and the other countless minutiae of being officially in business. We needed wise counsel and guidance to steer our growth.

Effective leadership begins at the top. There is no way any given person can successfully govern such a multi-pronged movement. Great organizations need great leaders to run a flourishing organization, and this starts with the Board of Directors (BoD) or a Board of Advisors (BoA). The approach to creating boards can take varied routes and its fomentation must be taken with great care. This integral body of organizational leadership must be cultivated wisely, iterated often, and include a vast array of thoughts and opinions.

The GO board of directors for the first two years was a paper tiger of governance. It solely consisted of Kyle and me, the same two people who were managing the organization. This organizational setup was poor at best and illegal at worst. Essentially, the board should strategize and the management should execute that strategy tactically. Though our initial approach to management raised a lot of eyebrows as we strode towards inflection, we had a specific reason behind this lack of governance. We did not know the culture of our tribe at the time we launched the company. As detailed earlier, defining a set of core values to unify the tribe were vital for scaling growth.

We had an aspiring vision and achievable mission. We had local leaders like Eric building schools and Peter building farms. We had Champions like Ben and Sarah raising funds and awareness for those projects. We had a ragtag group of volunteers that traveled to Africa to see the projects and then flipped sausages to raise money. But we lacked the core values that would unite us all. Collectively, we were like a blind Moses, climbing up Mount Sinai in search of the Ten Commandments that would bring our people together.

Once our organizational mission around transformative development became clearer, we started coalescing a culture to make our model thrive. While success loomed with its heavy hands of great responsibility upon our shoulders, Kyle and I spent weeks going back and forth on this pivotal code that would unite our tribe. Eventually, ten values were documented. The final door to find the right leadership opened.

Joe was the first person we called as he epitomized the humility within leadership. He listened, empathized, and gave more than he took. When he spoke, his words mattered. When we met with Joe to ask for his hand in leadership, all we had was a printout of our core values. That's all it took in those early days. As we matured, we developed a one page on-boarding process flow to outline the entire process, a ten-page deck outlining the roles and responsibilities to set expectations, a contract for the specifics, detailed financials, and our core values. We started somewhere and then grew accordingly. More astounding leaders subsequently joined our board, and gave wise although sometimes disparate thoughts about how to approach our growth and methodology.

Despite our growing board, my savings dwindled as we rarely met the mounting operational needs of the organization. I took the salary hit when the bills could not be paid on time. I felt at fault for not closing on major gifts so I doubled down on my networking efforts. I knew my weak point: the moment of "the ask". It is that pivotal time when the storytelling ceases, a slight silence hushes the conversation, and the forthright question that needs to be asked so you walk out with a signed check hits your conscience. I faltered at the moment of specifically asking for money and being clear regarding how much and when.

I often walked out empty handed even with opportunities aplenty. I attended other nonprofit galas, boozed it up at University of Illinois alumni events, schmoozed at random conferences, attended meet-ups, signed up for classes about growing businesses, then started *teaching* classes about those classes, and continually got the word out about GO. Interested ears mushroomed quickly. Yet the needle didn't move as I wasn't strong at making "the ask." Making "the ask" is an intrinsic and explicit art. While I had the colors on my palette, I lacked the refined brush techniques to paint a compelling picture that translated a nice story into dollars in the bank.

Eventually my story flew into the ears of Katlyn Torgerson and Lindsay Simonds. They saw the potential underneath my caked brushes and had the skill set to refine my technique. We met at The Board Match, an annual speed-dating event where thousands of working professionals who want to serve on boards meet with around 150 nonprofits. Katlyn and Lindsay both worked at CCS Fundraising, a strategic fundraising firm that partners with nonprofits for transformational change.

They took my dirty brush, laid it down, and gave me four key lessons on how to better use it:

Lesson #1: I was in sales. Get over it. Yes, this was the nonprofit sector and we were doing "good" work. But you still need money to eat and so you have to sell yourself and the company. Drive home the impact and the value. Sell, sell, sell. And make people feel *great* about their gift.

Lesson #2: Impact drives income, not the other way around. Figure out how to convey the impact of your work to any target, and any donor.

Lesson #3: Cultivating and prospecting transformational gifts take time. There is a science and a method to get from, "I've heard about your work" to "Did the $500,000 check come through okay?"

Lesson #4: Perfect your ask statement. When it's time to step up to the plate, *always* take the swing, and always *ask*. More details on the perfect "ask" follow below.

Once framed in simple and empowering terms, I had the ability to mentally envision any oncoming major gift engagement. We role-played in our conference room with Lindsay playing Mrs. Money Bags while

I told my story and then converted, at *just* the right moment, to my ask statement. We repeated scenarios over and over of big requests followed by various reactions. We practiced how to respond to a "no", how to create a sense of urgency for the dreaded "maybe", and how to build upon a "yes".

My brush strokes grew more confident and bolder. Rather than being nervous about asking for money, I could not wait for that moment when the "the ask" would be made. Now bolder with asking for help, the student became the teacher and I successfully asked Lindsay and Katlyn to helm advisory boards for GO so we could improve fundraising across the organization. Our Champions, local leaders, and board of directors all needed this critical information of how to make effective ask statements.

We hit our stride. Asking for money became oddly addictive and we began to blossom. Firstly, we started an operational budget with everyone working as 1099 contractors to get our administration organized. We then converted those contractors into full time employees once we could afford realistic salaries and benefits. Despite being a cofounder, I was actually the sixth person to be paid at GO. In my view, leaders eat last since the motivations to grow something vary widely, even across the earliest adopters. The top of the pyramid would never exist if you do not have a well-fed foundational base. Leadership is lonely and expensive in many regards, but it comes with the territory.

Crucially, this initial sacrifice motivated my hustle since my own livelihood was continually at stake. Failure came often and I improved with each rejection. I met a potential major investor through friends and invited him to a few exclusive events where he met local partners and Champions. And then we were drinking tea, in a trendy spot in the Fillmore district. I knew his tailor and how much he spent on clothes so I had a read on the amount to request. Our conversation flowed smoothly and I could tell we liked each other. Then the moment presented itself.

I leaned in, and made "the ask".

He laughed out loud while shaking his head.

"Hey, listen. That is a great ask. Really. But no," he said.

I stood undeterred in knowing how to handle his "No". I asked him to host events and introduce me to his friends. Six months later that investor would help me raise $10,000. He coached me with further neurolinguistic programming lessons to become a more confident fundraiser. Opportunities grew and the transformation happened. A few weeks later I made a $25,000 ask over lunch. The answer was yes and we both felt great about the experience of making such a large commitment to one another.

Then came a $50,000 gift.

Then our team hit their stride.

We became more confident in our abilities to grow and increased the scope, budget, and quality of our recurring events to draw more donors. We put a large focus on our annual gala, a springtime event that brought in 30 percent of our operational funding. We started small and thought big and I always strove to trust my team. Our first gala in 2009 had only 40 RSVPs a week before the event. We had expected and budgeted for over 100 guests. I felt embarrassed by the thought of a near empty room where listless guests made awkward conversations. I wanted to pull the plug. But our team stayed confident and calmed my nerves. The night of the gala, 100 people showed up (I learned that San Franciscans hate committing early) and we raised $35,000. We iterated and improved upon this pivotal annual event, focusing deeply on compelling storytelling paired with strong asks. By 2012, our galas were raising over $100,000 for our operational capacity to grow.

Our circle widened as our influence and impact increased. Galas not only brought in funding for the organization to grow, it also showcased our work to a wider network of influential people. To keep widening the net, we started hosting smaller events and salons at luxuriant homes in San Francisco and Beverly Hills so people could meet us in more intimate settings. Opulent doors opened. The hummingbird found himself in the company of elephants, and my little wings beat anxiously. I had never been around such striking wealth. Its striking contrast to the focus of our work anchored my heart in troublesome doubt. I had to project confidence and ease while masking incredulous feelings as my life experience swung wildly between the richest of the rich and the poorest of the poor.

Ironically, I entered these circles by significantly decreasing my own financial wealth. My meager nonprofit startup salary qualified as "low income" in San Francisco. I stood on the behalf of people that, at best, made a few dollars per day. Yet I routinely found myself in multi-million dollar homes whose garages housed cars that I had no idea how to even enter. I ate off Versace plates while tempering my intake of amazing champagne so my donation ask would be steady, not slurred.

While preparing for that moment of "the ask", my analytical brain could never stop dividing these luxuriant material goods against the impact in the field. I found myself sitting next to a prospective donor as he careened down Rodeo Drive in a McLaren P1. As the city of lights flashed by the gilded window, I calculated his car was worth 125 rainwater catchment systems. Enough to give nearly 1,000 people access to clean water for 50 years. These thoughts gave me power since it made my "ask" seem trite. If someone spends $150,000 on a mode of transport, surely they could invest $10,000 or $25,000 for a worthy cause?

Empowered by my analytical brain and the dedication within my heart, I kept making the "asks" and I kept closing. Our wider team, from our staff in San Francisco to our partners in the field, did the same and opportunities began to mushroom around us. Funding began coming in at a quickly increasing pace.

Then in one moment, I knew everything would change. I found myself standing in front of my neighborhood post office. A routine day, an ordinary place. I exited holding an envelope—regular size, regular weight, just like the gas bill. The return address bore the name of the Leonardo DiCaprio Foundation. Amidst the hustling foot traffic, I tore it open and stood still while a $500,000 check made out to GO floated into my hand. The congratulatory letter attached said two more checks would follow that would fund the ClearWater program in Ecuador. I had no idea how to process the feathery lightness of a check that contained so many zeros and commas. So much promise and belief lay written on this promissory note that would give thousands of people access to clean water while protecting their environment.

Our time had come.

When Kyle and I first started GO in 2009, we received our first batch of checks with the words "Groundwork Opportunities" written on them. This was the first physical product with our name on it. I marveled that it somehow qualified our existence and made GO 'real'. I tore out check number 1011, took out a pen, and wrote it out for $1,000,000. I had no idea how I would raise that amount of cash as I had never seen that kind of money.

I carried that check in my wallet every day, every hour, and every minute.

It was there every time an investor said, "No."

It was there every time a project didn't quite work out.

It was there every time I heard, "Sorry, maybe next time."

This paper based ideological goal went with me to every failed fundraising experience. It stayed with me as I got better at raising money. Then on the eve of 2013, GO stood with over one million dollars in assets.

I took out the $1,000,000 check that had been with me for the last four years.

I shredded it and shared the photo over social media.

Life seemed limitless.

It seemed like nothing could ever go wrong.

Then it all did.

TURN IT AROUND
THE ART OF THE ASK

There must be an "ask" before anything is given. The art of asking takes years to master and is easier written than executed. The right moment to ask someone for an investment— whether money, time, or both— requires skill and a belief in your convictions. Learning to calm your nerves, fully embracing the present moment, and understanding the subtle nuances of human attraction requires dedicated focus and humility.

It took me a long time to learn this vital skill as interest in GO piqued early from friends and family. These initial supporters inherently trusted me so donated money came with few questions asked. Yet beyond my personal social network, I struggled with raising money.

Practice and pressure forces sound execution and I failed my way forward. Shortly after Joe's random donation in the park, I knew we were onto something. I walked into the office of Patrick Meade, my boss at Slalom Consulting, and stated I was leaving to pursue my passion. He wished me all the best and I went all in on GO.

And I got knocked the fuck out.

Six months later, I walked right back into that same office and asked for my old job back. My saved nest egg was gone as I bumbled through my first few fundraising asks. Operational dollars trickled in unevenly. That feeling of failing to execute was far worse than any rejection I ever received in asking people for money. I never let myself forget that.

So when Katlyn and Lindsay came into my life, I doubled down on my efforts. I learned that I wasn't *asking* the *right people* in the *right way*. Once armed with the below lessons, I left Slalom for a second time, this time armed with a much more polished ask. And I never looked back.

Just Ask

This sounds ridiculous as advice yet it must be said since most people do not ask for *what they want*. They work diligently at their desks expecting a raise. They launch startups with an awesome product and believe investment dollars will magically appear. Wrong. You will not get what you deserve merely by creating impact. While that may draw attention, it will not compel action. You must ask *specifically* and *concisely* for that money or for whatever form of energy you need to succeed.

Preparation

Know your investor. People give to people and people love giving to people that they know. Getting to know people takes time and you must first cultivate the relationship and be *genuinely* and *authentically* committed to the relationship and the person first. This helps with understanding their giving priorities and how they would like to help. At GO, I knew in advance which donors were fascinated by educational versus agricultural programs. I knew which donors wanted to know all the minute details against those that liked to hear the visionary trajectory of the work. These details matter. The more you can know in advance of a meeting wherein you intend to make a big ask, the better your outcome.

Write Down Your Ask

I have my ask statement written and memorized in advance of my meeting. Always. When it comes to the right time to make "the ask", the statement must be delivered concisely and directly. Here is my ask template:

I would like for you to consider __(what)___ so/since ____(why)_____.
Examples:
I would like for you to consider investing $10,000 so we can launch our GO Champions initiative.

I would like for you to consider raising my salary by 15 percent so I can help our company thrive.

Why is this statement so effective? First, it starts with an option, as people love choices. By using the clause, "I would like for you to consider", I am offering you a choice. You can act or not. That gives me a psychological advantage since choices make people feel powerful.

Second, ensure the ask pertaining to the "what" is clear. I will use the first example to elucidate. At this point in the conversation, it should be clear about the impact $10,000 will have and how it will be leveraged. Perhaps I have a visual one-page business plan to convey my message. Perhaps I forgot this document while rushing from one meeting to the next so I draw it on a cocktail napkin. Either way, I must have clearly explained the impact about how extraordinary growth can come from a measly $10,000. Then, at the crucial emotional apex of "the ask", I just need to state the direct ask (in six words or less). For example, "invest $10,000, raise my salary by X%, a Y% discount, etc."

Finally, add a *brief* "why" at the end to close the loop (for example, "so I can help our company thrive"). Note the italics of *brief* in that prior sentence. I have seen countless botched asks that begin brilliantly only to end in a diarrhea of re-hashed *why* statements in a never ending run-on sentence, very much like this particular stream of thought, which I should have already ended, yet I continue to drill home the point of how annoying this thought becomes, and if you are *still* reading at this point while getting frustrated, you should get the point of brevity. If you cannot summarize your *why* in one breath, distill it down and try again.

After the Ask

First, say nothing when the ask statement comes out. Keep calm and stay quiet. Any justification made after "the ask" is put out there will weaken your position. Maintain open body language and strong eye contact. Don't blink, and stay focused. Subsequently, one of four responses will occur:

Agreement

Yes! I would *love* to invest $10,000 to help GO thrive. If that feels great, then do pat yourself on the back and realize you probably did not ask for enough. An immediate affirmation usually means you came in too low and did not challenge expectations. With immediate agreement, you'll never know if your request was not challenging enough. But well done, all the same.

More Time

This is the most common response as time is the most crucial element in negotiation. This response means your ask is challenging though desirable. Savvy negotiators will create space at this juncture and introduce a third party into the equation to buy them time ("I need to speak with my wife" or "Let me run this up the chain", etc.). The important thing here is to ensure you do not leave the meeting without specific follow-up meeting times. Ask questions to clarify their timeline. If you can, introduce a sense of urgency to narrow this timeline in your favor (For example, "I'd love to announce this gift at our board meeting next week", "I'm buying a home soon and really need that raise", etc.) And be grateful by thanking them for their time.

Less

My asks are direct and often catch people off guard, forcing them to do a notable blink-jump, where their eyes flutter as they surge backwards in their chair. I've had many people laugh out loud at my "ask" because I aim high. That's fine, as long I stay calm. After their initial shock, people will want to come in at a level wherein they feel comfortable. That's understandable but realize you are delivering impact, not asking for money. If you feel that your impact is worth the energy you just requested, stay close to that true value. Keep yourself and your "ask" in high esteem; you have a value of self and that is non-negotiable. That being said, if the same ask to many people *always* results in disbelief, perhaps it is time to tone it down.

Declination

No is only a trifle notion that closes one door while opening an infinite number of new ones. The trick is being able to quickly turn the "no" around in your mind to other possibilities. Prepare for the "no" with other options ready. If a prospective investor said no to funding, perhaps they could introduce you to someone that would be interested. Even better, perhaps they might be willing to host a dinner at their home to meet with their friends or associates. If you didn't get that raise perhaps an extended vacation is permissible. A no is just one closed road. Seek out other avenues that may still get you to your wider end goal. Be polite and confident by gauging the energy of the other person. If the receiver of the ask closes their body language and answers in monosyllabic terms, then it's time to move on.

CHAPTER 15

THINGS FALL APART

Success is not built on success.
It's built on failure.
It's built on perseverance.
And the most notable successes?
Those are built upon catastrophe.

As she surged, GO indiscriminately wove herself into the most intimate fabrics of my being. Nothing distinguished my personal and professional lives. Take my wedding day, a profoundly personal event that somehow became deeply steeped in many professional layers. Set in Zanzibar, an island off the coast of East Africa, I stood in the open-air ruins of a church once owned by David Livingstone. I pledged a life-long commitment to Heather, my best friend, in front of family, friends, and colleagues. The scene seemed magical in that remote corner of the world. I met Heather through GO as she was close friends with our first supporters and attended our earliest fundraising events. She was there from the beginning. And four years later, she became mine and I became hers.

Some of our guests were related by blood and others by belief, yet we all sat like sisters and brothers under the imperious African sun. Everyone was somehow connected to GO. Some had raised funds for our work and some had built schools. They were among our first family of supporters and partners and traveled in from America, England, Poland, Tanzania, Ghana, and Uganda. At the center of the ceremony stood our officiant and guiding light, Peter Francis Luswata. Kyle and I had trusted him in our foundation of GO when it was a mere budding idea scrawled on a napkin. Now Heather and I entrusted him with the sanctity of blessing the most important relationship of our lives: the one we held to each other.

I stood in wonder as the gospels of our African choir swelled the humid air. I could not believe how fortune had smiled upon me with this much love. After the ceremony in the ruins, our entire party sailed off into the sunset on a rickety dhow. I thought that I was capable of manifesting anything I wanted in life.

I returned from my wedding a new person with a higher sense of self, an evolved purpose, and a deeper passion for life than ever before. I lost a sense of humility. I sailed towards hubris and vanity. After years of pushing the wheel of organizational development towards any sort of movement, I let go and dizzily ran with it downhill. I became fearless in decision-making as my behavior steered towards dangerous pride.

The potential felt endless and I put in effort at every second to keep growing. I went to the gym and between sets would shoot out an email. Pump a set. Send an email. Pump a set. Enter data into Salesforce. Pump a set. Raise more money. I would leave the gym blasting, "Starting From the Bottom" by Drake, literally thinking my body was expanding immediately after lifting weights, allowing us to take on more growth.

Celebrities started sending in checks. People of influence joined our board. I found myself parroting slogans on commercials with our corporate partners, and our work got featured in mass media. I fulfilled a childhood dream of being featured on NPR by sharing my story on Snap Judgment. Our wedding got covered in a two-page spread in the *San Francisco Chronicle*. Things just kept getting bigger.

Nothing could go wrong.

And I was arrogant for believing that.

My confidence stemmed from working with a strong and dedicated team, albeit one that was encountering growing pains. Our financial situation had now stabilized though our leadership style had not. Our board of directors was coalescing slowly and I realized that I was at the center of a large problem in communications amongst its members. Since I had always been present during their recruiting and on boarding, they always conferred directly with me about a host of issues though seldom with each other. We lacked a crucial growth element of open and honest communication, the fertile soil where trust grows rapidly. Inadvertently, I created a pyramid reporting style that choked effective communications amongst our leadership. So our strategic vision stalled in its execution.

Likewise, our management team hit unexpected road-bumps. Shortly before my wedding Kyle had won two around-the-world airline tickets on Groupon. He took his life partner Jessie Curtner on an adventure of a lifetime, spending a year circling the globe. And so with a heavy heart, he submitted his resignation from managing GO.

Kyle's departure left GO with me at the helm though I was backed up by a capable crew to help steer our growing ship. Our motley staff of a few employees, many interns, and countless volunteers brought the nonprofit programmatic and fundraising strategy experience that Kyle and I lacked. They passionately shared our determination to grow and filled crucial spots on our growing team as we prepared for his departure. None more so than Amber Johnson, an intern from our earliest days that quickly rose in the ranks to lead alongside me during this pivotal inflection point.

While we were a small organization, our growth trajectory seemed limitless. I felt that in every fiber of my being. When GO could not afford the talent we needed to thrive, I even paid vital staff like Amber with cash from my own savings to keep us growing. Our tight knit team spent days, nights, and even weekends together. Interns became friends, and friends became interns. We were all in it together.

The bonds of friendship that grew around this inner circle of the original tightened closely around my life. As my entire life spiraled around GO, it eventually led to meeting Heather, a strong and beautiful woman that literally felt like love at first sight. Since Heather and I were both new to San Francisco, our social circles were small so we grew tight friendships around the GO team. Our personal and professional lives became intertwined in GO's rise, as Heather was a talented event planner. She volunteered countless hours alongside Amber to stage event after event, from rock concerts to fashion shows, to help raise money and awareness for GO. Year after year *after year*, we all spent long nights and weekends together, building deep bonds of friendship as our emerging team grew.

Everybody at our wedding party was somehow connected to those early days of magical thinking, when the hope and unbridled optimism of continual growth would never stop reverberating in our hearts and minds. We thought we were friends for life, dancing together like no one was watching under the pale moonlight.

Then somehow, it began to fall apart.

~

Two months after our wedding, GO was in full preparation mode for our annual gala. This vital fundraiser raised around $125,000 (around 30 percent) of our capacity funding that enabled our organization's growth. As unrestricted funding is among the most difficult money to raise, the pressure to execute weighed heavily on our 30-person event team.

Meanwhile, fomenting our board of directors to work as a collective whole left me challenged. I succeeded in recruiting talented people to join yet I couldn't quite manage to coalesce them into a productive team. I scheduled a board meeting for the last day of January 2014 to solve this challenge and to ensure a viable future. And that started with electing a strong chairperson of the board, a dynamic and executive position to steer us effectively towards a new horizon.

This pivotal meeting was set at noon on January 31st. The gala was four weeks away and a new fiscal year was dawning. I was up early, pacing the room reviewing my meeting notes. I nervously recited the motions, the formal method of putting proposals in front of the board that would decree their resolution. They would require a vote up or a vote down. Little margin for error existed. The key motion was to elect a new board chair, a nomination I had prepared but one I knew would come as a surprise to a few directors. I rallied support around Joe Richardson, who was both our first social investor and official board member. I would make the motion, knowing I had the votes to win. Yet

I feared hostility from certain board members not yet convinced that he would be the right choice.

My phone rang at 8:00 a.m. in the midst of my mental pacing. A familiar voice from our bank asked whether I could meet right away. I explained that my morning was *quite* busy.

She insisted, stating it was urgent.

I stuffed my board notes into my backpack and took the tram downtown, arriving before opening hours. After brief formalities from two bank managers that were unusually icily irreverent, they asked me about how securely I kept my password for payroll transactions. My heart froze. I knew this question spelled out a path that I had to take but did not want to follow. I grew impatient and told them to get to the heart of the matter. They slid over a one-page spreadsheet that concisely spelled out the following:

Amber was stealing money from GO.

I blinked and looked at the spreadsheet. Their questions about password security hazily floated in the air. I could not meet their eyes. I kept looking at the page.

Amber?

Stealing?

She had been there from the beginning.

Years of work and friendship flashed before my eyes.

Amber.

Stealing.

I iced up.

I opened my mouth to respond. Nothing came out. Internally, rage and sadness vied for my attention. How could someone so close and so dear to me do such a thing?

Foundation shattering information always takes time to process, often measured in weeks or months, not minutes or hours. I shook their hands with cold, sweaty palms. I said that I would be in touch. I looked at my watch. Two hours until the board meeting. Amber would be at the meeting, sitting by my side as I gave progress reports about our annual gala, which was on track to be our largest ever. Hundreds of our strongest supporters, staff, and board would be there, celebrating our fifth birthday. Ironically, a motion to increase our pay as peak performers also sat on the agenda.

I breathed in. And then out. I mentally placed the information on a cloud, watching it drift away in my mind.

I had no idea what else to do. I simply could not process the information with the right degree of thought it required. I walked around the block of our office over and over until the board meeting started. I entered in a state of shock, and felt like a car had just hit me. It's that odd feeling we get when we *think* we are fine though we truly are not. As I took the elevator up to the conference room, I erased the information from my mind.

Amazingly, the meeting went quite well. My motions passed and a new leader was selected. I tabled the discussion regarding pay increases as I thought my façade would break discussing this ironic topic.

I excused myself from the post-meeting happy hour and went home early.

I spent the weekend meditating. How could I tell the board? How could I tell Heather? Who should I tell first? The more I thought about it, the worse it got. Being gutted by a close friend and colleague lurched away the ability for me to reason or to trust. I turned the situation around and around in my mind with a merry-go-round of possible actions. It spun continuously, never stopping at something that seemed logical or appropriate.

I enjoyed a lazy Sunday at home with my newlywed wife. I pretended life was normal. I held on to one more calm afternoon for just a little bit longer. Then on Monday morning, I told Heather. She left shaken to work. I then called our new board chairman. Disbelief radiated out when the news struck and an emergency board meeting was telephonically staged. As I shared what I had learned, I could feel their shocked reactions.

Some knew the depth of our personal relationship. Some were new to the organization and saw the situation with a more austere light. After heated discussion, we decided how to proceed. We issued a mandate that we would act to increase the number of choices for all parties involved as we moved forward. Specifically, this meant that we would not accuse Amber of anything until we heard her side of the story. If we accused her of something, thrusting information we purported as evidence, no matter how conclusive it may have been, the number of responses she could give would be dramatically limited. We would learn nothing with accusation. So we framed it openly.

Essentially, we presented the information in her presence in a different frame. We were indeed having issues with a new payroll system recently installed at GO. Sometimes people got paid twice and sometimes not at all. These critical issues resulted in me reaching out to the bank to research what was going on. Their investigation found that most of the problems were software errors. Yet a few transactions were of a much different and more devious nature. Those transactions compelled the bank to call me on that fateful morning.

Amber knew of these payroll issues, so we selected the most gregarious and kind board member to meet with Amber and me about the bank's research. Together with Amber, we looked at ways to improve our current state of affairs with a misbehaving payroll system. We neglected to overtly mention the bank's conclusion that certain transactions had ended up in her account by her own volition.

And in this approach, we found Amber providing falsehoods. She made claims about her specific whereabouts during the specific times when money was transferred from our account to hers. Her claims were contradicted by her own social media postings and email time-stamps as to her whereabouts during those crucial transactions. I sat stunned as I watched her lie with impervious confidence. We created an opening for her to take the path of redemption, vastly increasing the number of choices she could make in our intertwined fate. She chose to limit her own opportunities by continuing on with further falsehoods. Our organization became limited in how to respond. The data on paper that coldly yet logically narrated a story of deceit had been confirmed. She would have to be fired.

The path in the execution of Amber's termination became mired in challenges as the board split into hawks and doves. Different viewpoints arose on how to handle the situation from both an internal and external perspective. Some actors on the board weighed in and suggested more punitive action. Some suggested grace and forgiveness. The professional deliberation stretched on for days and teetered on a fine balance of chaos and order. While the board considered her future, the personal consequences of this betrayal manifested themselves in acute and unforeseen ways. Rumors began to swirl amongst our inner circle of friends and supporters. Normal conversations quickly became awkward. We were now two weeks from our biggest event of the year and the abrupt disappearance of Amber, who had stopped coming into work during such a busy time, raised more than just eyebrows. I claimed she was having personal issues and dodged the question of her absence as best as I could.

I had to delegate tasks to people like never before given the chaos. Volunteers became empowered overnight with the capacity to make decisions and some were hired as contractors. In terms of resources, we were seeing numbers of Champions inspired, dollars raised, and the scale of programs launched growing at unprecedented levels. Our organization continued to thrive, which required even more of my attention to manage. The effort to sustain that growth went beyond merely putting in double the hours to make up for Amber's absence. I came from management consulting so the 80-hour workweeks weren't foreign to me. But this was different. The price paid for the organization's security felt like a pound of flesh taken from my side as the consequences began to ring out on a personal level.

I returned home daily weary from doing the work of two. Heather sat despondently on the couch, often in tears. Amber's actions had created a wedge between Heather and me since she was close to both of us. We chose not to talk about the situation amongst our close friends who were connected to GO. Virtually overnight, close friends became distant. On top of that, I had to request that Heather's volunteer role in helping to stage the gala double in size since I was so overloaded with work. No one else had the skill set to pull off such a large event in such little time. Once she got home from work planning corporate productivity seminars, she quietly helped me with seating charts, invite confirmations, alcohol permits, and countless other event minutiae until the wee hours of night. Exhausted tears would flow from her eyes against the unfairness of it all. Bitter guilt harrowed my tired body to bed in the evenings.

An unexpected catastrophe had wedged itself between us. Soon, our choice of quiet introspection became legally enforced as a letter arrived addressed to me from an expensive law firm. The terse words on the crisp white paper threatened legal action if I spoke to anyone about what was occurring with Amber. As advised by our board and legal counsel, I kept quiet on a personal and professional level. I quietly labored on for the greater good of what we had created and all to devastating effect.

My silence on the matter triggered a fallout of friends that began slowly and then swiftly. Rescinded invitations for social engagements arrived via email, voicemails, and austere phone calls. Both Heather and I were uninvited from trips, dinner parties, and even a wedding. The more we stayed quiet about what was happening, the more despondently we watched a large part of our social circle shrivel. Intimate friends that flew to the other side of the world for our wedding now quickly walked to the other side of the street when they saw me pass. Friends became strangers.

Heather and I canceled existing travels and personal events to avoid more awkward social interactions. We clenched our teeth while swallowing flight cancellation charges. In addition to loneliness, I felt a profound sense of guilt as I watched a bitter pain manifest in my wife as she watched friendships crumble into forlorn estrangement. Her empathy knows few bounds yet here, she was legally bound to keep quiet. Somehow, I could not shake the feeling that this was entirely my fault.

Fatigue began our days and tearful sorrow ended our evenings.

We were reaching a brink. More people yelled at me in those weeks of separation than in my entire career. The complexity of California's labor laws and the diversity of opinion on how to handle the matter made getting legal counsel a requirement. Risk averse, we erred on the side of caution at all intervals, no matter how much humiliation we had to endure. Being "mean" in any sense limits actions and exposes risks of lawsuits; grace always opens more doors, even when the inevitable final closure of termination is the only path.

Our legal counsel kept us dutifully on this interminable path despite its heavy toll on my personal life. The ordeal stretched from weeks into months, given that each side had retracted behind an iron curtain of legal ambiguities. From a professional perspective, light began to show at the end of the tunnel. I nervously anticipated the approach of our annual gala, which I considered to be a key litmus test of our future since it was a large gathering of our closest supporters. I had only communicated to our team as we approached the crucial date of the annual gala that Amber was no longer part of GO. As advised by our lawyers, no reason was to be given to any stakeholder (employee, contractor, or advisory board member) unless deemed absolutely necessary. Our lawyer wrote an official communiqué for me to send via email to this body of 30 people. Legally bland and tersely worded, these foreign words bore no resemblance to any email I had ever sent. I feared that the wider walls of GO would break. Did I deserve the trust of our tribe without being able to tell the truth? Amber had disappeared after years of building everything up.

Office rumors spread like wildfire.

And somehow, the wall held.

Despite the gala being held right in the middle of the ordeal, the event was a great success. The GO tribe stood steadfast at our finest hour despite the massive fissure in our foundation. Over 120 people attended and we raised 40 percent more in revenue as compared to the previous year. Overnight, we were flush with cash and ready to rebuild and reinvest in our future. Relief overwhelmed me.

This crucial burst of energy and resources gave us a much-needed boost. We were finally able to reach a separation agreement with Amber thanks to the wise legal counsel of Hanson Bridgett after three months of excruciating negotiations. We chose to take the higher road by merely parting ways despite a few recalcitrant voices that wanted vengeance for the wrong. There was no termination and no outside legal action. We would provide a professional recommendation as long as the stolen funds were returned. Then we would be a mere two ships passing each other in the night, separate and equal. The paperwork was formalized and sent out for signature across all parties. Finally, this would all be over.

With the gala and my frugal penchant to always save for a rainy day, we had just enough runway left to build upon this "crisis-tunity". Crisis forced cohesion. Our board had communicated amongst each other like never before and their dedication to ensuring the survival and long-term viability of our work was unparalleled in scope. I marveled at their resilience to meet day after day, making time in their busy professional and personal lives to craft a path forward. A sleeping giant of talent had awakened and dutifully sailed through a powerful storm.

Additionally, I began to fully leverage the extent and passion of our wide volunteer network. Before the crisis, I felt humbled when anyone would choose to volunteer their time by folding napkins at the gala, chipping in code to our site, or taking photos in the field. I rarely asked for more than what they gave. In this temperamental manner, I failed at leading since I did not challenge them. There was meaning and purpose in their actions; this is why they volunteered to begin with. I ultimately realized the power of delegation and trust that empowered them to move us all forward.

During the turmoil of Amber's dismissal, I had no choice but to rely on the strengths of others. I found myself saying to staff and volunteers: "I need you to manage this. You own it. Now deliver. Please and thank you." Some excelled in their challenges and others did not. Either way, it was a boon to figure out how much people could do when properly challenged.

We had strong leadership, a dedicated tribe, and cash to invest. We could shape a new future. Yet I felt gravely wounded as the crisis went beyond a professional challenge. It had struck directly at my recent marriage; a state of being that was then still raw in its formation. I felt so badly that the situation caused so much pain to Heather. A silly little eye accident that propelled me to create something that continually requested my sacrifice was one thing. It was entirely another matter to behold a beast that ultimately required us to sacrifice as a cohesive family unit. Then the beast that I could no longer control bared its teeth, and in a very public fashion.

The *San Francisco Chronicle* article about our wedding came out. We picked up the newspaper and saw photos of many friendly faces that had faded into strangers. Worse, they published an egregious error entirely discounting Kyle from our whole history! I had not been given a chance to proofread the final version and that public fame brought private anguish. A heated personal argument broke out between Kyle and myself. I apologized profusely and explained the situation since I could not bear to lose more friends.

He listened and forgave but things kept falling apart. More simultaneous fires kept starting. A project partner that we had worked with for years was publicly accused of corruption and child abuse. He denied the claims though became paranoid an assassination attempt was being made on his life. Simultaneously, another project partner, a man of humble origins from a very poor corner of our planet, claimed an intoxicated member of our leadership made sexually inappropriate comments while making unwarranted advances on him during a fundraising event. A similar incident repeated itself only a few weeks later at a fundraising event in Beverly Hills. During the event, another intoxicated member of our leadership demanded that my wife strip down to her underwear and jump into a pool with two men, who happened to be major donors. These young and wealthy players of Hollywood watched as this advocate of GO and I screamed at each other about this indecent proposal. They laughed as we traded fierce words and shoves in their gilded kitchen.

This all happened within weeks. I had lost my friends. I had lost my sense of decency. I thought I might lose Heather. Yet I kept waking up day after day, scrolling through emails and hoping to raise more money so we could provide more impact. I moved through the motions. Then one day, after another round of reading emails accusing me of this or that, I slowly closed my MacBook.

I was done.

I couldn't bear to have Heather see me this way.

I went to the guest bedroom, crawled into the same sheets that once housed the giant John Dau, and tucked myself into a fetal position.

I began to cry.

Heavy thoughts soaked in despair saturated my mind. Foremost, was I even worthy of these sufferings? Could I even really acknowledge them as such given the focus of our work? Yes, I had lost friends. My organization was losing control. I made little money to show for it all. My family was greatly hurt. I lost sleep and weight, and slugs of gin on the sly became a shameful crutch to end the day. Before our marriage, I lacked health insurance so I self-diagnosed and self-medicated when I got ill, which happened frequently given the stress within my life.

I was unwell.

That's undeniably a sacrifice.

Yet were these various hardships of launching a startup nonprofit in one of the world's most expensive cities comparable to the indignity of not having clean drinking water or basic human rights? I worked alongside people who had survived genocides, walked across the blistering deserts with bare feet, and who witnessed the butchering of family. Our beneficiaries faced suffering on a recurring basis. Could my emotional rupture situated in the coziness of the Western world truly compare to those living in extreme poverty?

Yet it *hurt*. That I cannot deny. Not without being honest to myself. Perhaps my comparison to those living in extreme poverty made my suffering even more acute since I often didn't feel the "right" to complain. As compared to my management-consulting colleagues, I made 40 percent of my previous salary. I lived paycheck-to-paycheck, gleaning financial stability and health insurance off Heather's corporate plan. Not only did she bear the insults and demagoguery of our shrinking social circle, she took the noble helm of being the familial breadwinner. Our home stayed afloat *through her resilience*, bearing the burden of the *how* while I struggled to figure out the *why*. So while I could internalize and process my sufferings, requesting others that I deeply loved to follow suit became an intense new challenge.

Ironically, things were growing quickly while I debated throwing in the towel. Donations were still flowing in, we were hiring, our work was published in mass media, our events sold out, and new projects cropped up in Kenya, India and Peru. Day in and day out, I continued to put on my game face by speaking about GO on stages big and small. I stuffed down my sufferings during this time of new growth. Externally, we flourished. Internally, the bleeding continued.

A colleague and dear friend, whose empathy knows few boundaries, wrote me one Monday morning during this time of conflicted solace. Like all great leaders, he had eerily prescient timing. He sensed I needed someone to listen. He had been acutely following the searing drama.

He wrote a thoughtful and kind email asking about my wellbeing.

I responded to his note with one sentence:

Everything I have is falling apart.

No signature, no other details.

In hindsight, reading this email now makes me see how ridiculous I was then. I had been given magnificent learnings and lessons that made me stronger. He called me via Skype and listened. I started to feel better just by the mere virtue of having another listening ear.

We are all tested at certain points in our lives and previously undiscovered weaknesses will rise sharply to the fore. They will cut, and they will hurt. Eventually, this too shall pass and you will gain priceless wisdom to move onwards. I had to face my responsibility for this damage. I learned that I often tend to see the best in people, which is a great strength as a founder but a weakness as a manager. There had been smoke before the fires and I chose to ignore the warnings until the situation escalated. I would have failed at getting us out of the mess on my own. Yet our community did not fail. Instead, the bonds of a brotherhood and sisterhood united under a vision of a just, equitable and productive global community were too strong. I see this now yet back then the truth was shrouded in the fog created within my own mind.

My unnecessarily heightened sense of self led to my silly 'woe-is-me' emails written to a friend who only wanted to provide their support.

I slowly started to feel better but my inner purpose that drove all of my action at GO still felt ruptured. I retreated away from the city and spent time with family in a small town on the coast. I watched the faint outlines of ships in the harbor bob up and down one cold and foggy Saturday morning in Bodega Bay. Dawn had just broken and only the navigation lights on the masts blinked through.

I felt physically and emotionally exhausted. I did not think I could go through with this any longer. Sitting cross-legged on the ground and looking out into the fog, I Skyped Peter in Uganda and relayed the entire affair. Detail after detail, I vomited out my toxic thoughts. I said how I felt that my world was closing in around me. I explained how the pain was striking my friends, my family, and my marriage.

In a virtual sense, he took his hand and struck me.

"Do you know how lucky you are to have found Heather? Do you not know how loving your parents are? Have you not met her family, her parents and strong brothers? How many friends did you have at the wedding? So what if ten of them are no longer around? You want children, yes? Once they are born, they will become your world. They will be your entire existence. I know. Believe me. I have two daughters. They and Cissy are my world now."

The words struck like bullets. I kept listening.

"Bart, think of everything you have. These stories around you, these 'things' that you label as despair, will change. They will continue to change all the time. They will heal. You have the power to determine when the healing comes. And you must do this quickly for the sake of your family. Listen. The love from my family radiates out into the world. It is my rock. My daughters show me the world the way it can be. How do you think my work is so successful? Does the farm grow food because of the soil? No, it grows because of the people's effort that plant the seeds. The power of people working together."

I watched the ships in the fog and let the words sink in.

"Do you see this?" he asked.

"Yes," I said.

He said "I love you" and we said our goodbyes.

He was right. He took the same situation and told a different story with the same facts. Sure, perhaps a third of the people that came to my wedding may never speak to me again. Yet the other two-thirds had now grown into much stronger relationships. Over and over, I turned the situation around in my mind and began to see how fortunate I was, and how deeply this experience improved my wellbeing.

Quitting it all then would last forever. The pain would be temporary. As Peter's words echoed in my ear, I realized I needed to find strength from my family and tribe. I could not quit and let them down due to personal misgivings expressed as pitiful stories that clouded my mind. I needed to rebuild the community around me as well as myself.

Community and the ties that bind found their foundational roots in my marriage. This was the center of it all—the one root that must be strong so my entire tree could thrive in the forest. I started there and discovered a story wherein these challenges had deep purpose and shone great light into my life. Despite the intense hardships, starting GO gave me the greatest blessing in my life: the fateful and irreversible introduction to my soul mate. *That* could never be changed or broken, no matter what happened; no matter who did what, and no matter how hard any challenge would be to endure. Heather and I built upon that moment of grace given to us from GO and our love grew stronger. This same love radiated outwards to our family, friends, colleagues, donors, board members, and countless others that wove themselves into the fabric of our community.

This includes you, dear reader.

All of us are interconnected. Whether it be the Ugandan farmer who wants a better future for his daughter, a local leader that guides others towards economic and communal viability, or a seventh grader from California who wants to share her resources. We believe in a universal bond that connects all of humanity.

What we started was bigger than any given individual. I could not run away from that.

I stood up.

The sun came out and the ships became visible.

I put one foot in front of the other and started back up the hill.

I felt light, ready for the day.

TURN IT AROUND
INCREASE CHOICES FOR ALL PARTIES

Nietzsche once wrote: "He who has a why to live can bear almost any how." Though things felt like they were crashing down in the aforementioned circumstances, the opposite was also true. Many new paths and thoughts were opening. Nothing about the *why* behind my motivations had changed. People still needed help improving their wellbeing and I still felt compelled to do something about it.

There are lessons to be learned in all experiences, and meaning to be found in pleasure and in pain. While I learned countless lessons through those magnificent failures, two summary lessons stood out from the rest.

Always Increase the Number of Choices for You and All Parties

From the moment I shared the bank's information about the situation, our board set out with a very important precedent on how to proceed: always to act as to increase the number of choices for you and all parties involved. This will empower every actor to respond in his/her own way. It enables a gamut of responses to guide and inform the involved parties. Hopefully, the process leads to a common agreement that is beneficial for all. Crucially, the notion also allows you to glean truth in times of great uncertainty. In a time when I doubted my own judgment, this precedent provided me with the footing to rise back up.

In the beginning, the stark and clear information on the Excel spreadsheet provided by the bank told one story. That information contrasted greatly against our long relationship. It didn't make any sense and I struggled on what next step to take.

In specific terms, this ideology meant that we agreed not to confront any party directly by accusing anyone with the bank's findings. If you outright accuse someone of anything, you greatly limit his or her choices on how to respond. Instead, our board framed this challenge as "let's figure this out together". Could we truly believe, without a doubt, that someone this close in our lives could betray our trust? So we framed the situation openly to present choices and learn more. Once devious steps were taken that further belabored trust, then the truth became disappointingly self-evident. Our course of action became clear.

This lesson is bigger than solely helping during times of conflict resolution. I also apply this method of increased choices in my personal life. My parents were frugal and instilled a healthy fear of debt. I never run a credit card balance I cannot pay off that month. A running balance means heavy interest will be accrued and more money owed. With more debt, I have fewer choices on what I can do in the future.

More acute usage of this lesson comes in legal matters. Lawyers have become an integral part of my life and while I trust their wisdom, I realize they are prone to being overly cautious in decisions. They have seen so many situations go bad that there are few, if any, paths on how to proceed without some sort of risk. The more you learn about every option in a legal quagmire, the more fear builds of a case going very wrong. Here, acting to increase choices for you and all parties, even when it may mean sacrificing something despite being the victimized party, is consistently the most successful route. Creating options for you and others in humility and unselfish grace rewards equitably and justly, even if meaningful things like money or property or people are lost in the effort.

Finally, this lesson also means I give back selflessly. I am undoubtedly privileged today. I may not be tomorrow. So what I have today I share with others. Sharing my resources increases their choices and mine simultaneously, now and in the future. Perhaps one day I will lose the fickle blessing of privilege and so will need others to share with me. And so the cycle of healthy and sustainable development will continue, building wellbeing in perpetuity.

Trust Yet Verify

One thing that became clear through these travails was that we, as an organization, needed to firmly establish our boundaries of safety, trust, and collaboration. The values of kindness and transparency inspire employees and volunteers to work at extraordinary levels of productivity. It empowers them to collaborate and work towards extraordinary goals that extend far beyond the means of a solitary individual. We as human beings need that sense of collaboration and it's biologically programmed into our brains to work with one another.

That said, I learned in difficult fashion that we must have limits to our kindness; we must accept the fact that certain malicious actions can occur that can threaten the existence of the tribe. Whether intentional or accidental, pathological by nature or devious by nurture, bad things do happen. And when they do, corrective actions must be taken so the organization can thrive.

Additionally, this situation exposed me to the curious nature of risk in the nonprofit sector. Our board commissioned a thorough review of our organization's risk management and security matters after this turmoil to prevent it from happening again.

Surprisingly, we learned that nonprofits actually are at greater risk of fraud, theft, misappropriation of funding, and other like malfeasances specifically because of their trusting nature. In addition to often lacking the resources to implement robust risk management protocols, nonprofits pay less attention to this vital organizational component because at some emotional level, we find it hard to believe that a person could "steal from charity". But it happens frequently within the nonprofit sector, as many people are simply gullible. Having shared this story with other nonprofit leaders, I can personally attest to some truly mind-blowing stories of how fallacious actors have siphoned vital resources from well-respected organizations. We collaborate and trust; yet we do not act and verify.

People are trusting by nature. We inherently want things to work out for everyone and mistake others' intentions of having this same goal. We believe employers when they tell us that they are 'people-focused' and have a great 'work-life balance'. We believe in people that join charitable causes since we believe they have the best of intentions for the work itself.

Yet people also have their own motivations, which can be deeply cryptic. Those motivations spill over into the companies they join, the political parties they support, or the organizations they lead. Even I have personal doubts as to the true intention I had when I started GO. Sure, I have the historical facts that could shape a motivation though given everything I know now, could I possibly think in the same mindset as I did in the past? The more I observe my own motivations, the more they begin to change. So how can I possibly project why others have joined, volunteered, or partnered in one form or another? Nothing is more perplexing in this world than attempting to project how others think about and see the world.

In the past, I misguidedly trusted that people's intentions equaled mine. I know better now and I am more careful in the decisions I make in life because of that notion. I trust people, of course, though I ensure that I verify that trust. In doing so, that often leads to more meaningful relationships since people value the effort put into the verification. Whether it is simply remembering a birthday (an act that validates the meaning of a personal relationship) or implementing a dual signature verification of expenditures (an act that brings transparency to professional relationships), these make a difference in how we value the people and the organizations we live and work with.

CHAPTER 16

END GAMES

Maybe it's not always about trying to fix something broken.
Maybe it's about starting over and creating something better.
It gives you another chance to make things right. Better, stronger.
An opportunity to find stronger leadership and see things anew.
Someone who could figure out where all this is going.
And, perhaps, why it started in the first place.

Kyle and I had always envisioned full transparency at GO. We would bare it all in hopes that success or failure would inspire action and learning. Now, given legal circumstances beyond my control, I was prevented from living up to that value. Binding legal agreements across an array of issues forced me to conceal details as to why various members of our leadership were no longer around.

I walked the line, stayed quiet, and reminded everyone about the 'why' of our work. The mantra was: *We are here to help leaders end poverty in their communities. This work is not about any given individual. It's about the team, the values, and the mission.*

We were ready to start anew after the successful 2013 gala that straddled these crises. I believed GO would persevere following countless phone calls and coffee dates with our key supporters. They expressed their unwavering faith in our work during those long conversations. They believed in our mission, which gave me the strength I needed to continue building our "Tower of Babel" to the sky.

This dedication was vital since in addition to the deeply divisive Amber situation, GO faced many simultaneous and consequential issues. The accusation of sexual impropriety by a new project partner during his visit to the states morphed into financial exaction to appease the situation. This seemingly quid pro quo request of hush money cast doubt on the scandalous claims and the board intervened, who were by now very scandal weary. Additionally, at the same time, another long-time project partner faced public accusations of negligence and fraud in Cambodia. That situation escalated so quickly that he feared for his life and claimed there was a conspiracy to assassinate him. I fielded Skype calls with an individual who sought my counsel about his impending execution. I felt lost as I wondered how on earth I could provide guidance about that?

And *all that* was simultaneously topped off with various alcohol-fueled and scandalous *Jersey Shore* endings to glitzy fundraisers, as mentioned earlier. In short, things were getting way out of control. We took swift action by enlisting various consultants and board members to put out the fires. The accused member of our leadership resigned to avoid further scandal, financial appeasement was denied to the project partner, a full audit of the Cambodian project was ordered (which steadfastly disputed the accusations of corruption while setting up a detailed action plan to remedy neglected programs), and a strict cap on alcohol consumption during events was implemented for GO staff.

We also survived the depths of these ordeals since we had cash in the bank. Disasters teach many great lessons, foremost being that they are *really* expensive to manage. Risk management consultants, auditors, and lawyers come with an impact that demands serious dollars. Fortunately during this troubled time, we cleared $1.1 million in donations in one month, which gave us over eight months of operational runway to transform our foundation.

Additionally, communications flowed at a much better pace at the board level. Despite being scandal weary, our board members actively organized around key focus areas without my direct involvement, which was instrumental in calming the turbulent seas. So with core values that kept the tribe united, active board involvement, and a surplus of cash, we weathered the storms. GO stood ready to invest in new leadership to build upwards and onwards.

That process started with finding a new leader to validate the impact and long-term viability of our work. This individual needed to become a trusted advisor to our social entrepreneurs and have a strong stomach for drama. A person who would be tough enough to spend weeks out in the field, void of life's creature comforts, and then be ready to engage with wealthy socialites to raise awareness. Someone who had khakis for the mud and formal wear for the galas. A difficult challenge though she finally appeared amongst a wide pool of earnest candidates.

I made her an offer she couldn't refuse and a new dawn for GO shined brightly when Sienna Moore joined our tribe. She was a dynamic, earnest, and innovative young leader ready to take our work to new heights following months of damage control. We wanted to capitalize on her strong international development background by building a systemic method to measure our impact. Raising money was no longer the biggest challenge and investing it wisely became the greatest task at hand.

Foremost, we wanted to track our holistic impact. While we were doing a good job on a micro level by reporting impact to individual GO Champions, we were struggling to do the same at the macro level. GO Champions raised funds for a diverse group of local leaders and their projects. Some raised money for water wells, others raised money for drill rigs to provide more wells, some raised money for schools, and some raised funds for scholarships for children to attend those schools. While it was easy to tell any given Champion that, for example, the $1,500 you raised built a rainwater catchment system, it was far more complicated to report this impact across many Champions who were raising funds for many types of ideas.

Since the individual impact reporting was good, GO Champions kept mushrooming. Many of these Champions became repeat fundraisers and excelled at influencing their network to join our tribe. They encouraged others to become GO Champions and to start their own fundraisers. Internally, we began delineating Champions as those that raised funds and Super Champions as influencers that not only raised money, but they also encouraged more Champions to join our fold. We focused attention on the Super Champions' passion by attending their events in person, sending them gifts, and inviting them to join us on delegation trips to Ecuador, Uganda, Cambodia, or Tanzania. We formed an entire advisory board to sustainably grow this body of well-engaged philanthropists.

Additionally, other early-stage nonprofits that lacked our fundraising technological focus began to showcase their development projects on our website. We became a channel provider for other nonprofits that shared our values and beliefs that lasting change happened when we supported local leaders. We worked together and helped them inspire Champions who could raise funds for their work. SHE-CAN—an organization that connects professional US women with young female leaders from post-conflict countries—raised over $15,000 on our site. ClearWater—a movement for clean water, rainforest protection and cultural survival in Ecuador's northern Amazon— raised over $150,000 for hundreds of rainwater catchment systems. Kibera Girls' Soccer Academy (KGSA)—an organization in Kibera, Kenya, which empowers girls to thrive academically and personally— raised nearly $300,000 for a girls' boarding school and community center.

This growing pool of money and partnerships brought many new challenges. For example, our promise of "100 percent of donations to cause for projects" struggled under the weight of our popularity. One thousand dollar, $5,000, and $10,000 donations were being made on a recurring basis. One Champion even got a $50,000 donation. With PayPal charging us 2.2 percent on all transactions made on our site, that one $50,000 donation cost us a whopping $1,100 in bank fees! In the early years, we had a partnership with Google Wallet who charged us zero percent fees to process credit cards. Once Google phased out that program, our bank fees reached perilous heights.

However, the 100 percent promise was a founding principle of GO. It fostered immediate trust and made us popular. Other nonprofit crowd funding sites charged up to 15 percent, so the demand for our "free" service was obviously high. We believed that this model could operate at scale. Many like-minded organizations like Charity: Water, UniversalGiving, Kiva, and DIGDEEP stood alongside us with a 100 percent giving model. Collectively, they leveraged this same structure to raise over one-billion in donations. Yet the challenge of raising operational funding to manage GO's growth took its toll on our over-worked and under-paid staff.

That same promise also prompted investment proposals to flood in from around the world. Some came directly from local leaders like Peter and some came from existing organizations like ClearWater or KGSA. Some projects even came from the GO Champions. When Champions traveled to the field, they often met many other local leaders with varying degrees of capability and trustworthiness. Altogether, this surge of proposals from many channels became greatly problematic as we had an immature strategy of which proposals to accept or decline.

This challenge was acute since given our size, we became a larger target for fraud. Many plagiarized investment proposals came in and required heavy vetting before any investment was made. And then, once funded, the projects became expensive to maintain. Inspections meant traveling to very remote areas of the world. And the farther you go, the more expensive it is to get there. Flying to Duk Payuel, South Sudan for a site inspection is *not* cheap.

Neither was the cadre of international development consultants we hired occasionally to do audits of our partnerships. Even our existing and good-natured partners struggled with the success of growth. Certain local leaders began to show signs of strain under the pressure, whether caused by mismanagement of operating at larger scales or becoming political targets since their success made them influential, or by just plain incompetence when too much was done at once. A great limitation in the funding of startup community based organizations is their desire to attempt to fix *everything* in their community. An organization that specializes in everything specializes in nothing. The local leaders that ran these organizations tried, but could not do everything well. Some lacked focus. When they started raising hundreds of thousands of dollars, their operational inefficiencies became radically apparent. This wasn't fully the social entrepreneurs' fault as after all, those local leaders worked in the most challenging environments in the world. They faced constant political, environmental, epidemiological, and fiscal risk. In short, not only did GO herself need better management systems, so did our portfolio of over 20 partners we had invested in.

Equally, issues grew on the funding side of the equation. Influential people came into our tribe for evasive reasons. And when celebrities and wealthy patrons offered us large amounts of money, I asked few questions, which was poor judgment on my part. Here's an example: at a house party in Beverly Hills, we met a very well-known actor's fiancé. Admittedly, I was star-struck as posters from his action films adorned my walls in college. Our relationship began wonderfully and she purported to be his trusted advisor when it came to philanthropy.

She stated that she loved our work and would influence the actor to give a major, six figure gift. I spent a lot of time cultivating her support via phone calls and trips to Beverly Hills to get everyone aligned. But once the money changed hands, his fiancé requested a fundraising commission from GO. When I explained that fundraising commissions made off charitable donations are highly unethical and potentially illegal, she unleashed her barking Hollywood agent upon me. This man took the word asshole to new levels and yelled at me over countless phone calls. Various insane emails and voicemails followed after I avoided his calls. I eventually ceased all communications and they came after us with a hotshot lawyer that represented, among other notable clients, Vladimir Putin. That resulted in our lawyer being entered into my list of *favorites* on my phone (Leslie, I am *ever* so grateful for you). I spoke to her daily to figure out how to get us out of the mess when celebrity egos are unleashed. Her counsel and strategy succeeded and the other party renounced their claims to any commissions raised off the actor's generous gifts. And while we were allowed to keep the funding to provide clean drinking water for hundreds of people, it came with an extraordinary expense of resources.

This is but one example of many regarding the curious proclivities and fancies of our major investors. Their luxuriant peculiarities proliferated my life. Most gave because they truly believed that sharing their vast blessings in life was the right thing to do. I loved these folks fiercely. However, there were those that gave to get access to fame and privilege, and who saw charitable support as a means to some obscure, selfish end.

Sienna saw all of these challenges and began to root out the reason of our existence with a fresh pair of eyes. We stepped back to the beginning. In the early days, GO's predominant focus was to support community led projects in areas of extreme poverty. In economic terms, these were places where people earned less than $2 per day. Every day brought a slew of macabre decisions that one had to face when living on the margins of human existence. One could either afford food or medicine, go to school or fetch clean water, live in fear of loan sharks or sell one of your children to pay them off. We saw emaciated children die of malaria. We heard stories from mothers who became prostitutes so they could afford medication to treat their HIV. Once you see poverty of this magnitude, you are compelled to act—to do something *NOW*. So listening to the local leadership became the first step and asking how we could help became the first question.

Then, a project of some sort would be conceived and somewhat vetted. Then a deal would be struck. We'd build a school or invest in a drill rig to provide clean sources of water. We'd give $1,000 or $10,000 or even $30,000 and then say, "see you later." Later was vague since we had no idea when we could raise enough operational funding to return and see the impact. To mitigate risk of the money being sucked down a black hole, we partnered with other, more experienced NGOs that worked in the area to informally observe and report on our funding. Soon, we witnessed more children going to school, families having roofs over their heads, healthy food to eat, clean water to drink, and in the best cases, earning more money for a brighter future. Anecdotal evidence of the impact was presented by our partners and through other international NGOs that worked in their communities.

We took that impact and weaved it into our marketing, portraying indigenous leaders in positions of power, and successful in their efforts to eradicate poverty through their projects.

We purposefully avoided the "poverty pornography" so prevalent in the nonprofit sector, which depicts starving children, forlorn men, or emaciated mothers that pull heartstrings via misery. We wanted to stop the pity and hopelessness and have our tribe believe in the strength of local leaders.

Our marketing strategy aimed to dispel misguided notions that the economic lack in countries like South Sudan or Cambodia was somehow the fault of the local populace being ignorant or incapable. We devoted all our marketing channels to showcase talented and strong leaders who were committed to and capable of starting something good in their communities. This strong message resonated and donors flocked to support. Yet as we grew, many of our supporters kept continually asking about our local impact. What were we doing for our own communities? After all, our local neighborhoods had homelessness, abuse of women, crime, and unsustainable usage of resources.

This question made me pause as my first instinct was dominated by logic. If I raised five million dollars, I could help a lot more people by investing those funds into areas of extreme poverty. As one example, one million people die from malaria every year with most victims being children. A mosquito net kit treated with quinine that comes with instruction of use costs $50. Therefore, with five million dollars, I could help 100,000 children live a better life. There is simply no better bang per buck in terms of investing my philanthropic dollars.

But logic sways the minds of few supporters. People give with their heart, not with their head. So we probed further. And inadvertently, this exploration of local impact led us to discovering something unseen within our own model. We invested a lot of resources into the growth of both social entrepreneurs and GO Champions. As both groups grew in size, we constantly debated which group got priority of our limited resources. There were no projects without the social entrepreneurs like Peter. But there was no funding and awareness for these projects without the Champions. Was their relationship solely based on the transfer of resources? Or was there something deeper at hand?

I probed my thoughts further and sought counsel from Sienna. This retrospective exercise had me reflect back on my own journey, wherein I discovered a personal transformational development since GO began. At the onset, I knew little about the social impact world and lacked purpose in life. Along the way, I was introduced to amazing leaders from around the world. I listened to their counsel and learned their methods of guiding others.

Whether visiting Muslim farmers in rural Uganda or meeting indigenous tribes that live within the Amazonian rainforest, I transformed through them. Their lessons have been amongst the greatest gain in my entire life. I learned humility, courage of thought, and gratitude. Rarely do I forget the miracle of having clean drinking water running from my tap, or the wonder of having a hot shower available. I use less and share more as these expressions of gratitude and grace increase my wellbeing greatly.

As the impact of GO grew, I focused on growing my network and began passionately collaborating with other nonprofit leaders in the Bay Area. People began to seek my counsel as GO matured. I realized the repeatable patterns that propelled our success and started to coach others that wanted to help improve our local neighborhoods. I never said no to a coffee, lunch, or drink to help local nonprofits improve their work. We shared ideas that would improve both local and international communities.

Then I looked across at my best friend, the person that began this journey with me over a random coffee in Berkeley. Our relationship inevitably stood bruised after the swells of growing an organization this large. Yet we persevered, stronger through it all. We met as naïve do-gooders in the middle of Madagascar. Now, we are both fathers and our families live right down the street from one another in Fairfax, California. We share the honor of being married to our spouses under the wise guidance of the same individual: Peter Francis Luswata. This man that transformed our lives, also empowered us to transform our families and our communities, local and global alike.

As noted earlier, Kyle's father concisely summed up the impact thusly:

"There was a Kyle *before* meeting Peter and then a Kyle *after* meeting Peter. These people were not the same."

In starting GO, the purpose of our lives had changed vastly for the better. We extended ourselves out into the world by exchanging ideas with local leaders, hoping our good intentions would lead to good outcomes. Sometimes they did, sometimes they did not. But when things clicked, our impact shined incredibly, locally and globally. When we found the humbly curious, those individuals in our social circle who came with open minds and full hearts, we offered this same experience of authentic connections. These altruistic interactions created a sense of "Ubuntu", a Xhosa term roughly translating to 'human kindness'. When a "Kyle" meets a "Peter" or a "Sarah" meets a "Costa", the spiritual bond of ubuntu is created. Desmond Tutu defined the concept as:

"A person that embodies the spirit of ubuntu is open and available to others, affirming of others, does not feel threatened that others are able and good, for he or she has a proper self-assurance that comes from knowing that he or she belongs in a greater whole and is diminished when others are humiliated or oppressed."

Simply put, ubuntu teaches us that when you do better, I do better. When you are not well, I am not well. This fundamental worldview is the reason we started GO. There is no concept of *Others*. There is no *Them* and *Us*. Only *We*. And *We* believed that wellbeing needed to be shared with the whole of humanity. And the most effective lever to make this change occur happens by connecting leaders. By looking back at our history with this new lens, we found that we actually did have a 'local impact' through our work.

At first, we saw the GO Champions as a means to raise funds and awareness for social entrepreneurs like Peter who was launching farming related ventures in Uganda. But as we peered deeper into the lives of the GO Champions after their experience working with these social entrepreneurs, we realized many had become change-makers and leaders within their own communities. Some began their own organizations or completely changed careers to continue driving social impact. For example, a Wall Street investment banker named Alex Silverman became a GO Champion for Peter to launch a micro-finance fund in Masaka. After witnessing Peter's impact first hand, she leveraged her financials skills by joining a nonprofit that provides funding for public schools in her community. Once more stories like those got discovered, the question of prioritizing one persona or the other, local leader or GO Champion, moved towards equity between the bodies of leadership. This meant focusing on the relationship, not the individual.

Specifically, our distilled reason for being was the transformative development that fosters when leaders interact with one another. When a social entrepreneur and a GO Champion were united in cause, the paths of both of their lives were changed forever. The local communities surrounding each iterated and improved. As Champions learned about the conditions of wherein our local leaders worked—whether via Skype or by traveling to the field—they conserved their usage of water, learned to grow their own food, wasted less, volunteered more, and shared their lessons with classmates or colleagues. They became more philanthropic with their time and energy. We were building a sense of global ubuntu one relationship at a time.

The major thing missing was an effective business model to continually replicate these transformative relationships. Crucially, that strategy must also mitigate the risk of nefarious motives prone to certain people that latch upon our movement. Those incidents spiked as we grew since we had few guardrails in place. As our tribe ballooned, we learned that we should no longer hurl any given person out into the chaotic streets of Nairobi. Nor could we partner with each and every local leader that had a bright idea. Nor could we cash six figure checks from well-known actors without asking clarifying questions.

While the nefarious individuals were a minority, they took an extraordinary toll of effort for two reasons. One, the psychological impact of somebody's dignity being affronted weighs deep so you must listen, calm the tempers, and then slowly diffuse the situation. Two, reputation is vital in the nonprofit sector. For a young organization like ours, one bad story could greatly damage your credibility. This problem became acute once we expanded beyond our own social circles of trust.

Here is an example to illustrate the problem. As we grew, both prospective GO Champions and local leaders met us through social media, mainly through our Facebook page. In 2014, two individuals named Adam and Jane (names changed for privacy) separately reached out to raise funds for local leaders. GO connected both of them to two separate social entrepreneurs in Eastern Africa. Both raised $10,000 in novel ways that gathered media attention. NPR and local newspapers covered their fundraising efforts and featured our work. Both then traveled to Africa, met their local leaders, and saw the impact of their support. Jane returned a new woman, determined to help more. Adam stayed. And stayed. And stayed. The partner was too polite to ask Adam to leave even though he had stopped paying for his food and board. Adam would also often come home drunk on village moonshine. And then he watched pornography at the project partner's home and exhibited lewd behavior. Eventually, when this information reached our attention many miles and weeks later, Adam was forced to leave. By then, trust had deeply eroded between our local partner and our home office.

Of course, the correct move here was to invest heavily in our operational budget to find more "Janes" and to screen out the "Adams". This was equally necessary on the project side of the equation since we received forged proposals or half-baked ideas, even via trusted channels.

Essentially, more monitoring and evaluation became necessary which is, frankly, expensive. In the beginning, we had two people who wanted to do something different to help the wellbeing of others. We had little idea what we were doing so we put in $2,000 of our own money and a lightning bolt of energy to give it a shot. In a blink of an eye, our work was raising millions of dollars and created all sorts of human interactions, good and bad. We also had a very business-driven mindset, striving towards efficiency, efficacy, and impact.

An honest look in the mirror was required. We asked ourselves a profound question at a leadership level: what was our endgame? There were stories to be proud of and lives that had been improved for the better, yet to what end?

That question changed everything.

TURN IT AROUND
DEFINE YOUR END GAME

I hear pitches for projects and companies all the time. To separate the foolish from the fantastic, I ask the question "And to what end?" Essentially, I would like to know that if you had an infinite set of resources to reach your goals, then what does achieving that vision look like? The purpose of any organization should derive from its inevitable conclusion. Once clear, the majority of the steps required to achieve this endgame make themselves apparent and you can reverse engineer the actions needed to achieve that goal.

In 2015, GO reached an inflection point. We were suffering from mission creep and had many investments shooting off in a variety of directions. My entrepreneurial brain constantly wanted to create and innovate. While this is a vital skill in start-ups, continual iteration and pivoting can become dangerous as the organization matures. Standardization of your product or service becomes a necessity as constant innovation drifts purpose towards unsteady waters. This is why an experienced board of directors is vital in all stages of organizational growth. Their collective wisdom keeps focus on the long-term. They set the strategic boundaries that govern the execution of the mission and vision. In short, boards should always be mindful of the end game.

In 2015, our leadership staged a retreat to identify our endgame. All fifteen participants were required to read, "What's Your Endgame", a paper by Alice Gugelev and Andrew Stern of the Stanford Social Innovation Review (SSIR). This pivotal paper on philanthropy was greatly needed since nonprofit endgames are more complicated than those of for-profit companies. The latter generally exists with a purpose to find a market gap, fill that gap with a product or service, and then profit.

Nonprofit endgames are unique since they operate in an area where there is often market failure. There is no ability, and perhaps no justification, to leverage a profit motive to drive impact. Helping a sick patient or finding shelter for the homeless should be driven by benevolence and empathy. But to do more good, we need to compare and contrast who is providing these services efficiently so we can wisely invest our resources. As millions of charities exist worldwide, uncovering their endgames is instrumental in our ability to evaluate efficacy.

Why do so many nonprofits exist? While for profit endgames are well documented and regulated which leads to many mergers and acquisitions, nonprofit endgames are murkier which facilitate an environment wherein they mushroom boundlessly. Indeed, there are 1.5 million active nonprofits in the USA alone, a number that is accelerating as the IRS made it even easier to start a licensed nonprofit in 2015. Additionally, the ease of making slick websites or creating dynamic marketing materials that capture donors' attentions are proliferating rapidly. With the advent of social media, it's easier now more than ever to get noticed.

In brief, it is very easy for anyone to start and grow a nonprofit and the barriers to mergers and acquisitions are great. Yet few social entrepreneurs ever ask themselves *why* they should exist. We know what to do and we know not why we do it. This is where endgame thinking drives leadership to take a wider and longer-term view.

SSIR's game-changing paper on endgame theory came at a crucial time in GO's evolution. It wisely posits six different endgames of a nonprofit:

- **Mission Achievement:** A discrete problem with a defined and achievable outcome. Think John Kennedy's call to put a man on the moon or ending the polio epidemic which was the original mission successfully driven by the March of Dimes.

- **Government Adoption:** A model with high coverage potential that can integrate into public service programs. An example is Room to Read, a nonprofit that builds libraries and schools in developing world countries while training governments how to manage them with long-term planning.
- **Commercial Adoption:** A product or service with profit potential that currently works in an area of market failure that must be subsidized to become economically viable. Think the Internet circa the 1960s when universities poured billions of research dollars to build the foundation of digital communications.
- **Open Source**: A breakthrough idea that is easy for other organizations to adopt or integrate. Think parklets, sidewalk extensions in metro areas that provide more space and amenities for people using the street. Or Wikipedia, which became the first free online encyclopedia that allowed anyone to edit articles.
- **Sustained Service:** A strong organization with a proven ability to sustain funding that fills a market or public service gap. Think hospitals.
- **Replication:** A breakthrough product or model that is easy for other organizations to deliver or adopt where you demonstrate impact and share it with other organizations. Think of charter schools. Think…GO?

With our board of directors coalescing over many concurrent failures and organizational struggles, we hired a professional facilitator to guide us towards discovering an endgame. Board members, advisors, and key staff were all invited to this retrospective. Walking into that fateful meeting, I became fixed on the idea that we should follow a replication endgame model. In addition to witnessing transformational development occurring on a person-to-person level, I had seen it happening on an organizational level. Many projects began with one social entrepreneur that had one idea. Then that idea grew, found funding, and matured into an organization. These partners mushroomed around GO quickly, our success became their success, and so we readily collaborated with them. When partners like KGSA or ClearWater grew their organizations, we provided legal, accounting, financial, and general organizational consulting services so they would thrive. We grew big and they grew big. We exchanged ideas, strategies, successes, and failures all along the way.

In some cases, our partner organizations were able to implement our counsel more effectively than us because they had a stronger existing infrastructure, a more focused mission, or greater trust within their certain community. Since they relied on their own marketing or websites to promote their individual missions, donor relations were frequently blurred since many would donate on GO's website merely to support KGSA or ClearWater. This challenge grew significant as our support widened in scope. We explained this issue in a mass email sent to our entire tribe shortly after this retreat:

GO started by focusing on raising grants of $10,000 or less on behalf of leaders in communities where we had a personal connection. It was a simple idea: to empower leaders to create sustainable change within their communities and to allow the local leaders to decide how best to make an impact. GO hoped to avoid the costly administration and infrastructure that plagued many larger organizations by focusing on small-scale grants with the goal of providing 100 percent of funds raised to cause.

As GO grew, we departed from our original operating model and our partnerships became more complex, while the size and scope of our grants expanded considerably. While failures were expected as part of the process and considered a valuable part of learning as we selected new leaders, our expanding size required more due diligence.

Earlier this year, GO's leadership evaluated the organization in the context of these changes and determined that to effectively manage our programs there was a need for significant investment in field presence, leader selection processes, more rigorous monitoring and evaluation, and impact reporting—all of which would require time, resources and capital to do well. Additionally, when GO began inspiring Champions to provide seed capital and visibility for local leaders in 2009, the field of crowd funding was new, and with your help, we were pioneering a movement that today has become a conventional method of raising funds for good causes. As such, our ability to continually inspire GO Champions requires an ever-increasing amount of investment to be fruitful.

Collectively written by our board, this wise letter spelled out that GO had outgrown its shell. Our services expanded vastly and needed about a million dollars of operational investment to provide the right safeguards to ensure the impact of our work excelled.

Then the question was asked again.

To what end?

CHAPTER 17

SAVING PRIVATE FAILURE

I finish typing the word "shutdown". My eyes well. My vision blurs. It's 1:30am. I am alone in the attic of my grandfather's home in Halinow, Poland. The darkness retreats from the dim lamp on the desk and the bright monitor in front of my face. It's very cold. The heat has been off for some hours now. October reigns with her cold rain and gloomy skies.

I look at a slide in my presentation deck. There are black numbers and bold red text everywhere. The graph dominating the slide reflects a harsh truth: a bent line, falling down, down, down. It represents our last bits of operational monies, tumbling down to zero in six months' time.

Eight years of an amazing group of people that believed we could craft a better world had been minimized to a slide about how to shut the network down.

I blink away the tears and rub out the fatigue. I need to keep going. The board meeting to discuss our fate is only hours away. A diminishing bottle of Macallan's sits by the lamp. I pour two fingers of her fermented wisdom.

I open Excel and ease into her spreadsheet logic. I shuffle numbers and the graph portraying our lifeline of resources tumbles downward on my screen. I find little solace in the austere budget numbers and envision them differently: people with salaries, protected by insurance plans to keep them healthy, and monies that give life to vital projects that ease the burden of poverty.

I weave from sheet to sheet of operational plans

After another hour, the slide "Plan F: Shutdown" is complete. I add the slide to a compiled Keynote deck that outlines five other operational scenarios.

Sitting in a chilly attic thousands of miles away from GO, I click save and send the presentation deck via email to the board.

I close my laptop and stare out the window.

It's dark out there.
Leadership is a lonely place, wherever you are.

~

Six months earlier.

I needed a break. My body physically, emotionally, and spiritually felt fatigue after seven years of wild growth, countless hours on the road, various international diseases, betrayals, fundraising galas, 48-hour bus rides across East Africa, crisis management, giving speeches, enduring lawsuits, spending evenings entertaining potential donors over dinners, following that evening by having morning breakfasts with advisors, writing endless emails, balancing, juggling, doing, executing, and fixing this, that, and the other thing.

Rarely did I give my body rest as I felt that so many things kept *happening* that needed my attention. I had lost significant weight and got sick frequently. The bittersweet speed of success is something I did not anticipate in terms of its impact to my quality of life. I did my best to hide the exhaustion.

From the outside looking in, I seemed to have it all. I helped build a successful nonprofit from scratch, created opportunities for thousands, married the woman of my dreams, lived well in a great city, had access to people of fame and means, and, in the eyes of others, appeared *always* well and *always* smiling. My role as Executive Director necessitated being a hyper extrovert that projected confidence and power. I believed that savvy donors, partners, and investors could sense weakness, so I bottled up my oncoming burnout.

This bottling of my raw feelings was incessant. Because of the public nature of my role, exacerbated by my narcissistic pursuit of being featured in media, I disassociated the vital difference of having separate public and private lives. I needed to be always "on". My life became a living Facebook feed where I felt required to tweak and edit the projection of success on a continual basis.

My mind became a pirouette, swirling ever faster as I kept turning around my thoughts to find gratitude in all that I had achieved. How could I lament about emotional suffering in the cocoon of the Bay Area when our partners in Uganda and Cambodia became targets for assassination or had their friends beheaded? How could I complain about my annual explosive diarrhea after getting back from field trips when I had access to sanitized toilets, and exquisite medical care at One Medical Group? How could I commiserate with the other social entrepreneurs I coached by wailing about how difficult celebrities were to deal with? Could I complain about my low income nonprofit salary when I still could make ends meet?

No, never. I believed that facing the guilt of uttering those complaints would prove to be worse than the suffering itself. I pushed it down deeper and imagined the gall it would take for me to complain about living the dream, even when that dream darkened.

My immediate colleagues at GO and the fellow social entrepreneurs we invested in suffered alongside. Some took pride in their scars as war stories were exchanged about catching malaria or dengue as a right of passage. Our American staff, volunteers, and GO Champions humbled me in their perseverance. On a field trip, Kyle got a stomach bug and spent a week drinking nothing but water. Another colleague developed jaundice and hepatitis C while losing nearly a quarter of his body weight. Despite his afflictions, he refused to take a salary for himself so his project would grow faster. I even watched my own wife suffer from a horrendous stomach infection in a Rwandan hotel that had no running water. She fought fever for days while bed-ridden. Outside her window, a street vendor blared a 30-second shrilling Afro-Cuban jingle over and over, hour after hour, till she approached insanity. At nights when I came back from work, I carried out buckets of her human waste. You know the meaning of true love when you carry your partner's fecal matter down a precarious flight of barely lit stairs.

I began to falter after years of being barraged by the juddering ups and downs the roller coaster of entrepreneurial "success". After the Amber incident, I lost a large swath of close friends. Leadership became a lonely place. Then I watched my significant other power through both the emotional and physical struggles engraved in the work of international development. Growing a family of our own became forefront on our minds and we began to wonder how this kind of life could continue. I didn't even earn enough to provide for a brand new Skorupa to join our world. *That* felt *awful*.

Additionally, my entrepreneurial skill set that drove constant innovation became a liability to GO. My board grew weary of my jumping headfirst into newer and bigger projects when other initiatives were stalling. Discipline, not growth, became the mantra at our leadership level. I struggled with this organizational evolution as my exhaustion grew. I needed a break.

An opening came in the form of tragedy. Both Heather and I lost all our remaining grandparents over late 2014 and early 2015. While all of their departures caused suffering, losing my grandfather, Henryk, struck deep. I had watched this man build—literally and figuratively— the foundation of our family over countless summers back in Poland. He worked tirelessly into his 90th year of life.

Nie jestem skonczony he would say with raspy laughter on every project he started.

I am not finished.

Then he was gone, finished off by a lightning strike of cancer.

A man that never understood the word retirement faded into the black of that infernal disease.

I had watched him mow the lawn of his latest property with vigor on a warm August afternoon in 2015. Then, three months later, he lay in a bed of suffering as cancer took its final grip. Fittingly, he died in a room that he had built with his own hands. With an air of eerie clairvoyance, he had converted our family home, a place whose walls inhabited so many family memories, into an assisted living facility for seniors.

This structural conversion was one of many projects in various states of disarray that he left behind. The properties fell into the hands of my father, his only child, who struggled under the weight of their responsibilities. A filial opportunity presented itself and together with Heather, we decided to move back to Poland to see where we could help.

I carefully disseminated this information at GO. I knew that we had a strong leader in Sienna and that she could take GO to new heights. Unlike me, she possessed the discipline of operational maintenance needed at our current stage. Additionally, she had nearly 10 years of international development experience so we congregated the board around this new path forward. We decided that the summary approach to 2015 would be to take a defensive posture against growth. If we grew, great, but we could not make that the goal given my indefinite absence. Fortunately, I left at a time when a unified vision existed across the board, while newer and more experienced individuals began to take charge of our growth. Most importantly, we had ample financial runway after yet another successful fundraising gala.

After two months of meetings, coffee conversations, Skype calls, and various transition tasks, I transitioned my managerial responsibilities to Sienna and only retained a seat on the board. My child GO had now grown up and I could only advise on her growth as she bounded away.

I departed with mixed emotions and settled into a large earth colored duplex where I spent my teenage and college summers. Both my grandfathers and father built this home together in the late nineties. My two sets of grandparents grew so close after my parents were married that in the dusk of their lives, they lived in this duplex altogether. Only inches of brick separated my mother's parents from my father's parents. My grandfather designed the third floor with multiple bedrooms for our summer retreats. Even though we lived in America, we always had a room with a familiar bed in Poland.

Despite feeling the emptiness caused by a lost generation, those familiar walls swaddled me in a feeling of inner protection. The nurturing feeling of being home released the tension in my body and I got incredibly ill. My body purged the staggered emotions and toxins. I sneezed out betrayals, coughed up humiliations, and vomited a bile of successes and failures. Heather and my parents watched in anxious trepidation as my body released and recovered over nearly two weeks.

When the purge finally ended, I felt calm, inspired, and new. My father and I set up a mobile office in my grandfather's attic to pursue a new mission. Seated next to countless boxes of papers, permits, and architectural renderings penned by my grandfather, I journeyed down a path of internal discovery to learn about the family business. I analyzed easements, rulings, and letters written by grandfather. Google Translate guided me through the nuanced legal nomenclature of Polish real estate laws. Heather took her side by us and plotted the launch of her new events planning company. The three of us sat in this small office, clicking and printing away while my mother was a floor below, incessantly cooking as always.

I had returned home to work inwardly and learn more about the foundation that empowered me with the privilege of giving back. I delved deeper into my paternal grandfather's work and considered his work and purpose. Why did Henryk start building? In my mind, he built so our family could build on. After all, he began by building a house for his wife and son.

Then he built another home. That drove income and gave his family more opportunities.

So he built another. And another. And so on.

Then my parents married. I came into this world and shortly thereafter, my sister Ania arrived. We all lived in my grandfather's first home, an extended family of six, living under a roof built by Henryk's own hands. Our special bond began from day one of my existence. We played together constantly in these cramped quarters. While Henryk kept building to keep his growing family together, he couldn't control the wider environment. The gray, withering politics of Communism drearily entered into our private lives, repressing our opportunities to grow.

My parents then made a fateful decision: we would be raised on foreign soil, in a country that would provide us with vast opportunities in life. Upon our departure, my grandfather and I fiercely embraced at Warsaw Chopin airport. Tears streamed down our faces as we desperately tried to hold onto our special bond for a few more moments. My father broke us free. And we left to America.

My parents did not let us forget the sacrifices made and we frequently returned for long stretches of time. These annual trips brought us closer to the foundation that gave our legs strength. In turn, both my sister and I spurned these altruistic values onwards through our personal lives and careers. I did so through GO and then my work in leadership development while Ania worked for Teach for America and then became devoted to being a teacher for youth in rural Arkansas. Given this precious gift of opportunity, we chose paths that would pay our gratitude forward in our newly adopted land and beyond.

The painful irony was that my grandfather intended his efforts to root the family in Poland. He built those properties with a firm belief that we would all one-day return back to manage them. Eventually, his plan worked but it was too late.

We had returned and he was dead.

His array of projects stumbled onwards after his death. Tenants raised complaints, building inspectors shook their heads while clucking about code violations, and legal actions manifested. The properties all stood on precarious ground and drove my father back home to sort out their mess. My father took on the responsibility of untangling the knot of dubious permits, unpaid rents, citations, and threats of condemnation. I joined to help and learned something vital about my existence.

I learned that I am not my father, a man whose skills I greatly revere. He is a trained civil engineer specializing in measuring the structural capacities of buildings and bridges. His diligence, prudence, and patience in craftsmanship know few bounds. During this trip, I observed him install sheer white curtains for the windows in my grandfather's living room. He bought the right length though they didn't *quite* fit right. Most people would never notice. He did. So he taught himself how to pleat and meticulously sewed ethereal layers of fabric precisely to fit the window. It took nearly two weeks for him to attain his precision. For *curtains*. Sheer and lily white, and as common as potatoes on a Polish dinner plate. This is the manner of how my father approaches all projects. I wish I could have this patience. As I've aged, I have trained with meditations to embrace this level of persistently calm patience.

But I am not there.

Perhaps never will be.

No, I am a reflection of a prior generation.

I am my grandfather. This man whisked projects with a tornado of energy, whirling them upwards towards a dreamy, hazy vision. A creator, he leaped from building one property to another without a strong focus on the maintenance of each solitary unit. Once a property had been built, it became time to start the next one and plan the one thereafter, and the next, and the next. The tower mattered more than the individual brick. He paid great attention to nurturing personal relationships with all who crossed his path. He loved family deeply, cared for all his workers—even giving jobs to the drunks in town—and somehow magically built rapport with even the most stalwart government officials. Even at the peak of communist shenanigans, with local officials worn down by foreign protocols, he managed to find the man behind the permit, or the woman behind the easement. His charm knew no bounds and whether Poland trudged through communism or flourished under capitalism, his work flourished because of his networks. He built relationships that increased choices for all parties, provided opportunities for all, and relied on a strong community of the willing.

He knew that while the law said one thing, the relationship that was created with the person reflecting that law told a different tale. Charm could bend the codices of rigid rules, which were so prevalent in the field of civil engineering. This is not to say he wasn't careful. Much like my father, he had a strong attention to detail. But he also understood when to challenge the status quo and drive things forward.

Wading through a myriad of building permits he had magically got approved, I pieced together conflicting realties. A nursing home filing stated that the entire top floor was 20 centimeters too short in one corner due to the slanted roof for office space. It could only be storage space. In reality, I knew that this floor buzzed with nurses on break and personnel filing expense reports. These contrasting realities were allowed only through Henryk's solid relationship with the town planning commission. Who could fault him? He broke an inane rule that decreed the entire top floor could only be storage space because in one corner, a moderately tall fellow would need to stoop. More space meant more seniors could find a home and that demand created more jobs. My grandfather forged his own path. In brief, he was an entrepreneur.

I learned in his wake and followed this same way of life. I defied rules and always strove to keep meaningful relationships at all costs. If an administrative rule stood in the way, I waived it away like a bee that could at best sting though not hinder progress. As I watched my meticulous father struggle with this inheritance of oblivious projects, I witnessed what happens when too much disruptive entrepreneurial thinking is unleashed too far. A bias towards action and a whirlwind of groundbreaking entrepreneurial activity is great. But eventually the weight of disregarded rules stresses the foundation. You must have operational safeguards and routine maintenance to ensure long-term success.

Henryk excelled at growing something from nothing yet faltered at the ongoing maintenance. With no transition plan, things were breaking loose. The time had come to pay down massive administrative debt from decades of neglected work.

Meanwhile, another organism of unbridled growth began to spill out of its Petri dish. Like my grandfather, I envisioned a project and started building it, inspiring people along the way to take part. Then I would move onto the next thing. I was very good at it. The greatest compliment and complaint I have received about my approach to projects is the same thing. A board member once said, "The distance between you *thinking* something and it *being* something is incredibly short". These conflicting words were meant to be cautionary as well as complimentary since she was correct that I drove ideas so quickly and empathetically that they often grew beyond my control.

GO started bucking way outside the lines of sustainable growth. I had the entrepreneurial ability that set her growth afire and now watched from afar at how big that blaze grew. Zero to $5.9 million raised is beyond anything I had anticipated in such a short span of time. We were building the plane as it flew off the tarmac and now found ourselves 10,000 feet in the air with hundreds of passengers aboard. While we back-filled the roles with people who had the required field experience to ensure a smooth flight, my long absence exposed cracks in GO's foundation. My deft ability to solve issues through established relationships could not be effectively replaced. The organization grew and iterated so fast that cracks shook the foundation. Here are a few examples.

Firstly, an American volunteer with influential ties to noted philanthropic bodies claimed sexual and cultural harassment occurred when she stayed with a highly trusted and long-term local partner in Tanzania. Our local partner retaliated against this claim and accused her of the same. Witnesses who were present sided with both versions of the truth. She was Jewish, a liberal, and fiercely independent. He was Muslim, a conservative, and a family man. The whole situation was overcast in gray shades of "he-said" and "she-said" versions of the truth. On both sides of the equation, we had failed at proper cultural immersion.

Secondly, another partner became opportunistic in our trusting approach. After receiving a loan to build a goat farm in Eastern Africa, he claimed a photo taken of a local woman from his village used in a marketing campaign had caused him to be sued by her family. He claimed the woman died in a flood and that the photo, which had never been shared online, had caused the family grievance. He insinuated we pay his incurred legal fees for this dubious claim. The request was denied though GO deleted the photo out of respect. A few weeks later he claimed to have been robbed, and that our donated office equipment (laptop, projector, etc.) was stolen. He requested we fund replacement materials. GO denied his request and these red flags prompted a review of his work. An onsite inspection was conducted to measure the impact of his work and to hopefully restore trust. During the trip, he fell asleep at the wheel while driving a GO employee home. While no accident happened, the incident begged the question about safety and evacuation procedures for staff and volunteers, something that did not exist. The resulting monitoring and evaluation report revealed that the farm project had created jobs for many people who never had a chance to work before in their live. But the relationship obviously remained severely strained.

These are only a few examples that required prudent mitigation strategies as GO settled into organizational maturity. We were no longer a scrappy startup that could fail forward. We needed to ensure consistent quality, safety, and impact. And ensuring the impact of our invested dollars was the foremost challenge since the projects in the field grew haphazardly. Without proper vetting and on-going support to ensure uniform quality standards, many projects were struggling for many reasons. We lacked the governance to ensure quality consistently. The fires began to grow. Accountability and trust eroded on many levels. Fatigue and frustration spiked.

Intense navel-gazing by the board began during my absence in Poland regarding how to approach these challenges. The board discussed what best operational investment(s) should be made to safeguard against such failures and ensure consistent impact. And then, communication stopped. Email briefings dried up and our monthly newsletter stopped.

The silence became deafening.

I sensed a bad turn.

The silence broke and board meetings began in earnest as summer faded into fall. I joined late evening conference calls to better understand how deep the fissures ran. Still, no conference call could replace looking into someone's eyes while they spoke, so I flew back to San Francisco for a week. I talked with our staff directly, and made Skype calls to our local partners around the world. The fog surrounding the truth refused to lift. I learned about the details of things gone wrong coupled with success stories. Stories conflicted which was maddening.

I debated remaining to help. But I had made a personal decision to commit myself to focus on my family and my wellbeing. The board encouraged my absence so I returned to Poland to help from afar. And then a few weeks later, a virtual board meeting cast an unexpected thought:

What would you think about a merger?

The idea resonated since I saw it as a natural extension of the replication endgame that we had envisioned earlier that year. I sat in front of my sleeping MacBook and looked around. It was 11:30pm. Everyone else was asleep. Alone in the attic, I began to rifle through my grandfather's renderings, permits, and scrawled notes. The work contained in those boxes had grown outside of their confines. Things were a mess. Any administrative burden could be fixed with an ample supply of funding and willpower. Attics could be raised higher to meet civil code standards; local field offices could be built to better monitor investments locally. New elevators could be installed to service the handicapped; cultural sensitivity courses could be provided to volunteers before they left for Africa. Polish lawyers could provide breathing room on overbearing European Union building laws; American lawyers could stop celebrities' crazed ex-wives from trying to sue our organization.

But to what end? And for what cost? Time, money, and energy were needed to create all of these institutional capabilities. Other organizations had surely already traveled down this path so why not seek a partnership opportunity? The next morning, the board requested I plot all our possible organizational endgames financially in preparation. We had cash though we needed to move quickly since restructuring is prohibitively expensive. I thought of six possible scenarios (plans A through F) where predicted responses from our support base could range from the ecstatic, "this merger is the best idea ever and here's a $25,000 check to help" to the slight, "this is outrageous and I won't stand for it" reaction. I drafted detailed financial models for each, where funding surged or plummeted, people got fired or hired, programs were cut or expanded, and every combination thereof. I saved the most painful task for last, the ironically lettered "Plan F" wherein everything failed and we would cease to exist.

As dawn neared, I wrote a long email to our board that explained the rationale of each analytical model. I attached a list of historical failures (Amber's stealing, partners accused of corruption, etc.) that while resolved, could wreak havoc on a nonprofit's reputation if they somehow reared their heads anew. They thanked me for the ideas and then voted me off the board due to conflicts of interest. Any official role I had in our future was severed. While logical, the decision still stung since I felt I had been kicked out of the very thing I started. I inadvertently learned a great act of leadership: the art of stepping down while others stepped up. It's a quietly disorienting and somewhat painful move to make.

Still, my voice had power and my unofficial role as an influencer carried great responsibility. First came the challenge of finding, vetting, and courting worthy suitors for this role while controlling the rumor mill. Organizational restructuring, dissolving, and merging are complicated, take time, and must be carefully communicated. I scanned emails anxiously and took part in various phone calls to learn more about what was happening. I felt somewhat proud to have formed a team that now consulted without me regarding the best future for GO. After all, it was their legal and fiduciary duty to do so. But it still pained me that I did not exactly know what was happening on a daily basis. As an analogy, I suppose that a good father should empower his daughter to become her own person so she can make her own decisions in life. And her decision at that time was to move on, find someone to marry, and share her gifts and goodwill with a larger family.

First, she created a list of suitors. Five organizations were considered. Then the dating game began. A conflict of interest arose early in the process since one board member, Lisa Kuhn, was also the Executive Director of the Foundation of Sustainable Development (FSD). As such, she was recused from any merger meetings. While I also didn't participate in these meetings since I was no longer on the board, I steered GO towards a partnership with FSD whenever I could. Foremost, I respected Lisa greatly and secondly, the pieces of what each organization brought to the table fit generally well. FSD was a social enterprise with a vast array of locally led international development projects in many of the countries where GO worked though they lacked our fundraising and corporate partnership prowess. At a high level, it seemed like a good fit though the road ahead was undoubtedly full of challenges.

In general, nonprofit mergers are difficult and expensive to navigate. They revolve more around intangible missions and heartfelt, highly nuanced methods and services that are complicated. Unlike for-profit mergers, no stockholders exist who stand to benefit financially when two nonprofits merge. In for-profit mergers, money leans in with its powerful energy and drives leadership teams to look past the challenges with financial incentives. Yet in nonprofit mergers, money wields its energy as a deterrent. At the pinnacle of leadership, a board member must almost always either donate or raise operational funding for the organization. At GO, it was expected that board members raise $10,000 per year, either by writing a check or encouraging their network to donate. If GO merged with a similar sized organization, it would then follow that the give/get amount would increase, perhaps double, in size. This is a large financial disincentive during an already difficult process. Assuming that challenge is surpassed, then the laborious integration of two cultures and ways of doing business begins. This requires *lots* of capacity funding, which most nonprofits do not have. Then come external challenges like the severe risk of donor loss given brand affiliation in the nonprofit sector is emotionally charged.

Perhaps most disadvantageous in GO's case was that we were approaching this mountain to climb with a leadership vacuum. While Sienna was acting Executive Director at the time, she was still relatively new to the role and was considering a move for personal reasons to another part of the country. I was in Poland watching the game from the sidelines. When originally pitched, I had been told that GO would retain our branding and structure to capture our sense of family. From afar, I sensed that lofty vision was quickly deteriorating.

Our operational savings dwindled as discussions lengthened. Social media posts and monthly newsletters ceased and cash flow withered. A generous board member pumped in more funds to keep things moving though discussions became strained. December approached and no strategic fundraising plan existed to leverage this crucial month when donors are in the giving spirit.

I returned to the USA as things reached a boiling point. On a Monday morning, my third day back home, two board members requested an urgent meeting. They sat me down in a neutral conference room in the basement of a co-working space. No courtesy greetings were exchanged.

The air felt cold. In a few minutes, they explained with a nervously practiced pitch that the board would be shutting down GO. Few details were given regarding why and there was no mention of the merger. My questions were dodged. They asked for my voluntary support in this move, which I rejected outright. The tactical execution caught me off guard and I felt no benevolence to find common ground. They walked out first to avoid the awkward quiet and I sat under the harsh office lights to gather my thoughts.

I sought counsel from internal and external parties. No actual rulings or meeting minutes about this organizational decision were shared. Since I had just arrived back from Poland, I had walked into that meeting tired and jet-lagged. I took no notes and had little idea what was going on. My communications with the board became tenser the more I tried to reach out to others regarding GO's state of affairs. I realized the board had a plan in place and they most likely feared my ability to influence matters against their desires.

Heather and I were staying at Kyle's home during this fateful week as we got acclimated back to San Francisco. He and I discussed what steps, if any, we should take as cofounders. We considered stances ranging from non-action to public revolution. My ego naturally found comfort in taking action as both Kyle and I had conceived GO within our minds. We were anchored towards an independent path. Kyle threw out the idea that we buy back the company ourselves, whether by our own financial means or by swaying public support. I still had relationships with major corporate donors and key project partners so perhaps I could foment enough support for such an action. While we definitely commanded enough ears to potentially win the public argument, I felt this proposition to be on dubious legal ground and too confrontational.

My initial instinct was not to lose what we had created. Partners and major supporters with whom I shared the breaking news asked me to fight for our existence. As the conversations with the board became nippier, this initial instinct became failure of true end-game thinking. I shed the emotional layers of thought and ego. I removed the memory regarding the board's poor communication approach. They were driven by a risk averse, corporately engineered thought process. I got that and after all, I recruited them so what else could I expect? I remembered our pivotal endgame board meeting.

If we as GO wanted to replicate and extend our impact in the field of transformative development on a wider scale, walking the lone path was the wrong direction. A full meeting of the board was convened in neutral territory and we met on amicable terms. I entered that meeting with a prepared statement to outline my thoughts in full. I transparently described all actions I considered taking and then I essentially pledged that I took faith in their collective counsel. We had gotten off on the wrong foot upon my return. Bygones to that and we hit the rewind button. Their aggregate experience had built disruptive companies, rescued bankrupt companies, and possessed decade of international development experience. I succumbed to their communal wisdom.

We shook hands and I got a bewildering forty-page contract to sign. The document outlined new responsibilities, compensation based on specific milestones, and a communication plan of what I could and could not say. I proceeded carefully and formed a personal board of advisors consisting of a lawyer, a life coach, and a human resource specialist to negotiate my position. As I said before, trust yet verify. Curiously, I found myself negotiating against the very entity I had created. Red lines were issued, clauses removed, and signatures were finally inked.

I became a contractor for GO, a worker bee with financial incentives to complete my tasks diligently at the behest of the board. I worked hard even though my tasks were rooted in taking apart something I loved. I trusted in the mission ahead and the aspiration driving the merger was still the right path. It presented the opportunity to grow our impact with a different organizational structure. While GO could raise funding to improve our operational infrastructure, we knew that other more experienced organizations existed with that infrastructure already in place. Why recreate the wheel?

As time wore on, the wider merger effort had lost steam. Why press on with the emotional and financial toll of a full merger when a simpler legal option existed? After deliberation, the board made the difficult decision to dissolve GO and continue its mission by handing over our assets and encouraging our base to support FSD as a sister organization. FSD had over 20 years of experience in international service and had field offices in Africa, Asia, and Latin America with local leaders doing the monitoring and evaluation of all projects. They had university partnerships for international exchange programs that provided both volunteers on the ground and a source of operational funding. Their website and marketing needed attention and their fundraising prowess was not yet unleashed. These were areas where GO's support network could be a value-add to their work.

Donors, corporate partners, and foundations were carefully groomed for the transition. Intellectual capital, cash, computers, event supplies, website code, and other assets were tallied on a list by GO's accountant and transitioned to FSD. A nonprofit law firm was hired to wade through the bureaucratic red tape. Our partner organizations that were not eligible to be supported by FSD (FSD only supports programs where they have local field offices and GO's countries of operation did not entirely map one to one) were given guidance on how to file their own 501c3 status or find shelter under other nonprofits that offered fiscal sponsorship. This work went on for over a year and required thousands of hours to perform.

Despite the expensive legal and accounting filings to various government bodies, we stayed the course. United under a common vision of doing good better, our leadership began communicating our decision collectively and individually to our entire support base. Some saw the potential immediately, while others felt great disappointment in the loss of something so dear to them. In my mind, nothing felt lost. The GO family remained in my life, the vision that guided their efforts were helmed by FSD, the core values that drove us to improve lives and communities didn't change, and only the structure beneath it all shifted.

I joined FSD's Advisory Board to help launch a new platform called Circles.org, which I viewed as an evolution of our GO Champions model. Circles.org relied on groups of donors to support quality international development projects. In GO's final year, we had been leaning towards this giving circle model since it became obvious that many hands make light work. For example, in 2015, a passionate do-gooder named Ryan Sarafolean connected with GO and rallied 25 GO Champions to raise $300,000 to help Abdul launch a women's boarding and community center in Kenya. Circles.org would operationalize this sort of community based giving while leveraging FSD's deep international development experience to ensure impact.

My circle of transformative development drew towards completion. After fifteen months of winding up GO, I steadfastly devoted my energy to FSD. Doors stood open to new rooms that I was eager to explore. I walked in and started raising funds for our first Circles.org campaign to benefit grassroots NGOs in Bolivia and Kenya. I found the same close friends from GO sitting by my side as we championed for women's rights and clean cookstoves.

The house was different.

But it still felt like home.

TURN IT AROUND
WHAT TO DO WHEN THINGS FALLS APART

In my leadership development workshops, I stage an exercise called 'Lemon/Lemonade', a purpose-drive icebreaker I learned from Seamus Harte, a San Francisco based designer and educator. I form everyone into a circle and say something negative to the person on my left:

"I showed up fifteen minutes late to my own workshop because I got a flat tire."

The student then must take this lemon and turn into lemonade. She will respond with something like:

"Well, at least you learned how to change a spare tire."

She then continues, handing a lemon to be made into lemonade to her neighbor. And so on. Often, some bold soul strikes a deeper chord. We hear:

"I saw so many homeless people on my walk over here."

"I recently got divorced and then fired from my job."

"My mother got diagnosed with cancer."

The room goes silent. We anxiously watch her partner, who inevitably responds with something akin to:

"Thank you for sharing that. We now have the opportunity to talk about it and to figure out a way we can help."

This response is a striking affirmation that we are all able to empathize as human beings when life takes unexpected turns. The Lemon/Lemonade exercise trains our mind that failure is really only rich compost for our next attempt. When things go wrong, the ability to persevere feels difficult, if not impossible. Yet within mere months, no matter how profound the failure may be, we can find the meaning in the struggle. We can leverage that experience to do better and be more mindful.

As GO manifested into a new state of being, I endured an internal reckoning that followed the well-known steps of grief, going from despair to hope. Eventually the empowering feeling of acceptance and understanding came. While this process of grief is healthy, there is a valuable technique that helps better frame the 'why' of mental sufferings, one I learned from a long-time friend and mentor, Costa Ndayisabye.

Our relationship began randomly. A mutual friend named Marion MacGillivray had brought Costa from his native Rwanda to Los Angeles so he could attend a trauma-counseling workshop. I was in town raising money for GO. We met at a gas station at dusk. In the waning light, his unbelievably bright eyes and a huge smile lit up everything around him. We shook hands, exchanged pleasantries, and like everyone that meets Costa, I instantly wanted to know more about him. We exchanged phone numbers and he called me that evening while I sat in my hotel room. As I sat in the spoiled comforts of business travel, he gently told me all the atrocities he endured over his life growing up in Congo and Rwanda. War, death, and genocides peppered his life. Our call lasted two hours. His 'sufferings' were profound and at the time my mind was so weak that when I hung up, I could only find solace in martinis at the hotel bar. He found solace that night in prayer and reflection.

Through his sufferings, a purpose was revealed to Costa and he discovered a love within the hatred. He knew he needed to share his enlightened message so he envisioned a powerful development project in his hometown of Muhanga. The project would build homes for survivors of the genocide while simultaneously facilitating workshops to heal their emotional wounds. The morning after our call, GO provided $2,500 for Costa's team to start this project of passion. He left the city of lights in order to build homes and spread the gospel of *The Work* in his native land. At this time, I only knew fragments about *The Work*, a reconciliation and trauma counseling process pioneered by Byron Katie.

One year later, Kyle, a volunteer named Ryan Gilpin, and I visited Costa in Rwanda to see the results from our first investment. His brilliant smile greeted us as we walked down an immaculately clean dirt path toward his home. We arrived in the capital city of Kigali just in time for Costa's graduation ceremony. He had completed his bachelor's degree in Business Administration and family, members of his parish, and neighbors came over to celebrate. Costa beamed confidence, gratitude, and love while draped in a glowing blue gown of an accredited academic. As evening came, the guests began to dwindle and a dinner of *chapati* (fried dough), avocado, and chicken was served. Over the wonderful food prepared by his wife, Bernadette, Costa explained what we would see on our journey. His radiance transformed into pensive thought as he outlined his vision. Even at this late hour, he continued wearing his graduation cap. He stood as an academic educating his acolytes.

Costa began by negating his organization merely built homes. While there was a home built for the most needy of community members as an output, it was a means to a wider end. The project's core focus was the healing of the deep emotional scars left after the genocide, wounds which affected the lives of all Rwandans. By design, each home built required the participation of local volunteers. Survivors and perpetrators of the genocide would work together side-by-side. Both still lived next to one another and so the home building process gave them an opportunity to work together as a communal unit under the auspice of a project. Before any physical construction began, Costa conducted facilitation workshops that wove the torn fabrics of the community back together. To guide this reconciliation process, Costa employed a method created by Byron Katie entitled "Doing the Work".

Our fateful encounter at the gas station was prompted by Costa's own journey in discovering the work of Byron Katie. Alongside four other Rwandan community leaders, Costa had been sponsored to attend a five-day intensive workshop in Los Angeles to heal their own emotional scar tissue. Costa chronicled this transformational journey in his book, *The Work That Brings Peace In Me,* and it covers the experiences of self-healing he encountered while at The School for *The Work*.

Essentially, *The Work* identifies and questions *the thoughts* that cause suffering in our lives. We cannot change what "is " (aka, reality) though we can change *the thought* around the reality we perceive. *The Work* outlines how to turn stories around in our minds so we can traverse any emotional valley. During Costa's workshops in Rwanda, every local volunteer, both victims and culprits together, went through a series of reconciliation exercises before any mud or concrete stained their hands. First, they had to remove the stain of war from their hearts before true development could begin.

While that sounds lovely, my cynical nature expressed doubt upon this process created by an autodidactic self-help guru from California. Yet I kept my mind open as Costa took us to nearby Muhanga, his boyhood home that lies 40 minutes west of Kigali, to see the first home built. His mother greeted us as we got off the bus, and together with Costa's staff, we headed to the rural outskirts. The lush green of the country erased the brown of the town as we trekked further up into the hills.

As we walked through the dense trees, I heard singing as we approached. Hundreds of people in dazzling colors surrounded a solid concrete home with an elegant roof and a tidy garden. There, in the doorway, stood Jeanne. Her hands were clasped as she looked meekly downwards at her feet. She stood in front of her community as they were softly singing and celebrating. Eyes of hope surrounded her. This was to be her home. These were the people who had built it alongside her. And just outside her door stood Bosco. He was the man who only a few years ago butchered her husband with a machete and then burned down her original home. He stood steadfast next to Jeanne and faced his neighbors. They stood together. Peacefully.

The community selected Jeanne as the first beneficiary of Costa's project because of this atrocity. She lost not only a home during the genocide but also her life partner. She had little means to support her children who witnessed the attacks. This difficult case was the prototype for Costa's first foray into community development and trauma counseling. As any bold leader, Costa found faith in his emotional faculties, skill in his instruction, and wisdom in his experiences.

Costa began *The Work* process with Bosco, Jeanne, and their neighbors four months before this home was built. The framework was roughly the following. During multiple workshops, Costa asked Bosco, Jeanne and their neighbors if the genocide was still occurring in their minds. After all, the war had ended fifteen years prior, so *was* the war *absolutely* true and *still* happening? Dumbfounded, nearly all said yes. Some were missing limbs, some had lost family, some lost homes, and some lost all of the above.

He asked again, "Is that *true*?"

"Yes," they said.

He asked, again, "Is that *absolutely* true? Is the genocide happening right *now*?"

People began to get confused.

"Well, no" they said, "It's not happening right *now* but the effects are still here!"

"My mother is dead!"

"My arm is cut-off!"

Costa began again.

"How do you react when they believe that *thought*?" he asked.

"Pain, suffering, anguish," they responded.

"Who would you be without the *thought*? Close your eyes. Picture yourself in the present moment. Your mother, who was killed then, she is no longer present. Now imagine looking at her, just for a moment, without the thought 'My mother should be here.' What do you see? What would your life look like without that thought?", he asked.

"Perhaps you would see that her values live through you."

"Perhaps you would see that her love bleeds into your heart."

"Perhaps you would see her light reflected in the eyes of your daughter." Costa said.

These turn arounds were repeated over and over, week after week. As the workshops proceeded, stories began to slowly yet surely turn-around in the minds of the participants. The genocide started its relegation to the past.

As the reconciliation efforts took hold, the community began the physical project of building the home for Jeanne altogether. Men and women of all ages volunteered to make mud bricks from the land. The only expenditures of the project were spent on workshop facilitation costs, fixtures (doors, windows, etc.), cement for the frame, and the roofing. Perpetrators and survivors of the genocide worked side by side, caking the dark soil into bricks that would build a bright future for their community.

During the first of my many trips to Rwanda, I witnessed the dedication and unbelievable raw strength of the Rwandan people while being immersed in the power of Costa's visionary approach. Even in our weakest and most desolate hour, we as humans can heal and rebuild ourselves. Costa had brought Jeanne and Bosco together by building a pacifying bridge over an unbelievably wide gulf of hate. Bosco, a trained architect, helped Jeanne design her new home, meager in its appearance yet rich in its significance. The same woman who lost her home and husband found a meaningful path forward. The same man who once killed now found solace and reconciliation. They found new versions of themselves during the journey of this project.

This was one of many stories I witnessed while observing Costa's powerful method to help people overcome the deepest of sufferings. These practices were by no means easy. They take patience and determination. Time and again, however, I have seen how they help people return to a state of wellbeing.

While observing GO break down into fertile compost, I never lost faith that I would find a new way to help impact the world around me. I took Costa's lessons and workbooks to write down and better construct my thoughts about the story transpiring around me. I turned stories of doubt and loss into ones of meaning and spiritual growth. Here were the three dominant stories that afflicted my being during this transition with their respective turn arounds:

Story #1: I am losing the company I founded.

Is this true? Turn it around.

The Turn-Around Story: We are evolving into something greater beyond ourselves.

Story #2: I am failing to lead and my failures have caused harm to others.

Is this *absolutely* true? Turn it around.

The Turn-Around Story: We all have an opportunity to learn from individual and collective mistakes.

Story #3: I have lost my friends.

Is this true? Turn it around.

The Turn-Around Story: I strengthened relations with family and true friends who I love with all my heart.

I did not lose the company I founded. I found a new family to grow our impact. I did not lose my job. I found new meaning within new endeavors. I did not lose my friends when things went sour. I strengthened existing connections. Over and over, I found ways to frame and strengthen my present state so I could move forward.

While stories of distress can haunt the mind, there is always a path forward. Failures and suffering are not easy to 'turn around' nor should the practice of flipping a story result in making the objectively true version of history into a false narrative. Simply calling one thing another can quickly lead to delusion of reality. Once mastered and balanced, the ability to turn stories around in our minds is a powerful tool that leads towards finding the beauty of what *is*. Turn-arounds empower people with the ability to learn from their circumstances by seeing 'negative' occurrences in different perspectives. This process leads one to acceptance of self by finding an inward and divine retribution from the mistakes of the past. Most importantly, it sways and influences others around you.

I find this power to be so vital for true community development since change begins with you, the individual viewing the unfolding story that you call life.

Reality is the story within your mind.

You have the power to control the narrative.

You have the means to lead.

This level of emotional intelligence only comes with failures of utter proportions. They are not learned by failing an exam or missing a bus that makes you late to work. Those are mere stumbles, training for the ensuing disruptive chaos that will unfold when one goes out of their comfort zone, the place where the magic happens. To fail properly, you must do something bigger by going beyond yourself.

Find solace in knowing that these stark failures will not break you. They will only make you bolder. They are experiences shared by all of humanity, as we are all broken at some time or another.

You will find grace within the suffering, the purpose in the occurrence.

CHAPTER 18

A HAVEN FOR HUMILITY

Over the past decade, leaders from all walks of life have taught me the art of doing the impossible. I learned from people who scavenged the burnt crumbs of the Earth and baked them into a wholesome bread that fed thousands. These trailblazers started things—whether projects, nonprofits, or businesses —that improved people's wellbeing and gave purpose to their own lives. Their visions inspired me; their humility softened my state of being.

In the moments of grace when they gave selflessly, I watched their wellbeing swell and perpetuate upwards and onwards. I cheered when they succeeded, I wept as I saw them fail. I strived to turn their failures into hopes so they would continue marching on. They did the same for me, revealing seeds of gratitude, which could be found even in the most rotten of fruits.

I studied under a Lost Boy refugee, one of 40,000 displaced during the Second Sudanese Civil War. He faced starvation, thirst, and fear of death from animal mauling while traversing the Sudanese desert by foot for three-months. After spending three years in a refugee camp, he is now a successful social entrepreneur and writer running a clinic helping millions of patients in his native South Sudan. I am humbled that he graced my home and enlightened my being. John Dau taught me **hope**.

I learned from a man who fled from not one but two genocides. He encountered more hatred than any one soul should ever have to experience. He endured and transformed. He now resides in Texas with his beautiful family and lives a life of peaceful joy. He's a successful social entrepreneur, an accomplished speaker, a published author, and began dozens of projects to help his native Rwanda thrive. Costa Ndayisabye taught me **love**.

I watched a Cambodian community leader scale his organization to magnificent heights. The Sao Sary Foundation was named after his assassinated father—a community leader in his own right. When his work hit an inflection point he hired over 20 employees, got his work featured on the BBC, and managed a massive budget. Unable to properly manage this rapid growth, his work deteriorated under operational failures. False accusations of abuse and corruption shattered his foundation. He tried and he failed. He is beginning yet again, starting something new. Vichetr Uon taught me **grit**.

I met a man and a woman in Tanzania. The AIDS epidemic ravaged their community, resulting in a never-ending supply of orphans in their community. So, the couple opened the doors of their own home to the youth who had lost their families. They built and now run one of the top primary schools in Tanzania educating 360 children yearly, a third of whom would otherwise not be able to afford education. They currently house more than 60 orphans in their home. James and Bernadette Nathaniel taught me **sacrifice**.

I gained knowledge from a blind Lebanese American who lost her sight at the age of seven. She founded a nonprofit as a result of her own personal experience and passion for empowering blind youth to be the catalysts for change in their communities. She is an internationally recognized advocate in the areas of disability inclusion and social entrepreneurship. Sara Minkara taught me **passion**.

I married my one true love in Africa under the guidance of a man who was born on a banana plantation. He knew farming from day one of life and grew determined to make Uganda the breadbasket of East Africa. He toiled under the world's longest running dictatorship and became a man of economic and political significance. This significance wrought grave injustice. Family members were attacked and close friends were killed. His health suffered. Yet he continued on, launching one farming-related venture after another. Peter Francis Luswata taught me to see grace within **humility**.

These leaders took their values of hope, love, grit, sacrifice, humility, and passion to start something good and make a positive impact. They resolutely toiled forward until an opportunity arose. Perhaps it was an open ear that listened to their story, or maybe an earnest volunteer that arrived at their project, or a wallet that opened. Whatever that one turn of fortune may have been, their diligent preparation latched onto the fickle swing of fortune and their life paths changed forever. Sometimes it took a week. Sometimes it took a decade. Some had to start all over again when massive failure arose. Yet they started something, began somewhere, and took that first step. Then that something grew. And grew. Then one day these great leaders saw themselves lauded as pillars of their communities. Some pillars grew so tall that they became targets of hostility as onlookers became jealous of the power they had acquired.

I've seen success turn into a smear campaign of corruption.

I've seen success steer noble minds into the darkness of selfish opportunism.

I've seen success cut short by death.

Despite all these barriers, I've seen their good work thrive. Even the most adverse conditions on the planet could not stop their impact. They took bare scraps and turned them into compost, a fertile soil to grow something new. They took their harrowing pasts, put them into a wider perspective rich with meaning, and manifested their backgrounds into stories of power. They were not afraid of suffering and understood its true purpose.

As the renowned Buddhist monk Thich Nhat Hanh said:

"Most people are afraid of suffering. But suffering is a kind of mud to help the lotus flower of happiness grow. There can be no lotus flower without the mud"

As I walked with them, our winding path towards something beyond ourselves traversed up and down sharply. The wild ups manifested ego and vanity. The humiliating downs broke down the vanity of self. Those inspiring leaders taught me how to eat last, to put others first, and to understand there was so much I did not know. They made me believe in a universal bond that connects all of humanity.

Through their collective eyes I learned of Ubuntu. This belief cries out that people are not isolated. There are no "Others". I am, because you are. And you are, because I am. Humanity is a quality we owe to one another. We create and belong to each other. There exists a great need to fully embrace this worldview of our innate interdependency.

Look around! War. Poverty. Hunger. Anger. Failure. So many have preciously few choices in life and so many struggles to bear. Yes, things are better than they ever have been in nearly the entire history of our world. As my grandfather built his first home in the 1950s, 75% of the world was living in extreme poverty. Today, it stands at less than 10%. Similar plummets have been documented in global illiteracy and child mortality rates. Meanwhile, surges in democracy, vaccinations, and literacy are continually propelling our society upwards.

But there is so much work to do to bring justice to all and end poverty within our lifetime. It may seem daunting and overwhelming but remember that the craziest thing we can do is nothing. With a bold motivation anchored by a steadfast belief of *Ubuntu,* we can shape a better and more just world.

When it seems too hard or too bold, find comfort in these words:

> *"Life can be much broader when you discover one simple fact. People that were no smarter than you made up everything around you that you call life. You can change it. You can influence it. You can build your own things that other people can use."*

I heard this notion from Steve Jobs at an early age and listened to the recording over and over. Its stark, striking simplicity burrowed deep into my psyche. These words guided me off the beaten path. I learned early on that poking the status quo of a predetermined life eventually blessed me (and those around me) with infinitely more possibilities in life. This can cause pain in the short-term as there are few roadmaps for walking this path. You will be put in situations that most people would consider as perilous jeopardy. I've been there. I've been detained in developing world countries. Friends have sued me. Deep relationships abruptly ended. I've lost an astounding sum of money. I've been fired. When my ideas lost traction or spun out of control, people lost jobs and were hurt. I've gotten lost many, many times.

Most would consider those experiences to be painful or difficult. I think of myself as blessed since they taught me great lessons. Success teaches you nothing. Failure teaches you everything. The harder the fall, the bigger the lesson. Failures or injustice may cause suffering but these experiences all have meaning. Once the meaning is discovered, the "failure" is then turned around to provide wisdom and strength. Suffering ends when meaning is discovered.

These lessons were harvested from working with compassionate and modest leaders from around the world. I walked alongside them for as long as I could. I wanted to become a better person, a provider that never forgot to share my blessings in life. Then one day I stopped walking outwards and directed myself inwards to care for my family. I prepared for a new journey in life. A new miracle arrived and she became the center of my world. I would now like to direct my thoughts to one of the world's newest disruptive leaders: a baby girl.

A person innocent in thought, fierce in being.

Her name is Haven.

I call her "boo bear".

And like you, dear reader, she can change the world.

My dearest boo bear,

You are ever so young as I write these words. Yet within my heart, I know you fully understand. Your watchful eyes shine as they take in the growing world. Your little feet wobble forward, determined to explore and discover. I watch as your little hands water the flowers in the yard. You intuitively sense that they need your help to flourish.

Amongst the babble of your language, I hear you repeat the word "Happy" over and over, bringing joy and laughter to those around you.

In your presence, hearts grow and expand; my love deepens to depths I never knew existed.

Your soul already creates so much good.

How can someone so small lift others up?

My child, you are truly a hummingbird with immense powers.

I hold a ferocious hope that your words and actions will continue to improve the world around you. It will not always be easy. Trying new things sometimes results in failure. You never get on a bike and start riding it. You fall down and it hurts. Don't worry; I will be there to catch you.

But then you must get back up, dust yourself off, and try again.

It will be a long time before the ideas and stories in this book resonate with you. Until then, we will need to practice trying and doing new things. You must put these lessons into action for it to matter.

My little rider, it's time for you to get on that bike, push off, and have a fall. Don't be afraid. Bumps and bruises build character. Character forms determination. Determination seeds grit, builds hope. These are the core ingredients to change the course of humanity.

Sound impossible? Then know this: impossible is only what you won't do. Life is too short to make small plans. Your great grandfather knew this. He built home after home and mowed lawn after lawn to make our freedom possible. Your grandparents brought us to a free nation that gave us boundless opportunities. With this great power comes great responsibilities.

So go.

Think different. Be unreasonable.

Take risks and fail miserably.

Again and again.

You will be all the better for it.

And so will I, and all those around us that we call humanity.

I love you.

Your Tata.

RISE TOWARDS A MISSION

Imagine a mountain. The air above the summit hovers near, just there, so close, yet always just out of reach. We can never reach the sky above the summit but we climb the mountain regardless because we make no small plans. The top brings us closer to the stars. Every mountain we climb is a bit different. Some require technical skills to traverse while others require only steadfast determination. We take steps forward even when the dusty sands of the peak sink your body backwards. Two steps forward, one step back. Then we reach the summit, achieve our mission, and glance upwards. There it is. That vision of the sky, brought closer by perseverance and testimony of inner will. We climb back down and scout another, higher mountain to summit and get us even closer the next time. It's impossible to reach the sky, yet it's worth striving for.

The great challenge of our lives is to understand our purpose. What mountains are we to climb? What stars do we yearn to touch? In founding and running GO for eight years of my life, I discovered a bridge to leaders of extraordinary character that grappled with the responsibility of having purpose in their lives. Their beliefs about religion, education, creed, and culture varied widely. Some were from tribes and some were from nation states. The main thing I witnessed that tied them all together was their conviction of self, which was driven by their purpose in life. This purpose was guided by their core values. Those core values were their guideposts and empowered them with the ability to know when to turn right and when to turn left. The path was always upwards towards the summit of the mountain they were climbing, and towards the mission that they could achieve. They continually found new and higher mountains to climb, and pushed their boundaries as they reached for their visions in life—the unattainable sky that was worth striving for.

A vision. A mission. Core values. These are the lights that help us navigate towards building purpose in our lives. I have these all written down as they cast light on my future horizons. They are the beliefs that are my anchor when the seas become turbulent, my guides when the next step needs more clarity and light.

Let's begin with my values as they guide my journey upwards. These are the core values that continually drive me to create a better human experience for my family, my community, and myself. The core value is in bold, the definition thereafter, and their source of thought and feeling are underneath.

Be humble

The dwelling place of charity is found when one strives towards modesty by stripping away pride.

Source: Grace.

Think differently

Because the people who are crazy enough to think they can change the world are the ones who do.

Source: Hope

Always be curious

Start by asking why and never stop questioning.

Source: Humility.

Embrace *Ubuntu*

No human is an island. Realize and champion the inter-connectedness of humanity.

Source: Passion and Love.

Give first

Lead with benevolence and rise by lifting others selflessly.

Source: Sacrifice.

With those values in my heart, I am then able to look up into the stars and seek my vision statement.

I exist to improve the wellbeing of people globally.

These eight words guide me as I share my energy with the world. They are my compass and guiding force in life. I am deeply indebted to Saul Garlick, a serial social entrepreneur, who guided me in a practice to discover this vision statement. This vision is bombastic, hopelessly naïve, yet one that brings both joy and wellbeing to my life. It guides my major decisions on what work I take on, what ventures I help start, what board I join, or which charities I support. While this vision is deceptively short, it is profound in its complexity.

- **I Exist:** Self-evident in every breath I take, I am alive and present.
- **To Improve:** The only thing everything can be is better. Everything that we do is another iteration that can be done better the next time.
- **The Wellbeing:** Wellbeing is the ultimate end goal of our existence. This thought is derived from a theory in psychology proposed by Abraham Maslow in his 1943 paper, "A Theory of Human Motivation", which is better known as Maslow's "hierarchy of needs". Maslow posited that human needs are arranged in a hierarchy where our base needs as humans start at the bottom of the pyramid with food, water and rest. Then as we go up the pyramid, we need security, friends and intimate relationships. Higher still, we have esteem needs fulfilled by feelings of accomplishment. And at the peak of the pyramid, we have self-actualization. To me, this is a state of wellbeing where we have continual personal growth and constantly fulfill our need to becoming all the things a person is capable of becoming. A state of harmony and of flow. Wellbeing is the end game of

both personal and community development and should always be the goal of designing a better human experience.

- **Of People:** I need people to thrive. Their motivations, psychologies, carnal drive, and ceaseless innovations to expand the potential of existence absolutely fascinate me. I always want to be with people and to learn how to craft them into leaders. While I love nature and have deep reverence for the animal kingdom, I fulfill my calling in life by focusing on the people that impact everything around them and therefore find joy in efforts that directly involve humanity.

- **Globally:** I don't care if a solution benefits merely the people of Gary, Indiana or Kampala, Uganda. I want to work with organizations that are providing services or products on a global scale that directly benefit the lives of people. I want to find solutions that benefit both Gary *and* Kampala. For me, the world is too small to work solely on local solutions; my focus must have some global or cross cultural aspect to it.

These words represent the stars that I reach out to grasp. As many mountains exist on the horizon, I leverage these words to find the right one to climb to come closer. So many missions, so little time. Can you lead this project? Will you help me launch my nonprofit? Will you join my board? Can you help us scale? The opportunities are endless and my energy is finite. My vision helps me delineate the many into the few.

Does your company, project, nonprofit, or idea serve people, seek to improve wellbeing, and do so globally? If so, then we can walk together. If not, I will wish you the best of luck and offer my best counsel as for what path you should take. I am mindful that many wonderful grassroots organizations operate solely on a local community level. I donate funds and give advice to these organizations frequently. But for anything more significant, such as joining a board or joining the team, I must find a global aspect related to human development for my heart, soul, and mind to be fully vested. This is my way of being and serving the world, an example so you can craft your own vision statement and start identifying the purpose in your life.

While helpful, a vision statement is by nature vague and aspirational, which makes it hard to concretely define the minute steps. This is where a mission statement comes into play. It represents the summit you can actually climb, the goal that can be reached.

A mission statement is defined in scope and is achievable. It blends the *what* into the *why*. The progress can be measured. And as one successfully summits mountain after mountain, those achievements influence our vision statement to be broader and bolder.

My current mission, re-defined on an annual basis, is as follows:

In 2018, I will be a nurturing father to my newborn daughter, a loving husband to her mother, a devoted coach to my colleagues, an accelerator in scaling a commercial business from $5 million to $10 million, a supporting co-founder of Button It Up events, and a published author.

This is a mountain I can climb. It's ambitious by design and may take longer than anticipated, as the path upwards may be more challenging than expected. I will proceed forward with deep sacrifices bestowed upon me by prior generations. My core values will guide my steps. I will draw wisdom from the tornado of my life experiences. I will remember the joys of launching ventures, the alarm of catastrophe, the grief of betrayal, the anxiety of putting my true self out into the public domain, and the humility of failure when things came crashing down. I will move forward with a passionate curiosity about the journey and be open to all teachings as I progress upwards and onwards.

I will balance professional endeavors by spending time with my soul mate and by joyfully playing with my beautiful daughter. They mean *everything* when it comes to restoring my wellbeing. I will serve them with a devoted presence in order to become a better leader myself.

I will never forget to lead a purpose driven life, one that continually evolves.

I will *never* stop trying to become a better version of myself.
This is a dream of being better, one that I want to share with you.
For if you and I share the same dream, it will become a reality.

Acknowledgments

My deepest gratitude goes to all the changemakers who grabbed ahold of my soul, challenging me to do better and to think differently. I am honored by your patiently instilled gifts of hope, virtue, and humility that empowered me with strength and conviction. You taught me to serve as best as I can and always strive to do better as a leader, a father, and a husband.

Every day, millions of people take on ambitious work to help make the world a better place to live. Traversing through comfort or pain, love or hatred, rain or shine, they show courage and grace in the face of extreme challenges like abject poverty and environmental destruction.

They do not look the other way.

They do what they can.

Their dedication inspired me to write this book.

To all those leaders starting something good, thank you for your noble hearts that inspire everyone to follow in the mighty flaps of your wings. I hope these words of gratitude propel forward the idea that every person can live a purposeful and productive life.

In addition, I would like to thank each of the individuals listed below personally as your contributions made this book possible.

Haven, I am blessed to be in your presence; you show me the beauty in our world.

Heather, I love you deeper than any metaphor can express; mere words will never suffice to convey my passion for our creations in life.

Mama i Tata, your sacrifices empowered me with the privilege of giving back to the world. I will never forget your lessons, courage, and conviction.

Dziadek Henryk, thanks to you, we continue to build onwards and upwards.

Dziadek Jasio, Babcia Zosia, i Babcia Hancia, may you rest in peace knowing that your sacrifices in life resonate onwards today, and through all of the tomorrows.

Ania, let's never agree. Our conversations would become ever so boring. And thank you for being a sister who continually inspires me to ensure the future minds of the world are educated in the best manner possible.

Doug, I think lemon and fierce intellectual discourse makes every dinner taste better as well. I am grateful you have become part of our family.

Kuba, keep digging. Who knows what treasure you will uncover?

Bob and Jeanne, thank you for raising such a strong daughter. She is passing on your values of hard work and loving affection to a new generation, while putting up with my overly meticulous nature on a *daily* basis. That is truly a fine balance.

Kyle and Jessie, let's always think differently about the world around us. Boundaries of thought were always meant to be pushed.

Arthur, listen to your parents. Haven thanks you for all the lovely hugs.

Peter, your humility and rolling tide of quiet power inspires everyone around you to be more virtuous. Through you, I learned a leadership path wrought from a meek soul, a thankful heart, and a giving spirit.

Costa, I will never grow tired of your unbridled optimism and joy for life. You continually show me the wonder of the Present Moment.

Eric, your sermons rocked me to the core of my existence. You taught me how to speak with burning fire in my veins. Your perseverance to progress forward, no matter how challenging the path may be, will never be forgotten.

Ibrah, you showed me that being a Tanzanian entrepreneur means being one cool cat, one smooth hustler, and a very caring father.

James, you are right. Education! Ed-u-ca-tion is the key to life.

Vichetr, we learned that unbridled growth needs devoted care lest the floor gives out from under you. I hope we both learn how to start something *better* the next time.

John, you are truly an awakened giant. No one has taught me more about grit and determination.

Sieng, your passion for and tenacity to provide for the education of young minds is infectious.

Vey, I am thankful Leah brought you into my life. No tour guide, photographer, entrepreneur, and ardent philanthropist makes me laugh so hard.

Mummi, I miss your matoke. You always served it with quiet wisdom.

Abdul, the hummingbird writing these words promises never to rest in service to the world. Thank you for inspiring me to be a better person.

Ana, I cannot wait for the Skorupa families' first steps to see Mis Primeras Huellas in person.

Shafii, you bring contagious joy and laughter to the art of selflessly lifting others up.

Mitch, I may never match your dedication to improving the world around me but I will never stop trying.

Shanti, you transformed my development, for better and always. I am deeply indebted to your teachings and I am mindful it took fortitude and great strength to wring out the wisdom from the most difficult of circumstances.

Violeta, one day I promise to show my family AMARNO in person so we can learn from the power of women's leadership groups who are leading the creation of sustainable economies.

Sara, you live in a world that you cannot see yet you have shown me the many wonders of life.

Lisa, you taught me to control the speed of my thoughts so that not everything that could be, would be.

Brian, the impact still resonates from your tremendous gifts and talents that took GO to new levels. The efforts of yesterday still continue to make an impact today, and will do so tomorrow. I miss our bike rides.

Todd, I *love* your passion for life and your unparalleled ability to find meaning in all experiences, whether positive or negative.

Horst, I will now always increase choices for all parties, now and in the future. Danke für Ihre hilfreiche Beratung.

David, you took a chance on us after a random, fateful encounter. The ride went wild as we bucked up and down. You have a *magnificent* ability to keep control with both hands on the wheel, even when the car is skidding on black ice.

Bobby, I love your acerbic wit and gifted mind. Few people have ever me made me laugh and think so hard at the same time.

Sarge, I love your attention to detail. That quality is the difference between something good and something great. Never lose that.

Lindsay, you halted me in my tracks when my "ask" became unclear. You built me into a better fundraiser and empowered me to give back at levels I never imagined.

Thomas, thank you for your dogged determination to do anything it took to help GO thrive. Even a bus could not stop you.

Kelly, you were are our first intern, the one who believed in us when the idea merely rested on my kitchen table, scattered in papers. Never lose that bravery.

Mags, you put so much cool and effortless style in the way shared our gift with the world. Through your guidance, our message reached the digital masses.

Kirstie, from writing grants to networking, you propelled our growth right from the beginning. Thank you for helping us get off the ground in those early days.

Jo and Michelle, I never knew that sumo wrestling and karaoke in Alaska could end up raising so many pigs for farmers in Uganda. Thank you both for being unreasonable with the status quo and more importantly, for *being* the change we wished to see.

Sara, who knew a drink on a breezy Saturday afternoon in San Francisco could lead to so much positive change in East Africa and within ourselves?

Vanessa, from England to America to Rwanda, doing something good is always best done with wonderful friends like yourself.

Ben, the school in Ghana keeps expanding and I cannot wait to hear from you once you see it in person.

Ryan, thank you for sharing Abdul's story and giving me the privilege to help KGSA thrive.

Erica, we'll never top that pre-dawn run in Cambodia. We got lost in the best way.

Lesley and Dena, I thank you with a full heart. Your courageous spirit brought our attention to things that could have been done better. The remedial action plan we put in place came directly from your determination to ensure quality programs.

Kari, you hurled yourself headfirst into East Africa, meeting our new cohort of partners and climbing Kilimanjaro. You pushed the boundaries of your comfort zone and blazed a trail for other women travelers to follow.

Apurva and Carly, I had no idea 7th graders could be so determined to make such a global impact while also running a ½ marathon. Rwanda awaits when you are old enough to venture out into the world.

Carlos, I never had your determination for equality of justice in high school. I have no doubt you will change the world. Stay ambitious, stay unreasonable.

Marley, with your mother's empathy and your strong voice, I see a great changemaker in you. Jill, you've raised an amazing and disruptive leader.

Madeleine, keep traveling, keep discovering, and you will continue finding ways to improve the world around you. Never forget to share your gifts, as you have so many.

Zoe, your ability to raise funds and awareness took our ideas to new levels. Thank you for trusting and challenging us with your passion for the indigenous people of Ecuador.

Rob and Jenny, can we all plan a family trip to Rwanda and Uganda? Our soccer team will not lose this time (right?) and we have so much more we can do to help rural agriculture thrive in East Africa's breadbasket.

Jenise, you always remind me to take shorter showers. Clean water, available on demand, is truly a precious gift.

Sophana, the way you give back to the world is laden with selfless humility.

Cheryl, what an adventure in Rwanda! You are a beacon of light that proves going beyond yourself to help on a global scale can be done at any phase of life.

Peggy, your travels with Judy to Rwanda opened doors and opportunities for so many. Thank you for taking a chance with us as you visited the land of a thousand hills.

Carolyn, your photography, fundraising, volunteering, and selfless spirit for helping with *anything* and *everything* continues to reverberate. You gave everything you could and that meant the world to us.

Amanda and Jessica, through your efforts, I had my first homecoming fundraiser event in Chicago. That meant the world to me.

Mike and Vina, you showed me that wedding registries can unite soul mates while giving clean water for hundreds. Thank you for sharing your special day. The good vibes are still resonating. The water is still flowing.

Toni and Lani, thank you for teaching me that dance is a powerful agent of change.

Zanoon, you took flash mob dancing to a whole other level. Never lose that fire.

Barbara, you proved not only She CAN but She WILL. I'm glad we could help your vision grow in our own small way.

Annie, your giving spirit humbles me. Thank you for leveraging your wedding to give back to the world.

Margo, through philanthropy we became great friends and that is a gift I will never forget.

Rebecca and Jon, you became Champions to provide clean water and bikes for hundreds in Cambodia. Until our next ride together, thank you.

Kevin and Jill, you found each other through selfless giving by funding clean water to hundreds in Cambodia. I can't wait to see when the twins witness this impact firsthand.

Nicole, you are right. Nightclubs in Chicago can raise a lot of money for good. And the school finally launched in 2018. Let's figure out how to tell all your students!

Michelle, when at an outdoor disco on a farm in Uganda, always remember that the phrase "I know Peter Luswata!" will protect you. Thank you for *everything*.

Vanessa, I have never seen someone harness the power of Facebook like you. As a university student, you found the time to visit Uganda and gave hundreds of people access to clean water. Always leverage your innate power to inspire and lead.

Shannon, Slalom connected us but it was GO that united our worldview that we can be audacious enough to build a better and more just world. When are we taking the kids to Uganda and Rwanda?

Nora, the morning yoga session in your backyard with Peter is among my most treasured memories in life.

Alex, you built the financial model that helped us thrive. I love how your career change empowered you to ensure all children find great public schools in their communities.

Tracy, though it took far longer than expected, the nursery school launched in 2018. Thank you for the patience, your impact continues on.

Sheena, the joy of running is so much stronger when you know that the finish line will also bring clean drinking water for those who need it the most. Thank you for being a champion.

Ojay, thank you for showing me the power of Salesforce to receive our first donation (which you matched!) and introducing me to the powerful intersection of technology and philanthropy.

Donna, thank you for learning how to edit a book alongside me. Through you, I became a better writer.

Lauren, you write beautifully and I look forward to reading your book about how you changed the world.

Barclay, I love your beautiful designs since they are always served with a warm Southern accent. I can even hear this accent while *reading* your emails.

Brian, your eye captures true light and reflects the real world.

David, your visionary guidance made this book really happen. I am filled with gratitude for your commandeering of this literary ship to a safe shore.

Chip, your guidance of writing this book will not be forgotten.

Saul, thank you for always being there to listen and provide apt insight. You are fearless in your convictions and continually inspire me to be a better social entrepreneur.

Glynn, thank you for fulfilling a lifelong dream of sharing my story on NPR. You inspire me to transform.

Seamus, thank you for being there when I need you the most. You are like my inner conscious, telling me the *right* thing to do, even when it's the last thing I *want* to do.

Momo, your arrival awaits. How will you serve the world and what can I do to help?

Made in the USA
Monee, IL
01 February 2020